3rd Edition

Upper Intermediate

MARKET
LEADER

Business English Teacher's Resource Book

Bill Mascull

Course components

Course Book with DVD-ROM
The key course component, comprising 12 units, four Working across cultures sections and four Revision units.

Teacher's Resource Book with Test Master CD-ROM
Includes step-by-step lesson notes and a photocopiable Resource bank of further practice exercises.

DVD-ROM
Included with the Course Book, the DVD-ROM includes the i-Glossary, extra self-study exercises, Course Book audio and scripts, interview videos and Case study commentaries and Grammar references.

Test Master CD-ROM
Included with the Teacher's Resource Book, this CD-ROM contains digital, customisable versions of the Test File tests, the audio for these tests and 12 further unit tests.

Vocabulary Trainer
www.marketleader.vocabtrainer.net
A personalised, interactive online tool which allows students to practise using target language from the Course Book in a variety of ways.

Test File
Six photocopiable tests including four Progress tests linked closely to the Course Book, an Entry test and an Exit test.

Practice File
A self-study workbook which provides extra practice for vocabulary, grammar and writing from every unit. Also includes activities to improve pronunciation and fluency through day-to-day functional English.

Active Teach
The digital version of the Course Book, with interactive activities and accompanying audiovisual resources for use in class with interactive whiteboards or on a computer.

Business Grammar and Usage
Provides clear explanations and targeted practice to strengthen any weak points your students may have.

Subscription website
www.market-leader.net
A source of information and extra resources for teachers to supplement their lessons, including exclusive FT content-based lessons.

Introduction

Market Leader is an extensive business English course designed to bring the real world of international business into the language-teaching classroom. It has been developed in association with the *Financial Times*, one of the world's leading sources of professional information, to ensure the maximum range and authenticity of international business content.

In addition to new authentic reading texts and listening material, the Third Edition features a number of exciting new resources:

- specially-filmed interviews with business practitioners for each unit
- *Case study commentaries* on DVD-ROM, with expert views on each case
- *Working across cultures* – regular input and tasks to develop students' intercultural awareness and skills
- four *Revision* units, one after every three main units
- an interactive *i-Glossary* on DVD-ROM
- additional photocopiable tasks in this Teacher's Resource Book
- *Active Teach* software to deliver the course digitally, through an interactive whiteboard or computer.

1 Course aims

This course is intended for use either by students preparing for a career in business or by those already working who want to improve their English communication skills. *Market Leader* combines some of the most stimulating recent ideas from the world of business with a strongly task-based approach. Role plays and case studies are regular features of each unit. Throughout the course, students are encouraged to use their own experience and opinions in order to maximise involvement and learning.

2 The main course components

Course Book

This provides the main part of the teaching material, divided into 12 topic-based units. The topics have been chosen following research among teachers to establish which are the areas of widest possible interest to the majority of their students. The Course Book provides input in reading, speaking and listening, with guidance for writing tasks too. Every unit contains vocabulary-development activities and a rapid review of essential grammar. There is a regular focus on key business functions and each unit ends with a motivating case study to allow students to practise language they have worked on during the unit. For more details on the Course Book units, see *Overview of a Course Book unit*.

After every three units is a spread called *Working across cultures*. Here students are introduced to key intercultural concepts, developing their awareness and skills in order to function effectively in international business situations.

There are also four *Revision* units in the Course Book that revise and consolidate the work done in the main units and culture spreads.

Audio and DVD-ROM materials

All the listening material from the Course Book is available on the audio CD. A number of these tracks provide students with exposure to non-native English accents which they may find challenging to understand, but which will help them build confidence in their own speaking. All of the audio files are also provided in fully-downloadable MP3 format on the DVD-ROM allowing transfer to personal computers and portable audio players.

The DVD-ROM is an integral part of the course. All 12 interviews from the Course Book can be viewed on the DVD-ROM with the option of sub-titles, depending on the user's preference. The interviews are accompanied by 12 video commentaries on the *Case studies* delivered by experienced business consultants. The interviews (which form the main listening focus of each unit) and commentaries provide an opportunity for students to get expert perspectives on the latest business practice through English. None of the videos are scripted and, as such, expose students to authentic examples of natural speech.

In addition, the DVD-ROM provides the students with interactive, self-study practice activities. These allow them to revisit problem areas and reinforce work done in class in their own time. The activities provide further listening practice, opportunities for task repetition and instant, personalised feedback.

The DVD-ROM also includes the *i-Glossary*, an interactive mini-dictionary which provides definitions and pronunciation of all the key vocabulary listed at the back of the Course Book and which encourages further self-study.

Vocabulary Trainer

This is an online, self-study tool that lets students take control of their own learning. Once students have created a personal account, the Vocabulary Trainer tests them on the meaning, spelling, collocation and use of vocabulary learnt in class. Their development is automatically recorded so they can chart their own progress outside the classroom.

Practice File

This gives extra practice in the areas of grammar and vocabulary, together with a complete syllabus in business writing. In each unit, students work with text models and useful language, then do a writing task to consolidate the learning. Additionally, the Practice File provides regular self-study pronunciation work (with an audio CD and exercises) and a valuable survival language section for students when travelling.

Teacher's Resource Book

This book provides teachers with an overview of the whole course, together with detailed teaching notes, background briefings on business content, the *Text bank* and the *Resource bank*.

The Text bank provides two extra *FT* reading texts per unit, followed up with comprehension and vocabulary exercises.

The Resource bank provides photocopiable worksheet-based communication activities linked to particular sections of the Course Book units.

- *Listening bank*: extra activities based on each Course Book Listening interview
- *Speaking bank*: extra activities based on each *Skills* section
- *Writing bank*: a model answer to the Course Book *Writing* task, together with an additional writing exercise

Test File

Six photocopiable tests are available to teachers and course planners to monitor students' progress during the course. There is an *Entry test*, four *Progress tests*, which test both skills and language knowledge and an *Exit test*, which reviews the work done throughout the course.

Test Master CD-ROM

Included in the Teacher's Resource Book, the Test Master CD-ROM is a useful assessment resource to accompany the course. It includes digital, editable versions of the Test File tests enabling valid, tailored assessment. It also contains the accompanying audio files and a further 12 unit tests. These tests assess students' progress in terms of the *Vocabulary, Language review* and *Skills* sections of their corresponding units. Full keys and audioscripts are also provided to make marking the tests as straightforward as possible.

Active Teach

The Active Teach software provides digital access to a range of course components via an interactive whiteboard or computer. Components include the Course Book, video and audio with printable scripts, the i-Glossary interactive activities based on the Course Book content, editable tests, the Teacher's Resource Book and the phonetic chart. It also includes the *Writing file*, which provides good models for product writing, and *Help* videos to make using the software as easy as possible.

Using Active Teach facilitates student engagement and enables clear giving of instructions and valuable feedback. It is ideal for use on a laptop in one-to-one classes.

3 Overview of a Course Book unit

A typical unit consists of the following sections:

Starting up

Students have the opportunity to think about the unit topic and to exchange ideas and opinions with each other and with the teacher. There is a variety of stimulating activities such as answering quiz questions, reflecting on difficult decisions, prioritising options and completing charts. Throughout, students are encouraged to draw upon their life and business experience as appropriate.

Vocabulary

Essential business vocabulary is presented and practised through a wide variety of creative and engaging exercises.

Students learn new words, phrases and collocations and are given tasks which help to activate the vocabulary they already know or have just learnt.

There is further vocabulary practice in the Practice File.

Reading

Students read interesting and relevant authentic texts from the *Financial Times* and other business sources. They develop their reading skills and acquire essential business vocabulary. The texts provide a context for language work and discussion later in the unit.

Listening

The authentic listening texts are based on interviews with businesspeople and experts in their field. Students develop listening skills such as prediction, listening for specific information and note-taking. They can, if they prefer, watch the interviews on the DVD-ROM.

Language review

These sections develop students' awareness of the common problem areas at upper-intermediate level. They focus on accuracy and knowledge of key areas of grammar. If students already know the grammar point, this section serves as a quick check for them and the teacher. If they need more explanation, they are referred to the *Grammar reference* at the back of the Course Book.

There is further grammar practice in the Practice File and in the Business Grammar and Usage book (see *Extending the course*).

Skills

This section helps learners to develop their communication skills in the key business areas of presentations, meetings, negotiations, telephoning and social English. Each section contains a *Useful language* box which provides students with the phrases they need to carry out the business tasks in the regular role-play activities.

Case studies

Each unit ends with a case study linked to the unit's business topic. The case studies are based on realistic business problems or situations and are designed to motivate and actively engage students. Students use the language and communication skills which they have acquired while working through the unit. Typically, students will be involved in discussing business problems and recommending solutions through active group work.

Each case study ends with a realistic writing task. These tasks reflect the real world of business correspondence and will also help those students preparing for business English exams. Models of writing text types are given in the Writing file at the end of the Course Book.

After students have completed each case study they can watch the *Case study commentaries* on the DVD-ROM. Here, a consultant talks about the business issues raised by each case. This may in turn lead to further discussion of the case in class.

4 Using the course

Accessibility for teachers

Less-experienced teachers can sometimes find teaching business English a daunting experience. *Market Leader* sets out to provide the maximum support for teachers. The *Business brief* section at the beginning of each unit in the Teacher's Resource Book gives an overview of the business topic, covering key terms (given in bold, and which can be checked in the *Longman Dictionary of Business English*) and suggesting a list of titles for further reading and information.

Authenticity of content

One of the principles of the course is that students should deal with as much authentic content as their language level allows. Authentic reading and listening texts are motivating for students and bring the real world of business into the classroom, increasing students' knowledge of business practice and concepts. Due to its international coverage, the *Financial Times* has been a rich source of text, video and business information for the course.

The case studies present realistic business situations and problems and the communication activities based on them – group discussions, simulations and role plays – serve to enhance the authenticity of the course.

Flexibility of use

An essential requirement of business English materials is that they cater for the wide range of needs which students have, including different areas of interest and specialisation, different skills needs and varying amounts of time available to study. *Market Leader* offers teachers and course planners a unique range of flexible materials to help meet these needs. There are suggestions in this book on how to use the unit material extensively or intensively, with fast-track routes through the units focusing mainly on speaking and listening skills. The lesson notes include suggestions on extending the classwork through the DVD-ROM and photocopiable materials in the Text bank and Resource bank sections of this book. In addition, this book gives suggestions on how to extend the course using components including the Practice File, the Business Grammar and Usage book, and the *Market Leader* specialist series, which develops vocabulary and reading skills (see *Extending the course*).

5 Case studies that work

The following teaching tips will help when using case studies:

1 Draw on the students' knowledge of business and the world.
2 Ensure that all students have understood the case and the key vocabulary.
3 Encourage the students to use the language and communication skills they have acquired in the rest of the unit. A short review of the key language will help.
4 Focus on communication and fluency during the case study activities. Language errors can be dealt with at the end. Make a record of important errors and give students feedback at the end in a sympathetic and constructive way.
5 Allow students to reach their own conclusions. Many students expect there to be a correct answer. The teacher can give their own opinion but should stress that there usually is no single 'right' answer.
6 Encourage creative and imaginative solutions to the problems.

7 Encourage students to use people-management skills such as working in teams, leading teams, delegating and interacting effectively with each other.
8 Students should identify the key issues of the case and discuss all the options before reaching a decision.

6 Extending the course

Some students will require more input or practice in certain areas, either in terms of subject matter or skills, than is provided in the Course Book. In order to meet their needs, *Market Leader* provides a wide range of optional extra materials and components to choose from.

Business Grammar and Usage New Edition

For students needing more work on their grammar, this book provides reference and practice in all the most important areas of business English usage. It is organised into structural and functional sections. The book has been revised and updated for the Third Edition and complements the *Language review* sections of the Course Book. Relevant chapters for further study are referenced throughout the lesson notes of this Teacher's Resource Book in the *At a glance* section at the start of each unit.

Market Leader specialist titles

Many students will need to learn the language of more specialised areas of business English. To provide them with authentic and engaging material, *Market Leader* includes a range of special-subject books which focus on reading skills and vocabulary development. Each book includes two tests and a glossary of specialised language.

Longman Dictionary of Business English New Edition

This is the most up-to-date source of reference in business English today. Compiled from a wide range of text sources, it allows students and teachers rapid access to clear, straightforward definitions of the latest international business terminology. The fully updated New Edition includes an interactive CD-ROM with 35,000 key words pronounced in both British and American English, together with practice material for both the BEC and BULATS exams, and is now available as an iPhone or iPod touch app to download from the Pearson Longman website.

Market Leader website: www.market-leader.net

The *Market Leader* companion website provides up-to-date information about the Course Books and specialist titles and offers a wide range of materials teachers can use to supplement and enrich their lessons. In addition to tests for each level, the website provides links to websites relevant to units and topics in the Course Book and also downloadable glossaries of business terms.

The *Premier Lessons* subscription area of the website has a bank of ready-made lessons with authentic texts from the *Financial Times* that have student worksheets and answers. These lessons are regularly updated and can be searched in order to find relevant texts for the unit, topic and level that students are studying. *Premier Lessons* can be used in the classroom or for self-study.

Contents

CONTENTS

Resource bank

Communication

AT A GLANCE

	Classwork – Course Book	Further work
Lesson 1 *Each lesson (excluding case studies) is about 45 to 60 minutes. This does not include administration and time spent going through homework.*	**Starting up** Students discuss what they think makes a good communicator and talk about different forms of written and spoken communication. **Vocabulary: Good communicators** Students look at vocabulary related to good and bad communicators. **Listening: Improving communications** Students listen to an expert on communications talking about good practice in the area.	Test File: Entry test Practice File Vocabulary (page 4) Practice exercises: Vocabulary 1&2 (DVD-ROM) i-Glossary (DVD-ROM) Resource bank: Listening (page 188) Practice exercises: Listening (DVD-ROM)
Lesson 2	**Reading: E-mail: for and against** Students read an article about the good and bad aspects of e-mail. **Language review: Idioms** Students do language awareness and practice activities on some common idioms.	Text bank (pages 114–117) Practice File Language review (page 5) Practice Exercises: Language review 1&2 (DVD-ROM)
Lesson 3	**Skills: Dealing with communication breakdown** Students listen to a phone conversation between a customer and a supplier and practise skills involved in dealing with breakdowns in communication.	Resource bank: Speaking (page 175) Practice File Survival Business English (page 55) Practice Exercises: Skills (DVD-ROM)
Lesson 4 *Each case study is about 1½ to 2 hours*	**Case study: The price of success** A company that makes and sells hi-tech electronic products has internal and external communication problems. Students role-play the firm's directors and accept or reject solutions suggested by consultants.	Case study commentary (DVD-ROM) Resource bank: Writing (page 204) Practice File Writing (page 6)

For a fast route through the unit focusing mainly on speaking skills, just use the underlined sections.

For one-to-one situations, most parts of the unit lend themselves, with minimal adaptation, to use with individual students. Where this is not the case, alternative procedures are given.

BUSINESS BRIEF

Within companies, communication falls into two main areas. There is the communication of information and technical knowledge needed to do the job at hand. Here, paper-based communication is being replaced by the company **intranet**, with internal company websites only accessible by employees. Some very large companies are appointing **knowledge officers** to exploit the information in a company to the full and facilitate its communication to those who need it. (But in this age of increasingly accessible information, there will no doubt always be the **information hoarders**, employees and managers who find power and pleasure in keeping information for themselves, even if it would be useful to their colleagues.)

There is also what might be called 'celebration-exhortation'. The internal **company magazine** is the classic **communication channel** here. It may be produced **in-house** by a 'communications department' or **out-of-house** by journalists who specialise in this area. It may try to demonstrate how the company is putting its **mission statement** into action: the management may try to change employee behaviour by exhortation and by praising the performance of particular departments and individuals.

Externally, **advertising** has been the most visible form of communication with customers. Usually this is designed to increase product sales, but there is also **institutional advertising** designed to improve **perceptions** of the company as a whole. Companies naturally like to be seen as human and environmentally aware. But the communication between companies and their customers is increasingly becoming two-way, with **customer service centres** designed to gather information, not just complaints, from customers about all aspects of use of a company's products. Ideally, this information feeds back into product modification and new product design. Additionally some companies are now using social software and micro-blogging sites such as Facebook and Twitter to communicate with their customers. See Unit 10 for more on **customer relationship management**.

Equally, a company must communicate with its investors, and **investor relations** are becoming an important specialised area of **public relations**. Investors want to know how their money is being used and what their prospects are.

Then there is the wider public audience to attend to. **Press conferences** may be called to announce important events such as product launches. **Press releases** may be issued to communicate more routine information. There is also the specialised area of **crisis management** and **damage control** (see Unit 11).

Whatever a company does, it has an **image**, so it should try to influence (some would say 'manipulate') the moulding of this image. This is one reason why the **communications industry**, in all its forms, is a multibillion-dollar business.

Read on

Paul Argenti: *Corporate Communication*, McGrawHill, 2009 edition

Joep Cornelissen: *Corporate Communication: A Guide to Theory and Practice*, Sage, 2008

John Doorley and Helio Fred Garcia: *Reputation Management: The Key to Successful Public Relations and Corporate Communication*, Routledge, 2010

Donald Hislop: *Knowledge Management in Organizations*, OUP, 2009

Thomas J Lauria: *Investor Relations: The Art and Philosophy of Effective Corporate Communications*, Lulu, 2008

LESSON NOTES

LESSON NOTES

Warmer

- Divide the board into areas and write one or two words in each area, like this:

drums pigeon post	painting
newspapers radio	language sign language

- Get the students, in pairs, to list all the forms of communication they can think of by adding to each group. Elicit their responses and complete the table on the board, perhaps to produce something like this:

drums pigeon post smoke signals semaphore Morse code telephone	painting sculpture music
newspapers radio television Internet interactive television	language sign language body language dance

- Invite comments and encourage discussion. (The students may come up with other responses, or organise them in other ways, but it doesn't matter.)

Overview

- Tell the students that they will be looking at communication, especially in the context of organisations.
- Ask the students to look at the Overview section on page 6. Tell them a little about the things on the list, using the table on page 8 of this book as a guide. Tell them which points you will be covering in the current lesson and in later lessons.

Quotation

- Write the quotation quickly on the board.
- Tell the students that it's from Ernest Hemingway, the famous American novelist. Ask if anyone has read his novels, e.g. *A Farewell to Arms, For Whom the Bell Tolls, The Old Man and the Sea.*
- Ask the students to discuss, in pairs, whether they think they listen enough when others are speaking.
- In a whole-group discussion afterwards, ask pairs for their opinions.

Starting up

These questions introduce the theme of communication and provide an opportunity for some speaking practice.

A

- Discuss the question in small groups or with the whole class. Rather than doing this in the abstract, take some well-known figures from television, politics, etc. and ask students what makes them good communicators (or not). Be tactful when discussing political figures. Students might mention body language, speaking style, ease that people have in identifying with them, etc. You could discuss what makes for charisma, the way that some people have a powerful attractive quality as communicators and leaders that makes people admire them and want to follow them.

B

- Ask the students, still in their groups, to choose the three most important criteria in the context of: a) native speakers and b) non-native speakers of a language. (The emphasis on grammatical accuracy will probably be different for a) and b)).
- Discuss answers with the whole class.

C

- Discuss the question with the whole class and write their ideas on the board. You may need to prompt them to think about such things as use of jargon, formality/informality, tone of voice, etc.

D

- Ask students to discuss the first question in pairs.
- Elicit feedback. Get students to give reasons for their preferences. (This will allow you to see who likes giving presentations and it will also give students the opportunity to talk about texting, e-mail, use of social networking sites such as Facebook, etc.)
- Ask the whole class to brainstorm question 2: the problems that can occur with the different forms of communication – a vast area ranging, for example, from the pitfalls of oral negotiations where each side has different interpretations of the outcome, to the

damage caused by indiscreet e-mails. Again, list their ideas on the board. (A topical issue that they might mention is the lack of privacy on social networking sites: for example, possible employers might have access to potentially damaging information.)

- Ask students to discuss, in pairs, how these problems can be solved.

- Elicit feedback.

- If you are doing this lesson at the beginning of a course and you have not done a needs analysis, this exercise forms a good basis for one. Agree with the students which communication forms are most important for them or need most practice. Note down what they say and refer to these notes regularly while you are planning and doing the rest of the course, so as to modify activities, emphasis of the course, etc.

One-to-one

This forms a good basis for a needs analysis, if you haven't already done one. It may give you ideas for role play of specific activities to complement those in the Course Book, based on your student's particular work situation.

Vocabulary: Good communicators

Students look at vocabulary typically used to describe good and bad communicators.

A – B

- Work on pronunciation of the words, without going into meanings at this stage. Get individual students to repeat the difficult ones after you, paying particular attention to stress: *arTICulate*, etc.

- Put the students in threes and get them to put words into groups: the good and the bad, and then into the more specific groups in Exercise B. If available, get each three to consult a good general dictionary, such as the *Longman Dictionary of Contemporary English*.

Exercise A

Good: articulate, responsive, coherent, sensitive, eloquent, extrovert, succint, fluent, persuasive, focused

Bad: hesitant, inhibited, reserved, rambling, vague

Exercise B

1 succinct
2 inhibited/reserved
3 rambling
4 articulate
5 coherent
6 persuasive
7 extrovert
8 responsive

C – D ◄)) CD1.1

- Get the students, in pairs, to read the talk and fill in the blanks. Play the recording for them to check their answers.

2 interrupt
3 clarify
4 confuse
5 explain
6 digress
7 ramble
8 engage

E

- Explicit examples of good communicators, either from pairs or the whole class. Prompt the students by mentioning different occupations: politicians, actors, news presenters, advertisers, etc.

◉ i-Glossary

Listening: Improving communications

Alastair Dryburgh is an expert on communication. He talks about:

- four key points about communication
- whether companies are communicating better with customers than before
- one example of bad communication

A – B ◄)) CD1.2

- Get the students to look at question A and listen once or twice to the first part of the interview, depending on their level. Elicit the answer.

- Get the students to look at the question in B and play the recording again. Elicit the four points.

Exercise A

No, he doesn't. He thinks it can make communication both better and worse.

Exercise B

1 People have limited attention, so communicate as succinctly as possible.
2 Recognise that communication is about meaning, so don't dump lots of data on people.
3 It's as much about listening as it is about telling things.
4 If communication is going to be effective, there's got to be some sort of emotional connection in it.

C ◄)) CD1.3

- Play the second part of the interview two or three times and get students to answer the question.

Amazon communicates well because you always know where you are – you get confirmation when you order something and further confirmation when the item is sent. They also make suggestions for things you might like to buy, based on what you've bought in the past or on what other people have bought.

D 🔊 CD1.4

- Get students to look at the questions. Play the third part of the interview once or twice and get students to answer the questions.

The company has introduced a computerised voicemail system that is very frustrating for the user: it is very difficult to speak to a real person, the options don't correspond to the callers' problems and the caller ends up going round in circles or hanging up. The company should simplify the system and make it easier to get through to a real person.

E

- Ask the students to work in pairs to find good and bad examples of companies as communicators.
- Then discuss the findings of the pairs with the whole class.

  ◎ Students can watch the interview with Alastair Dryburgh on the DVD-ROM.

  ➡ Resource bank: Listening (page 188)

Reading: E-mail: for and against

This article is about the advantages and disadvantages of e-mail.

A – B

- Get your students to discuss the questions in pairs. Discuss the findings with the whole group and ask the students about their personal experiences of using e-mail, particularly for communication within their company or institution.

C

- Get the students to look through the possible headlines and choose the best. Ask them to look through the article quickly, not in detail, and decide on the best title for the article.
- With the whole class, check that they have chosen title 3: 'A quiet word beats sending e-mail'.

D

- Get students to read the whole article in more detail in pairs. Go round the class and assist where necessary.
- With the whole class, list the advantages and disadvantages. Do this at a good pace.

Advantages: productivity increase; effective transmitter of documents and data; forces sender to think through arguments carefully and express themselves logically; allows swift replies to lots of different questions when time is short; don't have to allow for journey times or travel costs, unreliable postage or engaged phones/voicemail; economical for keeping in touch with distant contacts; available 24 hours a day; good for pitching discreetly and directly to someone powerful.

Disadvantages: business best done face to face or on the phone; recipient of e-mail doesn't hear tone of voice or see facial expressions; sender can't modify e-mail half way through to avoid causing offence; can't tell the mood of the e-mailer; easy to send an irritable response when angry; the e-mail is a more permanent form of communication; easier to be tough, get away with weak excuses, make things up or say no; less human; too much spam/junk; a distraction, e.g. in meetings.

E

- Do this as a quick-fire whole-class activity with the whole class.

1 face to face
2 causing offence
3 get away with
4 make things up
5 keeping in touch with
6 pitching to someone

F

- Get students to work in pairs. Go round and assist where necessary.

1 keeping in touch with
2 get away with
3 making things up
4 face to face
5 pitching
6 causing offence

G

- Get the students to discuss answers to the questions in pairs or threes for a few minutes and then to report back to the class. Deal with question 2 tactfully, for example, if you are dealing with people from different workplaces.

➡ Text bank (pages 114–117)

Language review: Idioms

In this section, the students look at different idioms. (Students usually love them.)

A – B

- Explain what an idiom is (an expression with a meaning that can be difficult to guess from the meanings of its separate words) and ask the students if they have any favourite idioms in English.

- Get the students to complete the exercise in pairs. Go round the class and assist where necessary, and then discuss the answers with the whole class.

Exercise A

a) nutshell **b)** point **c)** grapevine **d)** picture
e) stick **f)** wavelength **g)** tail **h)** purposes
i) bush **j)** mouth **k)** wall **l)** loop

Exercise B

1 g **2** f **3** a **4** e **5** l **6** d **7** b
8 c **9** j **10** k **11** l **12** h

C

- Do as a quick-fire activity, discussing the answers with the whole class.

---

1 get straight to the point **2** on the same wavelength **3** put you in the picture **4** talking at cross-purposes **5** beating about the bush **6** hear (*or* heard) on the grapevine **7** put it in a nutshell **8** got the wrong end of the stick **9** can't make head nor tail of it **10** talking to a brick wall **11** from the horse's mouth **12** keep me in the loop

---

D

- Ask the students, in simultaneous pairs, to take turns asking and answering the questions. Go round and assist where necessary.

- Bring the class to order. Get different individual pairs to repeat their exchanges for the whole class.

- Emphasise the fact that idioms have to be word-perfect (explain this expression) otherwise they can sound ridiculous. Work on expressions that have been causing problems, getting students to say the right thing.

Skills: Dealing with communication breakdown

In this section, the students discuss the kind of communication problems that can occur on the phone, and listen to two different versions of the same conversation.

A

- Get the students, in pairs, to brainstorm possible expressions for each situation, then to report to and discuss with the whole group. Draw their attention to the 'Useful language' box at the bottom of the page, which has expressions for all seven situations.

Suggested answers

a Could you slow down, please?
   Could you speak up, please?
   Could you speak a little louder, please?

b Could you hold on a minute, please?

c Sorry, what exactly does … mean?
   Sorry, I don't know what … means.

d Could you spell that for me, please?

e Could you give me a little more information, please?
   Could you give me some more details, please?
   Could you expand on that, please? (more formal)

f Sorry, I can't hear you. Could you call me back, please?
   Sorry, it's a bad line. I can't hear you.

g Let's see if I've got this right.
   Let me check if I've got this right.
   Could I just confirm what you've told me?

B 🔊)) CD1.5

Play the recording once and get the students to identify the problems the speakers have (all of them).

C 🔊)) CD1.6

- Play the recording once or twice and get the students, in pairs, to make notes on why this second conversation is better.

- Elicit feedback from the whole class.

- He asks Klebermann to hold on while he gets a pen.

- He says that he didn't understand what Klebermann said. He asks him to slow down.

- He asks for more information.

- He confirms what he has heard: *Let me check that.*

- He asks Klebermann to spell the name of the company.

- He checks the number of lasers that are required.

- Klebermann confirms the quantity of lasers that are required.

- He asks Klebermann to explain the meaning of *roll-out.*

- He mentions that the line is bad and that he can't hear Klebermann very well.

- He asks for more information.

- Klebermann suggests calling back, as he can't hear Koichi well.

D 🔊)) CD1.6

- Before students listen again, get them to work in pairs and try to predict (or remember) the missing words.

- Play recording again. Stop at points where students can complete the gaps.

> **1** hold on a second   **2** didn't catch that; slow down
> **3** check; Got   **4** spell that for   **5** did you say
> **6** does; mean   **7** a bad line; speak up   **8** call you back

E

- Read out each of the extracts in turn and ask the students to match them with the points in Exercise A.

> **1** b   **2** a   **3** g   **4** d   **5** g   **6** c   **7** e   **8** f

F

- Go through the expressions in the Useful language box, practising stress and intonation in particular.

- Get the students to role-play the situation in simultaneous pairs sitting back-to-back, using expressions from the Useful language box. Circulate and monitor.

- When the students have finished, praise strong points and mention one or two things that students should pay particular attention to. Then get 'public' performances from one or two individual pairs in front of the whole group.

- There are more situations like this to role-play in the Resource bank, on page 175 of this book.

 Resource bank: Speaking (page 175)

CASE STUDY

The price of success

In this case study, the students look at the communication problems at a manufacturer and distributor of hi-tech electronic products and make suggestions for improvements.

- Divide the class into three groups of students. Get one group to read the Background section silently, another the 'A product defect' section and the third group the 'Lawrence Discount Stores' section.

- Circulate and answer any queries.

- Quickly put the headings in the left-hand column of the table below on the board and elicit information from the group so as to complete the column on the right. Do this at a brisk pace.

Company	W. C. Hooper Inc. (WCH)
Activity	Manufacturer and distributor of hi-tech electronic products
Based in	Seattle
CEO	William Hooper
Key problem	Internal and external communication problems impacting on performance
Product defect, and key related issues	Cell phone became very hot and about to explode
	Customer service dept. sent replacement phone, but did not inform Marketing or R&D
	Phone withdrawn after a number of similar complaints
Lawrence Discount Stores	Richard Lawrence one of WCH's best and oldest customers
	Lawrence told Hooper he would probably order 5,000 EX-120s, executive toys (teach this expression).
	Hopper informed Regional Sales Manager (RSM) by phone
	When Lawrence ordered 5 weeks later, sales manager said it was out of stock.
	Lawrence complained to Hooper that his order was not given priority.
	RSM said he was waiting for confirmation.

- Make sure the students understand the situation by getting individual students to expand orally on different parts of the table, using complete sentences.

- At this point, get students to close their books and say what they think the most pressing communications problems are at WCH and what the solutions might be.

- Hopefully they will anticipate the communications problems in the panel at the top of page 13 in the Course Book. Get students to open their books again and run through the points there quickly.

- Point out that these issues are the ones that Betty Friedman, WCH's new Communications Director, has asked the consultants, Ward Associates, to look at.

◀)) CD1.7, 1.8

- Establish that the students are going to hear Hooper's reactions to the consultants' recommendations.

- Tell them they will have to make notes about Hooper's attitude to a) weekly reports, b) appointing a new account manager and c) dealing with defective products – write these up on the left hand side of a new table on the board.

- Play recording 1.7, pausing for the students to make notes after each point.

- Check answers with the whole class.

Weekly reports	Information overload (teach this expression)
Appointment of a new account manager	Will add to costs
	Customers like personal approach
	Wouldn't like to deal with new person
Dealing with defective products	Customer services to inform other depts. if someone complains – too bureaucratic, too time-consuming

- Explain that the students are going to hear one of WCH's sales reps talking to the company's head of communications.

- This time they will just have to give an oral account of the key idea.

- Play recording 1.8 once or twice and then check answer with the whole class.

The sales rep agrees with her CEO that paperwork is a waste of time that could be better spent on personal contact with clients.

Task

- Explain that in the task the students work in small groups as directors of WCH to discuss the consultants' recommendations. Underline the fact that students will also have to bring their own ideas on improving communications.

- Divide the class into groups of three or four. Appoint a spokesperson in each group who will report to the whole class after the activity.

- Get students to begin the task. Go round the class and assist where necessary.

- Circulate and monitor, noting strong and less strong language areas.

- Bring the class to order when the discussion is over in most of the groups.

- Get members from each group to summarise the discussion with the board's reactions to recommendations and the original ideas that they came up with.

- Praise the strong points that you heard in the small group discussions and talk about areas for improvement, getting relevant students to reformulate what they said with the corrections you suggested.

Students can watch the case study commentary on the DVD-ROM.

Writing

- The students write an e-mail from the communications director at WCH to the head of Ward Associates, with a summary of the decisions taken by the board. (These should be the decisions they came to in their own groups.)

Writing file: Course Book, page 127

Resource bank: Writing (page 204)

One-to-one

Go through the activities as outlined above. In the task, you could take the roles of different directors with different points of view, while your student sticks to just one role.

International marketing

	Classwork – Course Book	Further work
Lesson 1 *Each lesson (excluding case studies) is about 45 to 60 minutes. This does not include administration and time spent going through homework.*	**Starting up** Students discuss issues related to marketing. **Vocabulary: Marketing word partnerships** Students look at the vocabulary of international marketing.	Practice File Vocabulary (page 8) Practice exercises: Vocabulary 1&2 (DVD-ROM) i-Glossary (DVD-ROM)
Lesson 2	**Reading: Italian luxury** Students read an article about Italian luxury brands, discuss the issues raised and do an exercise on word partnerships. **Listening: How to market internationally** Students listen to two marketing specialists talking about international marketing strategies and the training of international marketers. **Language review: Noun compounds and noun phrases** Students work on the structure of noun compounds and noun phrases.	Text bank (pages 118–121) Resource bank: Listening (page 189) Practice exercises: Listening (DVD-ROM) Practice File Language review (page 9) Practice exercises: Language review 1&2 (DVD-ROM) ML Grammar and Usage (Unit 11)
Lesson 3	**Skills: Brainstorming** Students look at the principles of brainstorming, listen to a brainstorming session, and work on expressions used in sessions like this. They then put these ideas into action in their own brainstorming sessions.	Resource bank: Speaking (page 176) Practice File Survival Business English (page 57) Practice exercises: Skills (DVD-ROM)
Lesson 4 *Each case study is about 1½ to 2 hours.*	**Case study: Henri-Claude Cosmetics** A French cosmetics company looks at ways of marketing a men's fragrance worldwide. Students brainstorm ideas for a global product marketing strategy amd devise a promotional television commercial.	Case study commentary (DVD-ROM) Resource bank: Writing (page 205) Practice File Writing (page 10)

For a fast route through the unit focusing mainly on speaking skills, just use the underlined sections.

For one-to-one situations, most parts of the unit lend themselves, with minimal adaptation, to use with individual students. Where this is not the case, alternative procedures are given.

BUSINESS BRIEF

'The world's youth prefer Coke to tea, trainers to sandals,' wrote one marketing specialist recently. This implies that tastes everywhere are becoming similar and **homogenous**. But the watchword should still be '**Think global, act local**'. Acting local means having local market knowledge: there are still wide **variations** in taste, customs, behaviour and expectations between consumers in different markets, even markets that from the outside look very similar, like those in Europe. It means, for example, recognising attachments to local brands, how business is done in each place, and so on.

Of course, these are issues that a company with a **global presence** has to address. But even companies that seem as if they have been global forever had to start from a home base. For example, it took Marlboro 30 years and McDonalds 20 years to become truly global organisations.

How to enter overseas markets in the first place? Philip Kotler enumerates the various methods:

- **Indirect export:** Exporters use an **intermediary** such as an **export agent** to deal with buyers in the overseas market.

- **Direct export:** Companies handle their own exports, for example, by setting up **overseas sales offices**.

- **Licensing:** Companies sell the rights to use a **manufacturing process, trademark** or **patent** for a **fee** or **royalty.** In services such as hotels, the company may negotiate a **management contract** with a local business to run the hotels on its behalf.

- **Joint ventures:** Two companies, for example an overseas firm and a local one, may work together to develop a particular market.

- **Direct investment:** The company buys a local firm, or sets up its own **manufacturing subsidiaries**.

Of course, these different arrangements involve different levels of commitment, investment and risk. Kotler talks about the **internationalisation process**, where firms move (hopefully) through these stages:

- **Stage 1:** no regular export activities
- **Stage 2:** export via independent representatives/agents
- **Stage 3:** establishment of overseas sales subsidiaries
- **Stage 4:** establishment of production facilities abroad

This process will help them to progress towards global thinking and local action as they expand internationally. At different stages, companies will have different levels of understanding of the markets where they are trying to develop. Each step in the process requires different levels and types of support.

Read on

Isobel Doole, Robin Lowe: *International Marketing Strategy*, Cengage, 2008

Pervez Ghauri, Philip Cateora: *International Marketing*, McGraw Hill, 2009

Svend Hollensen: *Global Marketing: A Decision-oriented Approach,* Financial Times/Prentice Hall, 2007

Philip Kotler et al: *Marketing Management*, Prentice Hall, 2009

LESSON NOTES

Warmer

- Copy the table below onto the board. Ask students to consider the place of the international products on the left in relation to the products on the right in their own country/countries. For example:

  - Who drinks Coke or Pepsi? Is it all generations? What do people drink with meals?

  - Who goes to fast-food restaurants? Do families go there for snacks and family meals?

  - Who wears trainers? Is it only younger people? Do business people wear them to work and then change into shoes when they get there? etc.

Coca-Cola and Pepsi Cola	tea, coffee and local soft drinks
fast food	traditional food of the country
trainers	shoes or sandals
jeans	trousers
Western rock music	popular music of the country

- Discuss the place and use of the products with the whole class.

Overview

- Tell the students that they will be looking at international marketing.

- Ask the students to look at the Overview section on page 14. Tell them a little about the things on the list, using the table on page 17 of this book as a guide. Tell them which points you will be covering in the current lesson and which in later lessons.

Quotation

- Ask the students what they understand by the quotation on page 14. It should lead to some interesting discussion.

Starting up

This section introduces the theme of international marketing and provides an opportunity for some speaking practice.

A

- Get the students to discuss in pairs or small groups with one member of each group taking notes. Then ask the notetaker in each group to report their findings to the whole class.

Exercise A

Examples include:

- Cosmetics: Dior, Maybelline

- Soft drinks: Coca-Cola, Pepsi Cola

- Electrical equipment: Sony, Zanussi

- Clothing: Gap, Benetton, Zara

- Cars: Most cars are now marketed internationally. Ask students if they can think of any that aren't – perhaps ones they see in their own countries but never abroad.

B

- If the students run short of ideas, get them to research some brands for homework and report back in the next lesson.

C

- Discuss in pairs or as a whole-class activity.

Vocabulary: Marketing word partnerships

Students look at the vocabulary of international marketing and use it actively.

A – **C**

- Get students to work individually or in pairs on these three exercises. Go round the class and assist where necessary.

- Bring the class to order and elicit answers.

Exercise A

1 marketing   **2** market   **3** product   **4** customer
5 brand

Exercise B

1 marketing strategy   **2** market segmentation
3 product feature   **4** customer profile
5 Brand positioning

Exercise C

2 promotion   **3** market research
4 domestic market   **5** withdraw a product
6 slogan   **7** exporter

- Get students to talk about particular products, using these and related expressions. Don't ask the students to 'make up sentences' with the expressions, but get them to have a natural discussion incorporating them, led by you.

D

- Get students to discuss the issues in pairs.

- Go round the class and assist where necessary. Note how they are using the marketing vocabulary.

- Bring the class to order. Get individual students to say what they came up with in their pairs.

- Praise good use of marketing vocabulary and work on expressions that require this, getting students to say the correct forms.

 i-Glossary

Reading: Italian luxury

Students read an article about Italian luxury brands, discuss the issues raised and do an exercise on word partnerships.

A

● Get the students to discuss in pairs or small groups and then bring findings together with the whole class. (They are all names of designers and luxury brands.)

B

● Get the students to read the article quickly, scanning it for the information needed to do the exercise.

---

1 Palazzo Della Valle, Corso Venezia, Milan
2 leather shoes and bags 3 Diego Della Valle
4 Louis Vuitton, Hermès, Chanel 5 China and India
6 To complete the globalisation of Tod's

C – D

● Get the students to do these exercises in pairs and then check the answers with whole class (the correct information is underlined).

Exercise C

Tod's Group wishes to convey the charms of the Italian lifestyle to the world's rich. To do this, it focuses on ~~celebrity and glamour~~ its traditional, hand-made, century-old heritage, and its new advertising campaign will feature Italian ~~celebrities~~ families. The Chairman says he wants to expand into India and China to capture consumers there who appreciate the Italian lifestyle. To enter such big markets, Tod's will need to think about ~~quantity as well as quality~~ quality not quantity.

Tod's is primarily a ~~fashion~~ luxury-goods company and needs to be much bigger. China and India have more possibility for growth than Tod's traditional markets. The Chairman is <u>not</u> worried ~~because~~ that China will be able to produce luxury goods more cheaply. In future, Tod's will look to ~~lower production costs by manufacturing in low-cost countries~~ maintain the concept of excellence.

Exercise D

1 c 2 a/b 3 d 4 b/a 5 e

E

● Get students to discuss the issues in questions in pairs or groups of three.

● Go round the class and assist where necessary. Note how they are using the marketing vocabulary.

● Bring the class to order. Get individual students to say what they came up with in their groups.

● Again, praise good use that you heard of marketing vocabulary and work on expressions that require further practice, getting students to say the correct forms.

Text bank (pages 118–121)

Listening: How to market internationally

Students listen to two marketing specialists: Svend Hollensen, Professor of International Marketing at the University of South Denmark, talking about international marketing strategies, and Darrell Kofkin, Chief Executive of the Global Marketing Network, on training for international marketers.

A 🔊 CD1.9

● Get the students to listen once or twice to the first interview.

● Elicit the answers.

---

1 a) where you have one product and you sell it all over in the same format

   b) where you try to adapt your product to the different cultures, to different countries that you are in.

2 a) It has marketed one product concept for the whole world and this product is actually selling all over in the same format. It is a small company, based in Denmark and in Sweden. It is 'born global', i.e. it is getting into the global markets very fast by setting up production in Uganda in Africa. From there, it tries to sell in other countries of the world. So, by setting up a website from where they also sell these coffee products, they can sell to all kinds of hotel chains and to airline companies and to different retail chains.

   b) It's one example of a global brand that will sell all over the world.

● Encourage discussion of any points that arise, particularly if any of the students have experience of attempting to market a product globally.

B 🔊 CD1.10

● Play the second interview once or twice, stopping at convenient points to allow students to write down the answers.

---

1 marketers 2 practices 3 knowledge
4 techniques 5 international 6 report
7 business plan 8 presentation 9 webcast
10 internal briefing paper 11 worldwide
12 capabilities 13 global business

● Ask students what they think of the approach to training in this context.

◎ Students can watch the interviews with Svend Hollensen and Darrell Kofkin on the DVD-ROM.

Resource bank: Listening (page 189)

Language review: Noun compounds and noun phrases

This section looks at an area of grammar which can cause difficulty, particularly for those from some language backgrounds such as Latin-based ones.

● Go through points 1 and 2 with whole class, commenting where necessary.

A – C

● Get the students to work on these exercises in pairs.

● Go round the class and assist where necessary.

Exercise A
1 advertising campaign 2 chief executive
3 fashion producers 4 luxury-goods company
5 growth potential

Exercise B
1 leader 2 check 3 market 4 exchange
5 contract 6 conditions 7 product

Exercise C
1 really impressive advertising campaign
2 new customer relations department
3 highly competitive mobile phone market
4 incredibly successful product launch
5 loyal customer base
6 extremely thorough sales report
7 absolutely brilliant global campaign
8 increasingly competitive marketing environment

D ◀)) CD1.11

● Play the recording and check the answers with the whole class. For Exercise C, practise stress and intonation of the compounds, e.g. 'It was a *REally imPRESSive ADvertising camPAIGN*'.

Skills: Brainstorming

The idea here is to introduce the students to the concept of brainstorming (if they are not already familiar with it). Students look at the principles behind it, listen to a brainstorming session and work on expressions used in sessions like this. They then put these ideas into action in their own brainstorming sessions.

A

● Get the students to go through the points in pairs or small groups. Circulate and monitor.

● Round up the findings with the whole class. There are no right or wrong answers, but some of the issues below may emerge.

1 Yes, but sometimes it is good to be vague about the purpose of the meeting, so that participants don't look immediately at the specific situation. This will keep the discussion more open-ended and throw up ideas that otherwise might not have occurred.

2 Theoretically, no. The idea is to get everyone involved as equals. However, people in some cultures would always expect the most senior person to speak first, whatever the type of meeting.

3 Probably a good idea.

4 This should be one of the main features of brainstorming, in order to encourage as many contributions as possible, although sessions where this actually happens may be rare.

5 In theory, yes, but extremely bizarre suggestions would probably be seen as wasting time.

6 Easier said than done, but it's probably more acceptable to interrupt in brainstorming than other types of session.

7 Theoretically, the speculation should be as wide-ranging as possible, but most participants would probably set limits as to what is relevant.

8 Probably a good idea. Details can come later when developing particular ideas.

B ◀)) CD1.12

● Play the recording once or twice and get the students, in pairs, to answer the questions.

1 To come up with suggestions for the location, accommodation and leisure-time activities for their international sales conference

2 Amsterdam, south of Portugal, Florence

C ◀)) CD1.13

● Play the recording once or twice and get the students, in their pairs, to note the answers to the questions. Then check with the whole class and explain any difficulties.

1 Four-star hotels or boutique hotels

2 A half day to see the sights; a gala dinner; an hour a day for networking and for people to meet and discuss anything

D

● Get the students, in pairs, to match the expressions.

Stating objectives: **1**
Expressing enthusiasm: **2, 5, 6, 8**
Encouraging contributions: **3, 4, 5, 9**
Agreeing: **2, 7, 8, 10**

● With the whole class, work on the stress and intonation of the expressions where necessary, e.g. 'That's *GREAT!*'

- The idea here is to put some of the principles of brainstorming into action. (Bear in mind points 1–8 in A above.)

- Organise the class into groups of three or four for maximum participation.

- If there is more than one group, get different groups to do different situations in parallel. Appoint someone in each group who will note down the ideas produced, ready to report them to the whole class at the end of the activity.

- Make sure students are clear about the background to their situation.

- Start the activity. Circulate and monitor.

- When students have finished, get the notetaker in each group to say what ideas they came up with.

- Praise strong points from your monitoring of the brainstorming sessions and mention language points that the students should pay particular attention to. Get individual students to go back to the context where the mistake occurred and say the new, improved version.

One-to-one

Encourage the student to come up with ideas for each situation as quickly as possible. Do not interrupt. Afterwards praise and correct language as in the final bullet point above.

➡ Resource bank: Speaking (page 176)

CASE STUDY

Henri-Claude Cosmetics – creating a global brand

A French multinational company wants to launch a men's fragrance for the global market.

- Get the students to look at the background of HCC and Key features of *Physique*.

- Circulate and answer any queries. Discuss common queries with whole group.

- Quickly put the points in the left-hand column of the table below on the board and elicit information from the group so as to complete the column on the right. (Point out that the information here is not in the same order as in the book.)

- Make sure the students understand the situation by getting individual students to expand orally on a part of the table, using complete sentences

Background: HCC

Company	Henri-Claude Cosmetics (HCC)
Activity	cosmetics and personal care
Based in	France

Background: Physique

Ingredients	redwood, cedar, spices, fresh, woody, long-lasting aroma
Sales	HCC's best-selling product
Pricing	premium, top-end
Target audience in France	men aged 30–40
Qualities	Men feel confident, attractive, sophisticated; very appealing to women
Global launch plans	To be launched in 10 countries next year Aim: international recognition Campaign theme: '*Physique* for the Urban Man'

🔊 CD1.14

- Write the points in the left-hand column of the table below on the board.

- Play the recording once or twice and ask the students to make notes on the six points shown.

Physique

Target audience	Change from older, sophisticated, aspiring men to younger, masculine, adventurous, energetic men
Brand image	Change in image required
Name	Name change required
Positioning	No longer premium but high-volume, mass market
Packaging	Create new look with universal appeal
Slogan	Marketing dept. must start thinking about one

Product details

- Get students to look at notes individually. Go round the class and assist where necessary.

- With the whole class, get students to expand on notes orally in complete sentences, e.g. 'The bottle for *Physique* is tall, round and solid. It's black, and it's got the brand name in the centre. It's got a silver top and comes with (teach this expression) a screw-top or as a spray.'

- Continue with the whole class asking different students to continue the description.

- Work on any remaining difficulties that have cropped up so far.

Task

- Divide the class into groups of three or four. Explain the purpose of the brainstorming session and remind them that they shouldn't spend too long on each point.

- Circulate and monitor, noting strong and less strong language areas.

- Bring the class to order and get a representative from each group to talk about their ideas for the whole class.

- Praise the strong points and talk about areas for improvement, getting relevant students to reformulate what they said with the corrections you suggested.

- Then get them to move on, in the same groups, to the second part of the task. If there is an overhead projector in the classroom, hand out pens and transparencies so that each group representative can make a presentation to the whole class.

- Bring the class to order. Get group representatives to make their presentations.

- Again, praise the strong points and talk about areas for improvement, getting relevant students to reformulate what they said with the corrections you suggested.

   ◉ Students can watch the case study commentary on the DVD-ROM.

Writing

- Get the students to write the action minutes of their particular brainstorming session for homework. (Bring their attention to the format of action minutes in the Writing file, Course Book page 130.)

  ⇨ Writing file, page 130

  ⇨ Resource bank: Writing (page 205)

One-to-one

Get your student to glean the information to complete the tables and then have a one-to-one brainstorming session, where you both come up with ideas. Move on quickly from point to point.

UNIT 3 Building relationships

AT A GLANCE

	Classwork – Course Book	Further work
Lesson 1 *Each lesson (excluding case studies) is about 45 to 60 minutes. This does not include administration and time spent going through homework.*	**Starting up** Students discuss how good they are at building relationships, listen to an interview and do a quiz about their ability to build relationships. **Vocabulary: Describing relations** This deals with the vocabulary of relationships, looking at some typical word combinations. **Listening: Business partnerships** Students listen to Alison Ward, head of Global Corporate Responsibility at Cadbury, talking about building good relationships.	**Practice File** Vocabulary (page 12) **Practice exercises: Vocabulary 1&2** (DVD-ROM) **i-Glossary** (DVD-ROM) **Resource bank: Listening** (page 190) **Practice exercises: Listening** (DVD-ROM)
Lesson 2	**Reading: Business networks in China** Students read about the importance of connections when doing business in China.	**Text bank** (pages 122–125)
Lesson 3	**Language review: Multi-word verbs** Students look at multi-word (phrasal) verbs and practise them in context. **Skills: Networking** Students study networking language in a series of situations, and practise the language in role plays.	**Practice File** Language review (page 13) **Practice exercises: Language review 1&2** (DVD-ROM) **ML Grammar and Usage** (Unit 9) **Resource bank: Speaking** (page 177–178) **Practice File** Survival Business English (page 59) **Practice exercises: Skills** (DVD-ROM)
Lesson 4 *Each case study is about 1½ to 2 hours*	**Case study: Al-Munir Hotel and Spa Group** An Arab hotel group wants to strengthen customer loyalty by getting to know its visitors better and encouraging them to return to its hotels. Students come up with a plan for building relationships with guests.	**Case study commentary** (DVD-ROM) **Resource bank: Writing** (page 206) **Practice File** Writing (page 14) **Test File: Progress test 1**

For a fast route through the unit focusing mainly on speaking skills, just use the underlined sections.

For one-to-one situations, most parts of the unit lend themselves, with minimal adaptation, to use with individual students. Where this is not the case, alternative procedures are given.

BUSINESS BRIEF

BUSINESS BRIEF

When someone works for an organisation, employers and employees have expectations about what is reasonable behaviour in a work context. There is a certain level of **trust** between people, and even if the news is full of stories of breakdowns in this trust, we think of them as exceptions to **established norms** in **social relationships**.

Business-to-business relationships

Networking events can be a good way to make new contacts – in some industries, **trade shows** are ideal for this. Some say that first impressions count. Others think that someone's character can only be judged after a lot of contact in business contexts and socially. This is why deciding on a **supplier** or **distributor** takes varying lengths of time in different cultures. To emphasise the importance of relationships like these, companies may refer to each other as **partners**.

When firms work together on a particular project, they may enter into a **strategic alliance**. This may take the form of a **joint venture** between two or three companies, or a **consortium** between several organisations. An alliance may be the prelude to a **merger** between companies. Journalists often use the language of betrothal and marriage to describe situations like this.

Companies may overcome legal and other barriers in order to merge, but, as in marriage, there is no guarantee that the relationship will work and last. The cultures of the two companies may be so incompatible that the promised increase in profitability and **shareholder value** does not materialise.

Relationship networks

Stakeholder theory holds that society is made up of a web of relationships, and that each member of this arrangement has its **stake** of interest and of responsibilities. In a company, the interested parties are its owners (shareholders), managers, employees, suppliers, distributors, and customers, who may or may not be end-users of its products or services. A large company's activities have an effect on the places where it operates (think especially of **company towns** dominated by one company) and on society as a whole. Some companies publish an independent **social audit** that goes beyond the traditional **annual report** and attempts to give a bigger picture of the company's place in society, the benefits it brings, the effects of its activities on people and the environment (see Unit 1: Communication). Some say that social audits give a false sense of **social responsibility**. Optimists reply that pressure from stakeholders such as shareholders and customers can bring positive changes in the way companies work, and benefits to society as a whole. Companies are increasingly sensitive to accusations of causing pollution, tolerating **racism** or using **sweatshop labour**. Companies are increasingly aware that their overall image, negative or positive, will eventually be reflected in their share price, an ultimate indicator of building good relationships, not just commercial ones.

Read on

Francis Buttle: *Customer Relationship Management*, Butterworth-Heinemann, 2008

Richard Gibbs and Andrew Humphries: *Strategic Alliances and Marketing Partnerships*, Kogan Page, 2009

Jeffrey S. Harrison et al: *Stakeholder Theory*, CUP, 2010

Rawn Shah: *Social Networking for Business*, Wharton School Publishing, 2010

LESSON NOTES

Warmer

- With the whole class, build up a 'mind map' on the board of a typical individual and their relationships. Draw a circle in the centre of the board showing the individual, with 'spokes' going out to other circles representing family, colleagues, boss, friends, clubs the individual belongs to, etc.

- Invite comments and encourage discussion of the map.

Overview

- Tell the students that they will be looking at building relationships, especially in organisations.

- Ask the students to look at the Overview section at the beginning of the unit. Tell them a little about the things on the list, using the table on page 25 of this book as a guide. Tell them which points you will be covering in the current lesson and which in later lessons.

Quotation

- Ask the students to look at the quotation and say what they think of it. (It would be hard to disagree with it!)

Starting up

This section focuses the students on the subject of the unit. There is also a brief listening extract.

A

- Get the students to discuss the quiz questions in pairs.
- Go round the class and assist where necessary.
- Bring the class to order and get representatives of pairs to say what answers they gave to each question.

B

- In the listening activity in Exercise C, the students will listen to Gillian Baker, the Business Relations Manager of an international training organisation, talking about how companies can build good business relationships.

- Before listening to the recording, tell the students specifically that Gillian Baker is going to talk about the key factors companies must consider when communicating with their clients. With the whole group, get the students to say what they think the key features of this communication might be and write them on the board. Some examples are:
  - they should get to know each other well
  - they should talk to each other regularly.

C ◀)) CD1.15

- Play recording 1.15 once or twice and get the students to:

- check which of the points they came up with were mentioned, and in what order, marking this on the list prepared on the board in Exercise B.

- note the points they didn't anticipate, adding them to the list.

- note the details of the example (company, situation, result).

Points mentioned:

Give the customer/supplier superior value and satisfaction; exceed customer's expectations; satisfy and delight customer to create product loyalty, which will lead to better company performance

Details of example:

Company: Lexus

Situation: mechanic tuned customer's radio to the same stations as the car he traded in

Result: customer delight and satisfaction

- Play the recording again. Confirm the key points about communication and work on remaining unfamiliar vocabulary.

D

- With the whole class, get individual students to answer the questions, giving their reasons.

Vocabulary: Describing relations

This section deals with the vocabulary of relationships, looking at some typical word combinations, and prepares the students to talk about relationships in the later activities in the unit.

A

- Ask the students to work in pairs, getting them to say whether the words they know are positive or negative. With the whole class, put these verbs into a table on the board.

- Then, with the whole class, explain the verbs they don't know, using full sentences, like this:

If something *jeopardises* relations, it puts them in danger.

If people *resume* relations, they start them again after a period when they had stopped.

- After each of your definitions, ask the students if the expression is positive or negative and put it on the table on the board.

Positive meaning: cement, cultivate, develop, encourage, establish, foster, improve, maintain, promote, restore, resume, strengthen

Negative meaning: cut off, damage, disrupt, jeopardise, sever, sour, undermine

B

- Get the students in pairs to discuss the sentences and choose the correct verb in each one.

1 damage   2 establish   3 strengthened
4 undermined   5 improving   6 disrupted
7 broke off   8 jeopardised   9 building up
10 fostered

C

- Explain any unfamiliar words, e.g. *imposition*, to the whole class.

- If the students are unfamiliar with this type of matching exercise, point out that they can look for clues like full stops at the end of the numbered elements, indicating that the following element will be a new sentence. Here, there are no full stops, but in 4, for example, the plural *excellent relations* shows that the continuation must have a plural verb, so a) or b) must be the continuation, but only a) makes sense.

- Get the students, in pairs, to match the two parts of the expressions quickly.

- Round up the results with the whole class.

1 e   2 d   3 b   4 a   5 c

D

- Get students to think and talk about companies they admire (and also ones, perhaps, that had good relations with customers in the past, but no longer do, analysing why this is). This is probably better as a whole class discussion, where you can ask leading questions. Ensure that your students use the verbs above in Exercise A correctly, and work on those that need further practice.

◎ i-Glossary

Listening: Business partnerships

Students listen to Alison Ward, Head of Global Corporate Responsibility at Cadbury. She talks about building good relationships and gives some examples.

A ◀)) CD1.16

- Go through the five points with the whole class (pointing out the pronunciation of 'cocoa' – two syllables, not three). Then play recording 1.16 and ask the students to make notes on each point.

- Get the students in pairs to compare notes on each point. Play the recording again if the students need you to.

- Have a whole-class round-up, checking the answers to each point. (If necessary, explain VSO – Voluntary Service Overseas – and what it does – a UK charity working on aid projects in the developing world.)

1 2008   2 70%   3 40%   4 50
5 United Nations Development Programme, Care, VSO, World Vision

B ◀)) CD1.17

- Play recording 1.17 and get students to complete the sentences.

1 Fairtrade certification   2 ethical choice
3 very powerful; understood; cocoa-farming communities

- Ask students if they have heard of Fairtrade and what they know about it.

C ◀)) CD1.18

- Play the recording and elicit the answers.

1 With milk farmers in the UK
2 They have been working to change the animal feed, the investment and the way the feed is delivered to the milk farmers, in order to make the farmers more efficient and reduce their carbon footprint.

- Ask students how they could reduce their own carbon footprint – driving less, flying less, etc.

◎ Students can watch the interview with Alison Ward on the DVD-ROM.

➡ Resource bank: Listening (page 190)

Reading: Business networks in China

Students read about the importance of connections when doing business in China.

A

- Get the students to answer this question before looking at the article. Answers will depend on students' industries, or ones they plan to enter; networking events, trade fairs, conferences and so on.

B

- Get students to skim through the article individually or in pairs to find the answers. Check answers with the whole class.

1 A Hong Kong businessman who has used his *guanxi* astutely to win licences and building permission
2 An ex-INSEAD student who has used his connections from there to build his company, Tudou
3 An INSEAD graduate and partner at Granite Global Ventures who helped Gary Wang to raise $8.6m
4 A businessman who runs the Chinese operations of a South Korean systems company and who did an Executive MBA at the Cheung Kong Graduate School of Business in Beijing
5 Person in charge of McKinsey's China practice in Shanghai

- If there's a Chinese-speaking student in the class, get them to give the correct pronunciation of *guanxi*!

C – D

- Get students read the article in more detail, individually or in pairs, to find the answers.
- Go round the class and assist where necessary.
- Check answers with the whole class.

Exercise C

1 paragraph 3 **2** paragraph 1 **3** paragraph 2
4 paragraph 5 **5** paragraph 4 **6** paragraph 6
7 paragraph 8 **8** paragraph 7

Exercise D

1 *Guanxi* means 'connections' and is key to getting things done in China.

2 You can secure a business licence, land a distribution deal, find a colonial villa in Shanghai and make a fortune.

3 They can improve their understanding of the marketplace, hire the best talent and find potential business partners.

4 Networking that once happened in private is taking place at more public, informal events.

5 To keep in touch with previous employees who now work for the company's clients and provide a valuable network

E

- Allow the students to read the article again and find answers to the questions.
- Go round the class and assist where necessary.

1 tapping into **2** loyalty **3** accountability
4 obligation **5** connections **6** networking
7 perseverance

F

- If you have Chinese students in the class, ask them (tactfully) to say what they think of the article.
- Ask the students to work on the questions; then discuss them with the whole class. Be tactful in dealing with question 3!

➡ Text bank (pages 122–125)

Language review: Multi-word verbs

Students look at verbs made up of more than one word, otherwise known as phrasal verbs, and study them being used in context.

- Go through the different types of multi-word verb, pointing out the differences.

A 🔊 CD1.19

- Tell the students to look through the sections of the conversation. Answer any queries about meaning.
- Get the students, in pairs, to put the conversation in the correct order.
- Play the recording once or twice, stopping at convenient points, so that students can check their answers.

1 f **2** e **3** b **4** g **5** j **6** a **7** d **8** i **9** h **10** c

- Ask the students to read the conversation in simultaneous pairs, looking at the script on page 155 of the Course Book. Circulate and monitor, especially for realistic intonation.
- Ask one or two pairs to perform the conversation for the whole class.

B – C

- Get the students, in pairs, to underline the multi-word verbs in the conversation and then match them to their meanings.
- With the whole class, elicit the answers.
- Then get students to look at exercise C.
- Check the answers with the whole class.
- Point out the separable multi-word verbs, for example *put off something* and *put something off*. Point out that when using *it* as the object, the verbs must be separated; for example, you can say *put it off* but not *put off it*.

Exercise B

1 get on **2** checked in **3** build up
4 turn […] round **5** putting […] off **6** turn up
7 let […] down **8** set up **9** carry on
10 called […] off

Exercise C

2 They've put off the presentation until Thursday. / They've put the presentation off until Thursday.

3 I'm sorry I've let you down.

4 She's set up the conference call for nine o'clock. / She's set the conference call up for nine o'clock.

5 This is a crucial meeting. Make sure you turn up on time.

6 Everyone carried on working as if nothing had happened.

7 You'll need to check in at the Hilton around four o'clock.

8 I get on (well) with my new boss.

- If there is time, your students could discuss the questions below in pairs. Write them on the board, and invite different pairs to talk about different points. The idea is to use as many multi-word verbs as possible (not just ones from this section) when answering the questions.
- Try to have a phrasal verb dictionary to hand, for example the *Longman Phrasal Verbs Dictionary*.

Questions for further discussion

1 How can businesses build up market share?

2 How can companies hold on to their most valued employees?

3 What preparation should be made before setting up a meeting with an important potential customer?

- Circulate, monitor and assist if necessary. Note how each pair is using multi-word verbs.

- With the whole class, go over the multi-word verbs you have heard, correcting problems where necessary.

Possible answer for question 1

Of course, before companies can *build up* market share, they have to *get into* the market in the first place. They have to *find out about* how the market works, how distribution is *set up* and so on. When they have *put together* enough information, they can *set out* to attack the market, perhaps *starting off* in just a small area to begin with. They may try to *set themselves apart from* competitors by offering a product with special features, or they may compete on price.

Skills: Networking

Students look at networking language in a series of situations and use it themselves to role play two situations.

A ◀)) CD1.20

- Tell the students that they are going to listen to a series of conversations in the context of people networking.

- Ask them to look through the statements as preparation for listening, saying they will have to decide which statements are true and which are false.

- Play the recording and stop at the end of each situation to give time for the students to make their choice.

- Ask the students for their answers.

1 True

2 False (They don't have the expertise to redesign it themselves.)

3 False (She says that he travels quite a lot and is often in meetings or giving presentations.)

B ◀)) CD1.21

- Ask the students to look at the questions.

- Play the recording once or twice and ask for the answers.

1 Because they've had complaints from customers saying it's not working properly, it's hard to navigate, they can't find what they want and the product information is insufficient.

2 He's very interested and would be available to discuss it further in two weeks' time.

C ◀)) CD1.20, 1.21

- Before playing the first recording again, ask the students to look at items 1–5, and to think briefly about what the missing words might be.

- Play recording 1.20 again, and have the students fill in the blanks.

- Repeat the process for recording 1.21.

1 met **2** help you out; don't you contact
3 by any chance **4** mention
5 try to reach; for the contact
6 given **7** interested **8** meeting

D

- Before role-playing the situations, tell the students to look at the Useful language box.

- Get the students, in pairs, to practise saying the expressions using friendly intonation.

- Students take turns to say one of the expressions from the Useful language box, and to give an appropriate reply. For example:

A Haven't we met somewhere before?
B Yes, it was at the group sales conference in Portugal last year.
A Oh yes. Very good conference, wasn't it?
B We both went to that presentation on networking skills.
A That's right! It was one of the most interesting at the conference.

- You can demonstrate with one student to give the students the general idea. Then get the students to practise in pairs.

- Praise and correct as usual, concentrating on friendly intonation.

- Keep the class in pairs. If you are short of time, some pairs can role-play situation 1 and others situation 2.

- Make sure that the students understand the situation they are going to role-play before they start.

- Start the activity. Circulate and monitor.

- Praise good points and correct weaker ones, again concentrating on intonation.

- Ask for one or two public performances of each situation.

➡ Resource bank: Speaking (page 177–178)

CASE STUDY

Al-Munir Hotel and Spa Group

An Arab hotel group wishes to build customer loyalty by getting to know its visitors better and encouraging them to return to its hotels.

Background

- Instruct the students to read the section on the company's background in pairs.

- Circulate and answer any queries. Discuss common queries with the whole group.

- Quickly put the points in the left-hand column of the table below on the board and elicit information from the group so as to complete the column on the right.

- Make sure the students understand the situation by getting individual students each to expand orally on a part of the table, using complete sentences.

Company	Al-Munir Hotel and Spa Group
Countries	Oman and UAE
Director of Customer Relations	Vanessa Schultz
Her task	Build better relationships with guests Encourage repeat visits
Company's problems	Turnover (=sales) has fallen by 22% Occupancy rate has fallen from 81% to 62% Increasing customer dissatisfaction Retention rate (=guests returning) has fallen from 25% to 8% Low customer loyalty Rating has fallen from 4* to 3*
Vanessa Schultz's plan	To build long-term relationships between customers and the hotel

Customer Satisfaction Survey 🔊))) CD1.22

- Get students to look at the results of the survey undertaken by Mr Hamdi before they listen to the recording.

- Ask them to give specific examples of why there might be dissatisfaction in different areas. For example, the amenities might not be well-maintained, equipment might be broken, cleaning may be an issue, etc.

- Play the recording and get students to compare what they hear with the possible reasons that they just gave.

Reasons given by customers include:

- they don't feel they've had a memorable experience during their stay.

- they aren't made to feel special and valued.

- they want more attention paid to their needs and to be treated as individuals.

- they're looking for a more personalised service.

- no room facilities for making coffee.

- no vegetarian options on the menu.

- lack of facilities for children; no special menus for them; no play area, etc.

- staff need to be more responsive to customer requests and more positive in dealing with them.

- business area not open for the full duration of advertised hours.

- staff don't appear motivated and don't appear to enjoy their jobs.

Task

- Get the students to look at the agenda for the meeting with the Guest Relations and Marketing Departments and explain anything that they are unclear about.

- Tell them that in the initial stage of the task they will be in a discussion involving either the Guest Relations (GR) Department or the Marketing Department.

- Divide the class into groups of three and say which groups are members of the GR department and which the Marketing Department.

- Start the first stage of the role play. Go round the different groups and assist where necessary.

- When they have finished, put each group of GR people with a group of Marketing people, making six students in each new group. Tell one member of each group of six to drop the role (GR or Marketing) they have had so far and to take the role of Vanessa Schultz and to chair the meeting.

- Have each group of six discuss the various ideas, under the chairmanship of Vanessa Schultz. Point out that the objective is to come up with a concrete action plan at the end of the meeting.

- Go round the class and assist where necessary. Monitor for good and not-so-good use of language.

- When most groups have finished, bring the class to order.

- Get a member of each group to say what their action plan consists of. Compare the action plans of each group.

- Praise good use of networking language that you heard in the role plays. Then go over points that need more work, getting individual students to say the right thing.

Students can watch the case study commentary on the DVD-ROM.

Writing

● Students write to an existing customer of the hotel company, in order to make an offer that will increase customer loyalty.

● Ask for possible openings to the letter, for example: *Dear Ms Wise, You are one of our most valued customers. That's why we're making you this special offer ...*

● The students could write letters in pairs collaboratively in class. Circulate, monitor and assist. Alternatively, set the activity as homework.

One-to-one

Use these points for the task as the basis for a discussion about existing customers and a possible loyalty programme.

➡ Writing file, page 126

➡ Resource bank: Writing (page 206)

WORKING ACROSS CULTURES 1 Doing business internationally

As this is probably the first *Working across cultures* unit that you are doing with students, explain what cultural awareness is: the idea that people should be aware of different attitudes, ways of behaving, taking decisions, using time, etc. that other cultures may have, and how these must be taken into account in doing business in different cultures.

A – B 🔊 CD1.23

- Get students to look through the questions.
- Play the recording and elicit the answers for Exercise A.

Exercise A

1 He didn't agree with David's suggestions and wanted to impose the company's existing business model on the Chinese market.

2 He means they expected the pizza business to become successful quite quickly.

3 He decided that there was no point in continuing with them and advised the company to sell the restaurants.

- Get students to listen again and elicit the answers for Exercise B.

Exercise B

- Not adapting the business model to the Chinese market.

- Not making sufficient use of David Li's business knowledge.

- Selling a product that was unsuitable, as it didn't appeal to Chinese tastes.

- Making the pizzas too expensive compared to those of the competition. They were not considered value for money.

- Gaining a reputation for unreliability because of late deliveries.

- Setting up a take-out business rather than offering customers pizzas in an American-style restaurant with an attractive décor.

Task 1

- Students can initially compare their ranking results in groups. Then do the ranking with the whole class, comparing different students' answers and discussing any disagreements.

C

- Get students to discuss the question in pairs, bearing in mind some of the points from Exercise B above. Go round the class and assist where necessary.

- Bring the class to order and get representatives of each pair to talk about their ideas and compare them.

D – E 🔊 CD1.24

- Again, get the students to look at the questions before listening to the recording.

- Play the recording and elicit the answers.

Exercise D

1 She went to negotiate an agreement with Mumbai Enterprises, to distribute their products nationwide.

2 An important company owned by the Duleep Singh family, one of the richest families in India.

3 A visit to the president's home for dinner – Christina took gifts that were well accepted and they discussed non-business topics that interested them both.

Exercise E

- She made a false assumption that an agreement had been reached based on the president's vague answers and positive body language (smiling).

- She came across as impatient – she was pushing to close the deal based on a short-term timescale. This made them think she was rude and insincere.

- She made a mistake with some of the figures she gave them. This made them think she was incompetent and untrustworthy.

- Play the recording again and elicit the answers about the cultural mistakes.

Task 2

- Get students to discuss the question in pairs. Go round the class and assist where necessary.

- Bring the class to order and get representatives of each pair to talk about their ideas, and compare them.

- In India, it is likely that there will be some general discussion before people get down to business. Such discussion helps both sides to get to know each other better.

- Decision-making may take longer in some Asian countries than in Western ones. It's important to be patient and not become frustrated by the slower pace of discussions.

- Foreigners doing business in India should look for long-term benefits rather than short-term advantages.

- Indian people need to trust those they are doing business with. They need to feel that the other side is sincere.

- It takes time to build up relationships with business contacts in India.

F

- Explain the idea behind the exercise and get students to read the blog together in small groups.

- Go round the class and assist where necessary.

- Bring the class to order and go through the answers with the whole class.

- Melissa should have realised that there is a lot of bureaucracy to go through to set up a joint venture in Russia, and she should not have pushed Georgy to commit to figures that he wasn't ready to give.

- She should have realised that Georgy was giving her advice on the organic products, not being rude.

- She should have appreciated that Georgy felt safer using a lawyer he knew rather than a large firm he was not familiar with.

- She ought to have delayed her flight home so that she could have attended the meeting with the Minister.

G 🔊 CD1.25

- Make sure the task is clear.

- Play the recording. Students compare what Galina Koznov is saying with the notes they made in Exercise F.

- Elicit the answers from the whole class.

- Galina Koznov not surprised that Georgy (G) didn't want to give Melissa (M) a five-year sales forecast as there are so many certificates and permissions surrounding setting up a joint venture in Russia.

- G also probably didn't want to give figures that he'd have to change later in their relationship.

- M should have realised it would take longer to set up a joint venture in Russia than in other countries.

- Relaxing and socialising is very important to Russians so the weekend trip to G's *dacha* was a good opportunity to develop their relationship.

- Russians tend to be abrupt and direct when talking in English so M shouldn't have been offended – G was trying to be helpful and friendly with his advice.

- Personal relations are important in Russia – that's why he wanted to use his school friend, who he knew and trusted, as his lawyer.

- M made a big mistake not changing her flight – the meeting with the minister would have been an important step in setting up the joint venture. The minister felt devalued because M sent a lower-ranking colleague on her behalf – the only acceptable people to attend the meeting from her company would have been her or her boss.

Task 3

- Get students to do this for homework and check in the next lesson. (Or they could e-mail their work to you, and you could provide feedback by return e-mail, or in the next lesson.)

UNIT A Revision

This unit revises and reinforces some of the key language points from Units 1–3 and from Working across cultures 1, and links with those units are clearly shown. You can point out these links to your students.

1 Communication

Vocabulary
- This recycles and revisits vocabulary relating to communication.

> **1** articulate   **2** rambling   **3** succinct
> **4** extrovert   **5** coherent   **6** persuasive
> **7** eloquent   **8** fluent   **9** interrupted
> **10** digress   **11** engage   **12** listen

Idioms
- Students get further practice with these. Point out again that it's important to get idioms exactly right, or they can sound very strange indeed.

> **1** bush   **2** grapevine   **3** stick   **4** mouth
> **5** wall   **6** wavelength   **7** loop   **8** picture

Skills
- Work on correct stress and intonation of the expressions after students have done the exercise.

> **1** g   **2** c   **3** h   **4** i   **5** b   **6** j   **7** a   **8** k
> **9** m   **10** f   **11** l   **12** e   **13** n   **14** d

2 International marketing

Vocabulary
- Students get further practice in the vocabulary of international marketing.

> **1** j   **2** a   **3** e   **4** b   **5** i   **6** h   **7** d   **8** g
> **9** f   **10** c

Noun compounds and noun phrases
- Get students to work on the correct order of words in compounds and work on stress and intonation of the sentences when students have completed the exercise.

> **1** We're launching a really impressive product range.
> **2** The sales forecasts are very good.
> **3** We want to increase brand awareness.
> **4** We're doing extremely thorough market research.
> **5** They created a hugely successful advertising campaign.
> **6** We've just introduced a new customer loyalty card.
> **7** He thought of an absolutely brilliant advertising slogan.

> **8** They're entering the highly competitive online shopping market.

Skills
- Again, work on stress and intonation when students have completed the exercise.

> **1** purpose   **2** achieve   **3** think   **4** suggest
> **5** great   **6** best   **7** back   **8** mind   **9** stage
> **10** absolutely

3 Building relationships

Vocabulary
- With students, work on the process of spotting the 'odd one out', ensuring that students are clear about the meanings of all items.

> **1** cement   **2** create   **3** begin   **4** endanger
> **5** promise   **6** disrupt   **7** establish   **8** allow

Multi-word verbs
- This is a tricky area for many learners, so take time to work on this exercise thoroughly, pointing out the clues that indicate which sentence halves match.

> **1** c   **2** h   **3** d   **4** b   **5** g   **6** a   **7** f   **8** e

Writing
- This exercise can be done as homework, with students possibly e-mailing their work to you for individual correction, followed by general feedback in the next class.

> **Possible answer**
>
> Dear Mr Pereira
>
> Judy Milligan, an old friend of mine, suggested I get in touch. I'd like to talk with you about Brazil's petroleum industry. I'm a business journalist and I'm doing research on how various industries are coping with the current economic climate. I plan to produce a documentary film for television. I wonder if you could give me some facts and figures? I'll be in São Paulo next month. Would it be possible for us to get together?
>
> Thank you.
>
> Yours sincerely
>
> Tom Jordan

Cultures 1: Doing business internationally
- Students get further practice in intercultural vocabulary.

> **1** local   **2** product   **3** rip-off   **4** reliable
> **5** patient   **6** relax   **7** direct   **8** flexible

UNIT 4 Success

AT A GLANCE

	Classwork – Course Book	Further work
Lesson 1 *Each lesson (excluding case studies) is about 45 to 60 minutes. This does not include administration and time spent going through homework.*	**Starting up** Students look at language for describing successful people and organisations and talk about success symbols in their own culture. **Vocabulary: Prefixes** Students look at some common prefixes.	**Practice File** Vocabulary (page 16) **Practice exercises: Vocabulary 1&2** (DVD-ROM) **i-Glossary** (DVD-ROM)
Lesson 2	**Listening: Successful businesses** The managing director of a technology company talks about what makes a successful business. **Reading: Carlos Slim** Students read a profile of Carlos Slim, one of the world's richest men.	**Resource bank: Listening** (page 191) **Practice exercises: Listening** (DVD-ROM) **Text bank** (pages 126–129)
Lesson 3	**Language review: Present and past tenses** The tenses are compared and contrasted. Students look at how they are used in the Slim article and then use them to write about another company's history. **Skills: Negotiating** The language of bargaining, checking understanding and signalling is examined. Students analyse how it occurs in a negotiating situation and use it themselves in a role play.	**Practice File** Language review (page 17) **Practice exercises: Language review 1&2** (DVD-ROM) **ML Grammar and Usage** (Units 1–3) **Resource bank: Speaking** (page 179) **Practice File** Survival Business English (page 61) **Practice exercises: Skills** (DVD-ROM)
Lesson 4 *Each case study is about 1½ to 2 hours.*	**Case study: Kensington United** A major English football club needs to agree a new sponsorship deal to ensure its continuing success. Students take part in the negotiations between the club and a big media company.	**Case study commentary** (DVD-ROM) **Resource bank: Writing** (page 207) **Practice File** Writing (page 19)

For a fast route through the unit focusing mainly on speaking skills, just use the underlined sections.

For one-to-one situations, most parts of the unit lend themselves, with minimal adaptation, to use with individual students. Where this is not the case, alternative procedures are given.

BUSINESS BRIEF

People are fascinated by success. Business commentators try to understand the **success factors** that make for successful individuals, products and companies, and for economically successful countries.

People

Different types of organisation require different types of leaders. Think of start-ups with their dynamic entrepreneurs, mature companies with their solid but hopefully inspirational CEOs, companies in difficulty with their turnaround specialists. Each also requires managers and employees with different **personality make-ups**. Think of the combination of personality types needed in banks compared to those in advertising agencies.

Products

Successful products are notoriously hard to predict. There are subtle combinations of social, cultural and technological circumstances that mean that something will succeed at one time but not another. People talk rightly about a product 'whose time has come'. The technology to meet a particular need may exist for a long time before the product on which it is based **takes off**. For example, photocopying technology was around for years before photocopiers were commercialised on a large scale. In the beginning, cost may be a factor, but after a time a **critical mass** of users develops, costs come down, and no one 'can understand how they could have done without one'.

Companies

Success factors here include **energy, vision** and **efficiency,** but many of the companies that were thought to possess these attributes 30 or even five years ago are not those we would think of as having these qualities today. **Management fashions** are a big factor: **gurus** and management books have a lot to answer for. Once something becomes a **mantra**, everyone starts doing it, but objective measures of the relative efficiency of each type of company are hard to find. Different types of activities require different approaches to deliver strong financial results, the one measure of success that people usually agree on.

Countries

Economic success stories such as Japan, Germany and Sweden became models that everyone wanted to imitate. In the 1970s, government experts and academics went to these places by the planeload looking for the magic ingredients. In the 1980s and early 90s they went to the emerging economies of the so-called 'Asian tigers'. Now China is seen as the country to watch. At various times, commitment to **self-improvement, entrepreneurial flair**, efficient **access to capital**, vibrant **institutions**, a good **education system** and good **infrastructure** are held to be important factors for success, but the countries mentioned above possess these to very varying degrees.

In any case, how can companies and countries imitate others? Companies have a particular **culture** that is the result of their history, short or long. If managers and their consultants change them radically, for example by downsizing them, they may be ripping out the very things that make them tick. On the other hand, change may really be necessary, and companies with cultures and structures that were successful under earlier conditions are very hard to change in a genuine way, even if they go through the motions of adopting the latest management fashion.

With countries, how do you imitate social structures and habits that have evolved over centuries elsewhere, often with an entirely different starting point? The old joke about not wanting to start from here if you're going there is applicable. Also, by the time the model has been identified as one worth imitating, the world economy has moved on, and your chosen model may no longer be the one to follow.

Ability to **adapt** is key. Here, the US is world leader in adapting old organisations to new conditions – McDonald's and IBM, for example, have had amazing **turnrounds** from earlier difficulties. But radical **innovation** is equally important. The US is also good at generating entirely new companies that become world leaders. Though not as dominant as it once was, the US economy seems to be particularly good at producing these companies – witness Microsoft, Intel and Google. China, for all its new-found economic power, has yet to produce a company in this league.

Read on

James C. Collins, Jerry I. Porras: *Built to Last: Successful Habits of Visionary Companies*, Random House, 2005

Michael Hoyle, Peter Newman: *Simply a Great Manager: The 15 fundamentals of being a successful manager*, Marshall Cavendish, 2008

Michael E. Porter: *Competitive Advantage of Nations*, Free Press, 1998

LESSON NOTES

Warmer

- Ask the students to name the most successful business person/people in their own country/countries. (In a multi-nationality group, this is a good chance for students to learn about each other's business heroes.)

Overview

- Tell the students that they will be looking at success in business people and in organisations.

- Ask the students to look at the Overview section at the beginning of the unit. Tell them a little about the things on the list, using the table on page 36 of this book as a guide. Tell them the points you will be covering in the current lesson and in later lessons.

Quotation

- Get the students to talk about the quotation. Ask them if they think it's true.

- This is not to encourage their cynicism, but you could mention another Vidal quote: 'Whenever a friend succeeds, a little something in me dies.'

- Invite some quick comments, but don't anticipate the content of the rest of the unit too much.

Starting up

In this section, the students look at the vocabulary for describing successful people and organisations and talk about success symbols.

A

- Get the students to discuss the words in pairs. Tell them that they can add vocabulary that came up during the warmer session to their lists if they want to. Circulate, monitor and assist, for example, by explaining *charisma, nepotism* and *ruthlessness,* helping with pronunciation and suggesting words where necessary to describe particular character traits.

- Ask individual pairs to give their five most important characteristics and ask them why they have chosen them.

- Invite comments and encourage discussion. The students may say, for example, that the characteristics depend on the type of person. The characteristics of a successful novelist overlap with, but are not identical to, those for a successful chief executive. (Drive and discipline might be common to both.)

B

- Ask the students, in pairs, to talk about individuals they know, perhaps in relation to the five words they chose in Exercise A, and report their findings to the whole class. Say that they can relate the characteristics to the people that they mentioned in the Warmer activity if they want to.

C

- Get the students to work on the success indicators in pairs. Ask them also to name the particular cars, jewellery, holiday destinations, leisure activities, etc. that successful people choose at the moment. Invite comments and encourage discussion with the whole group. Of course, where there are different nationalities in the class, treat the status symbols of each culture tactfully.

D

- Get the students to work again in pairs, this time changing partners. Ask them to complete the statements with the words in the box. Check answers with the whole class.

Note:

Orientated is used in BrE only; *oriented* is used in both BrE *and* AmE. It doesn't matter which the students (or you) use as long as they are consistent.

> **1** profits **2** leader **3** innovation **4** workforce
> **5** customer **6** brand **7** shares **8** headquarters
> **9** subsidiaries **10** people

If you have time, get pairs to think of a successful company that they admire, and ask which statements in the exercise apply to this company. (In the case of successful recent start-ups, it may be that not many of the points apply.) Round up the discussion with the whole group.

Vocabulary: Prefixes

Students look at some common prefixes.

A – B

- Ask the students to find prefixes in the article.

- Get the students to complete Exercise A in pairs. Circulate, monitor and assist.

- Check the answers with the whole class.

- Ask the students what other words they know that use these prefixes or get them to use dictionaries to find some (e.g. *reapply, overreaction, outdo, co-author, underdeveloped, ultra-efficient, misaddressed, ex-teacher, decommissioned*).

- Then do Exercise B as a quick-fire whole-class activity.

> **Exercise A**
>
> **re**named, **over**confidence, **out**perform, **co**-founder, **under**estimated, **ultra**modern, **mis**informed, **ex**-business, **de**valued
>
> **Exercise B**
>
> **1** over- **2** out- **3** mis- **4** ultra- **5** ex- **6** de-
> **7** co- **8** under- **9** re-

C

Do the first one as an example with the whole class and demonstrate that the odd one out in each group is the word that cannot take the prefix in bold at the beginning of the line. Ask the students to complete the exercise in pairs. Circulate, monitor and assist.

2 boss **3** decide **4** lose **5** look **6** win
7 big **8** staff **9** grow

D

- Get the students to work either individually or in pairs to complete the sentences.
- Check answers with the whole class.

2 co-authors **3** relaunch **4** overestimated
5 mismanaged **6** outbid **7** ultramodern
8 ex-boss **9** deregulated

E

- Get students to discuss the statements in pairs. Circulate and monitor the language being used, especially prefixes.
- Bring the class to order. Get representatives of each pair to report their conclusions. Encourage discussion with the whole class.
- Praise good language points and work on three or four points that need it, especially in relation to prefixes.

◎ i-Glossary

Listening: Successful businesses

The managing director of a technology development company talks about what makes for a successful business.

A 🔊 CD1.26

- Get students to read the text to anticipate the words that might go in the gaps.
- Play the recording once or twice and ask the students for the missing words.
- Then play the recording again, stopping after any words that have caused difficulty.

1 successful **2** manufacture **3** sell
4 product **5** service **6** sell **7** cost
8 produce **9** technology **10** increasing value
11 venture capital

B 🔊 CD1.27

- Explain the task. Play the recording, stopping at convenient points, and get students to write a summary of what Tom Hockaday says.

Suggested answer
Natural Motion was set up in 2002 and its workforce has passion, vision and clarity. It has gone on to be a very successful software animation company, whose software tools are used in the film industry and in the computer game industry, to help make software characters look more realistic in those formats. Those involved have worked together from their early vision for what this company might be and have seen that being delivered with passion and enthusiasm. There have been some challenges along the way, but the team have taken forward their vision with impressive clarity.

- Get two or three students to quickly read out what they have written and compare the different versions.

C 🔊 CD1.28

- Play the recording and elicit answers from the whole class, explaining any difficulties.

1 environmental technologies, low-carbon technologies and alternative-energy technologies
2 a smart-metering technology company, a project for tidal energy, a project for wind energy, a project for lightweight electric motors

- Ask students if they have heard about these technologies and applications in other contexts, and if so, where.
- ◎ Students can watch the interview with Tom Hockaday on the DVD-ROM.
- ➡ Resource bank: Listening (page 191)

Reading: Carlos Slim

Students read about one of the world's richest men, Carlos Slim.

A

- Explain the task and get students to look through the summary before they read the article.
- Students read the article individually or in pairs.
- Go round the class and assist where necessary.
- When most students have finished, bring the class to order and get students to say what the errors are.

Carlos Slim is probably the richest man you have **never** heard of. The major influences on his life were his father, Julián, who was born in **Lebanon**, and Jean Paul Getty. He studied **civil engineering** at **university in Mexico City** and on graduating set up as a stockbroker. He made a lot of money in the Mexican recession of 1982, **buying** his assets in the middle of the crisis. In 1990 Slim gained control of Telmex, which owns 90% of Mexican telephone lines and is **one of** the largest parts of Slim's empire. Slim is also involved in charity through his Carso Foundation.

- If you have Latin American students in your class, it might be a good idea to point out that Carlos Slim is not well-known in the English-speaking world, hence 'the richest man you have never heard of', even if he is very famous in Latin America – an example of the Anglocentricity of the English-speaking world!

B

- Get students to match the pairs before reading the article again.

> **1** b **2** g **3** e **4** f **5** d **6** a **7** c

- Get students to read the article again and find where and how the pairs are used.

C

- Get students to work on this individually or in pairs.

> **1** buying spree **2** annual sales
> **3** turning point **4** economic crisis
> **5** global recession **6** retail outlets
> **7** business acumen

- Go through the expressions with the whole class working on any remaining stress/pronunciation problems, e.g. 'business *ACumen*'.

D

- Get students to work on this individually or in pairs. Go round the class and assist where necessary.
- With the whole class, elicit some of the ideas that they came up with. Insist on correct pronunciation of *I'd*.

➡ Text bank (pages 126–129)

Language review: Present and past tenses

The tenses are compared and contrasted. Students look at how they are used, then use them to write about Apple.

- Go through the rules with the whole class, elaborating on them where necessary. This is a tricky area, even for students at this level.

> **1** present simple **2** past simple
> **3** present continuous **4** present perfect
> **5** past perfect

- Point out the grammar reference section at the back of the Course Book if the students have not already seen it. They can look at the material on these verb tenses for homework.

A

- Do as a whole-class activity, re-explaining rules where necessary.

> **1** Present perfect: announcing news
> **2** Past simple: completed action in the past
> **3** Present simple: situation which is generally true
> **4** Past perfect: action completed before a time in the past
> **5** Present continuous: describing current situation

B

- Get students to do this task in pairs in class to practise the grammar before doing Exercise C for homework. Circulate and assist where necessary.

C

- Students do this exercise for homework. Make sure that they hand it in in the next lesson or e-mail it to you to correct.

Skills: Negotiating

The language of bargaining, checking understanding and signalling is covered. Students analyse how it occurs in a negotiating situation and use it themselves to role-play a situation.

A

- Go through the three points in A and the expressions in the Useful language box with the whole class. Get individual students to read the expressions, working on intonation.
- Explain briefly the role and importance of these expressions in structuring negotiations.

B – **C** 🔊 CD1.29

- Prepare students for the situation by looking at the questions in B, play the recording and get students to answer the questions.

> **1 a)** 150 rugs **b)** 10%
> **2** She wants the goods by the end of the month; it is not certain that she will get what she wants.

- Get students to look at the sentences with gaps in C and anticipate what might go in them.
- Play the recording again, stopping at convenient points and get students to say what is in the gaps, working on any difficulties.

> **1** discount **2** standard; in mind
> **3** double; willing; reasonable **4** asking a lot
> **5** proposal; prepared **6** a deal; the list price

D

- Get students to look at the script on page 157 of the Course Book in pairs, identifying the expressions in each category.

Checking language: *Are you saying you don't have that quantity in stock?*

Signalling language: *I'd like to ask a question now …* or *I'd like to make a proposal.*

E

- Explain the situation.

- Put the students into pairs and appoint the Sales Managers and Chief Buyers. Make sure that everyone knows who they are.

- Ask the Sales Managers to turn to page 133 and the Chief Buyers to turn to page 142.

- Get the students to study their information carefully.

- Tell the students they should:

  - start the negotiation with some small talk

  - get into the negotiation itself, trying to use the expressions for bargaining, checking understanding, and signalling

  - write down what they agree.

- Answer any questions the students may have, then tell them to do the negotiation in pairs.

- Circulate, monitor and assist. Note language points for praise and correction, especially in relation to the expressions for signalling, checking understanding and summarising.

- When the pairs have finished their negotiation, ask the different pairs what they decided. Summarise the results on the board, so that students can see the range of results.

- Ask one or two pairs to summarise the stages of their negotiations, the tactics each partner was using, particular difficulties and sticking points.

- Do a round-up of language points for praise and those that need correction. Focus on five or six language points, for example, in relation to expressions for signalling, checking understanding and summarising, and get individual students to use the correct forms.

One-to-one

This role play can be done between teacher and student. Don't forget to note language points for praise and correction afterwards. Discuss with the student their negotiating plan and the tactics they were using.

Resource bank: Speaking (page 179)

CASE STUDY

Kensington United

Students study information about Kensington United football club and take part in the negotiations between the club and a big media company about a new sponsorship deal.

Background/Current situation

- Divide the whole class into two halves, A and B.

- Get As to read the section on Kensington United's background and get Bs to read the section on Kensington United's current situation.

- Circulate and answer any queries.

- When students are ready, put them into pairs, with one A and one B in each. Students summarise their information for their partners.

- While students are doing this, put the points in the left hand columns of the two tables below on the board. Students work in their pairs to complete as much information as they can.

- Elicit answers and add them to the board. There will be some information missing.

🔊 CD1.30

- Play the recording once or twice and get students to make notes of the missing information.

- Round up the answers on the board with the whole class.

Kensington United (KU)

Recent performance	Very successful in UK and mainland Europe
Recent business performance	Commercially very successful
Footballing success due to	Marco Conti, its Italian manager
Commercial success due to	Ingrid Tauber, Commercial Director, and her work on diversifying into: • club travel agency • hospitality facilities • joint venture with insurance company • training courses on leadership • football boot manufacturing company.
Problems	Spectator (teach this word if necessary) behaviour

Current situation

Current sponsorship deal with	Insurance company (about to end)
Possible new broadcasting/ sponsorship deal	Universal Communications (UC)
Key factors in negotiations between KU and UC	Big audiences in UK and Asia Universal communications wants to boost sales of its mobile phones in Asia

- Check that the situation is clear to all the students by asking a few quick questions.

- Once you are satisfied that the situation is clear, move on to Stage 2.

Task

- Divide the class into groups of four to six. Within each group, half the students will represent KU and the other half, UC (two to three students on each side).

- Ask the whole class to look at the agenda for the negotiations and elaborate briefly on each point.

- Before the students read their role cards, make it clear that each side will have to work out its objectives, priorities, strategy and tactics, and think carefully about what concessions they are willing to make.

- KU negotiators turn to page 133 and read their role cards.

- UC negotiators turn to page 141 and read their role cards.

- Get each team to work together to develop an effective strategy for the negotiations. Circulate, monitor and assist.

- Make sure that each side has a chief negotiator who will be the first to speak. The chief UC negotiator will outline the purpose of the negotiations and the chief KU negotiator will reply. The chief negotiators should make sure that the discussions move on smartly, so that participants do not spend too long on each point.

- The negotiations can begin, in parallel where there is more than one group.

- Circulate and monitor, noting strong points and those that need correction. Do not intervene in the negotiations themselves unless the teams are completely stuck.

🔊 CD1.31

- Just before the negotiations seem to be coming to a conclusion, stop the class and tell them that a news report has just come on the radio. Play recording 1.31. Then ask the students to continue their negotiation.

- When time is up, ask the students on different sides what happened in their particular negotiations: what their objectives were, what tactics they used, whether they achieved their objectives, etc. Ask them what effect the news report had on their negotiations.

- Praise strong language points and correct ones that need correcting, getting individual students to rephrase what they said earlier, incorporating the corrections.

One-to-one

This negotiation can be done one-to-one. Ask the student which side they would prefer to represent. You represent the other side. Don't forget to note language points for praise and correction later. Afterwards, discuss with the student their negotiating plan and the tactics they were using. Praise and correct your student's use of language as appropriate, and highlight some of the language you chose to use as well.

 Students can watch the case study commentary on the DVD-ROM.

Writing

- This writing exercise can be done as pair work in class or for homework.

- Make sure that each student knows which type of writing they are going to produce: a press release from the point of view of the company they represented, or a letter, if the negotiation was unsuccessful.

➡ Writing file, pages 126 and 128

➡ Resource bank: Writing (page 207)

Job satisfaction

AT A GLANCE

	Classwork – Course Book	Further work
Lesson 1 *Each lesson (excluding case studies) is about 45 to 60 minutes. This does not include administration and time spent going through homework.*	<u>**Starting up**</u> Students discuss what motivates people at work. **Vocabulary: Synonyms and word-building** Students look at synonyms and word-building in relation to the language of motivation and job satisfaction. **Listening: Staff motivation** A Human Resources director talks about how her company creates job satisfaction among its staff.	**Practice File** Vocabulary (page 20) **Practice exercises: Vocabulary 1&2** (DVD-ROM) **i-Glossary** (DVD-ROM) **Resource bank: Listening** (page 192) **Practice exercises: Listening** (DVD-ROM)
Lesson 2	**Reading: Working for the best companies** Students read about two companies that are very good to work for.	Text bank (pages 130–133)
Lesson 3	**Language review: Passives** Students work on the passive forms of a range of verb tenses. <u>**Skills: Cold-calling**</u> Students look at the language used in cold-calling, and apply it themselves in a role play situation.	**Practice File** Language review (page 20) **Practice exercises: Language review 1&2** (DVD-ROM) **ML Grammar and Usage** (Unit 7) **Resource bank: Speaking** (page 180) **Practice File** Survival Business English (page 63) **Practice exercises: Skills** (DVD-ROM)
Lesson 4 *Each case study is about 1½ to 2 hours.*	<u>**Case study: Just good friends?**</u> A chief executive is worried about relationships between employees and their effect on the company. Students suggest what action the company should take.	**Case study commentary** (DVD-ROM) **Resource bank: Writing** (page 208) **Practice File** Writing (page 22)

For a fast route through the unit focusing mainly on speaking skills, just use the underlined sections.

For one-to-one situations, most parts of the unit lend themselves, with minimal adaptation, to use with individual students. Where this is not the case, alternative procedures are given.

BUSINESS BRIEF

'Happiness is having one's passion for one's profession,' wrote the French novelist Stendhal. The number of people in this fortunate position is limited, but there are all sorts of aspects of office and factory work that can make it enjoyable. Relations with colleagues can be satisfying and congenial. People may find great pleasure in working in a team, for example. Conversely, bad relations with colleagues can be extremely unpleasant, and lead to great dissatisfaction and distress.

Basic work on what motivates people in organisations was done by Frederick Herzberg in the 1960s. He found that things such as **salary** and **working conditions** were not in themselves enough to make employees satisfied with their work, but that they can cause dissatisfaction if they are not good enough. He called these things **hygiene factors**. Here is a complete list:

- Supervision
- Company policy
- Working conditions
- Salary
- Peer relationships
- Security

Some things can give positive satisfaction. These are the **motivator factors:**

- Achievement
- Recognition
- The work itself
- Responsibility
- Advancement
- Growth

Another classic writer in this area is Douglas McGregor, who talked about **Theory X**, the idea, still held by many managers, that people instinctively dislike work, and **Theory Y**, the more enlightened view that everybody has the potential for development and for taking responsibility.

More recently has come the notion of **empowerment**, the idea that decision-making should be decentralised to employees who are as close as possible to the issues to be resolved (see also Units 7: Management styles and 8: Team building).

But where some employees may like being given responsibility, for others it is a source of **stress**. People talk more about the need for work that gives them **quality of life**, the **work-life balance** and the avoidance of stress. Others argue that **challenge** involves a reasonable and inevitable degree of stress if employees are to have the feeling of **achievement**, a necessary outcome of work if it is to give satisfaction. They complain that a **stress industry** is emerging, with its **stress counsellors** and **stress therapists**, when levels of stress are in reality no higher today than they were before.

Read on

Richenda Gambles et al: *The Myth of Work-Life Balance,* Wiley Blackwell, 2006

Douglas McGregor: *The Human Side of Enterprise – annotated edition*, McGraw Hill, 2006

Stephen Palmer, Cary Cooper: *Creating Success: How to Deal with Stress,* Kogan Page, 2007

Neil Thompson: *Power and Empowerment*, Russell House, 2006

LESSON NOTES

Warmer

- Write *job satisfaction* and *motivation* on the board. Ask students, in pairs, to discuss and define each of them.

- Ask each pair for the results of their discussion, and their definition. Invite comments from the whole class. (The *Longman Dictionary of Contemporary English* defines *satisfaction* as 'a feeling of happiness or pleasure because you have achieved something' and *motivation* as 'eagerness or willingness to do something without needing to be told or forced to do it'.)

Overview

- Tell the students that they will be looking at job satisfaction.

- Ask the students to look at the Overview section at the beginning of the unit. Tell them a little about the things on the list, using the table on page 44 of this book as a guide. Tell them which points you will be covering in the current lesson and which in later lessons.

Quotation

- Ask the students to look at the quotation and say if they agree with it, giving reasons.

Starting up

Students discuss motivating factors at work and do a quiz on professional burnout.

A

- Go through the list of words and expressions. Get individual students to explain the less obvious ones (there's no need for them to explain *bigger salary* for example). Explain terms that the students don't know. Work on pronunciation where necessary, e.g. *colleagues*.

B ◀)) CD2.1, 2.2, 2.3

- Get students to look at the questions.

- Play the recording once or twice and elicit the answers.

1   supportive colleagues, commission, threat of redundancy
2   promotion opportunities
3   praise, more flexible working hours

C – **D**

- Get the students to discuss the questions in pairs or threes. Circulate, monitor and assist. Note language points for praise and correction.

- Get the representatives of the pairs or threes to say what their findings were. Encourage whole-class discussion, comparing the results from each group.

- Praise good language points from the discussion and work on three or four points that need improvement, getting individual students to say the correct forms.

- If you have time, get the students to look at the 'Are you in danger of burning out?' quiz on page 134. They can do it in pairs in class, or for homework. In both cases, ask individual students afterwards for their 'profile' and ask if they agree with it. Invite comments and encourage discussion.

Vocabulary: Synonyms and word-building

Students look at ways of developing their business-related vocabulary through synonyms and word-building.

A

- Go round the whole class and get the students to read out the words and expressions. Correct stress and pronunciation where necessary, for example *assESSment*, *emPOWerment*, but don't explain meanings at this point.

- Get the students to do the exercise in pairs. Circulate and monitor.

- Check the answers with the whole class.

2   Most people like to have control over their work and therefore put **empowerment** near the top of their list of motivating factors.
3   **Red tape** is a very time-consuming, demotivating problem which affects large businesses and organisations.
4   Overwork can lead to **breakdown** if not spotted early.
5   Many job satisfaction studies, perhaps surprisingly, have found that often **remuneration** is not the most motivating factor for many employees.
6   Offering **fringe benefits** rather than a salary increase can be a way of retaining employees in traditionally high staff turnover industries.
7   He received a very generous **severance payment** when he left the company.
8   One way for managers to monitor and develop staff is by using **assessment**.

B

- Ask the students to complete the sentences in pairs. Circulate, monitor and assist.

- Go through the answers with the whole class.

- Work on stress of different forms, e.g. *SATisfy* versus *satisFACTion*.

1 b) dissatisfied   c) satisfaction   **2** a) motivating
b) demotivated   c) motivation   **3** a) frustration
b) frustrating   c) frustrated   **4** a) unrecognised
b) recognition   c) recognised

C

- Ask the students to complete the exercise in pairs. Circulate, monitor and assist.

- Get a representative of each pair to say what their answers were, and what their reasoning was.

- Praise good language points that you heard students using, and work on half a dozen that have caused problems, particularly in the area of job satisfaction.

◎ i-Glossary

Listening: Staff motivation

Students listen to Madalyn Brooks, Human Resources Director at Procter & Gamble (UK), talking about issues of job satisfaction and motivation.

A ◀)) CD2.4

- Ask students what they know about Procter & Gamble. (P&G is known as one of the world's best managed companies. Its products include health, cosmetics and cleaning products. For homework you could ask them to research the company on http://www.pg.com/).

- Play the recording once or twice. Explain any difficulties such as *two-pronged approach*, and get students to answer the questions.

1 attracting, retaining and motivating employees
2 a) It seeks to be a business that is committed to its people. Most of its leaders of the organisation have grown up through the organisation and have come through individual, personalised career paths and development plans.
  b) It rewards and recognises people for their individual contributions. It drives their connection to what they work on to the reward and recognition that they get.

- Discuss any issues that arise.

B ◀)) CD2.5

- Get students to look at the questions here. This is quite a long section, so get students to take notes. Play recording 2.5, stopping at convenient points and explaining any difficulties.

- With the whole class, elicit the answers.

1 Stronger demand for flexibility in *when* people work, *where* they work and *how* they work. Driven by the changing role of women in the workplace. As more women entered workplaces, demand for flexible hours/timing started. Emerging generations in the workplace demanding greater flexibility of where they work through new technologies/remote communications. Demand for sabbaticals and opportunity to take time out increasing.

2 People want to take personal control of their growth. They don't expect to stay with the same company or do the same type of work all their lives. Stronger drive towards growth, development and learning.

3 People want to work for companies that are committed to green/environmental issues (e.g. reducing carbon footprint, recycling) and are committed to supporting local communities, getting involved in charitable work and other voluntary areas.

C ◀)) CD2.6

- Explain the task to students. (Tell them that some points will be mentioned more than once.) Play the recording again (twice with lower level groups), pausing at convenient points, but without allowing students to write down the answers.

- Ask individual students to talk about their answers and compare with those given by others.

Desire for ...
- training and self-actualisation
- building self and skills as lifelong learners
- growth and development through training and challenging assignments
- leadership and ownership
- feeling that a company is socially responsible
- time out for voluntary work – putting back into society
- pride in workplace that can be shared with families and friends
- voluntary work, such as working in schools and local communities (repeats earlier point)

◎ Students can watch the interview with Madalyn Brooks on the DVD-ROM.

⇨ Resource bank: Listening (page 192)

Reading: Working for the best companies

Students read about two companies that are very good to work for.

A – B

- Ask the whole class for examples of what they would look for in the ideal company to work for. (You could teach the equivalent expression *ideal employer*.)

- Put students in pairs and explain the task. Ensure that students understand they have to be ready to take notes on their article so as to be able to talk about it without referring back to it.

- When students are ready, get students to read their articles. Go round the class and assist where necessary.

- When pairs are ready (no need to bring the whole class to order at this point) get them to tell their partners the five key points from their article.

C – E

- Explain the next three tasks and get students to work on them in pairs. Again, go round the class and assist where necessary.

Exercise C

1 True   **2** False (M = 77%, K = 75%)   **3** True
4 True   **5** True   **6** False (K = 47%, M = 52%)
7 True
8 False (75% of M workers earn less than £15,000)

Exercise D

basic salary, role models, performance review, paternity leave

sporting career, childcare vouchers, medical insurance, pension scheme

Exercise E

1 medical insurance   **2** pension scheme
3 performance review   **4** paternity leave
5 Basic salary

- Bring the class to order. Work on any remaining difficulties.

F

- This task could be done in pairs or small groups. Again, go round the class and assist where necessary.

- Bring the class to order and get groups/pairs to report on their findings.

➡ Text bank (pages 130–133)

Language review: Passives

Students work on the formation and use of the passive forms of a range of verb tenses.

- Go through the three language review points with the whole class fairly quickly. Don't spend too much time on them now, but come back to them in relation to later activities in this section (see below).

A

- Ask the students, in pairs, to match the sentences a)–h) with the tenses 1–8. Circulate, monitor and assist.

- Ask the pairs for their answers.

1 c **2** e **3** h **4** b **5** d **6** g **7** a **8** f

- Work on any difficulties with the whole class.

Discuss the sentences with the whole class, in relation to the three points in the Language review, for example:

a) We're more interested in the employees than the people encouraging them.

c) We're more interested in the fact that minutes are taken than the person taking them, etc.

B

- Ask the students to work in pairs on the extract. Circulate, monitor and assist (for example with *determine*).

- Ask pairs for the answers.

1 has been defined   **2** is determined   **3** are driven
4 can be seen   **5** was created   **6** are satisfied
7 be satisfied

C

- Explain that the points form the basis for sentences from a report on an employee incentive scheme. Relate this exercise to the initial point about the passive being used to describe processes and procedures.

- Explain any words that require it, for example, *incentive*.

- Bring the class to order. Go round the class quickly and get answers from individual students.

- Union representatives were interviewed.
- Meetings with all Heads of Department were held.
- Management have been ignoring suggestions/complaints.
- Staff are not encouraged to take on new tasks.
- (Since April) staff have been encouraged to do various tasks.
- An open-door policy has been adopted.
- New performance reviews for managers to be introduced from 1st December.
- Research into new employee incentive programme to be carried out.

Skills: Cold-calling

Students look at the language used in cold-calling and apply it themselves in a role play situation.

A

- Explain to students that they will be looking at language for dealing with cold-calling, and explain what this means (phoning or visiting someone you haven't had contact with before in order to persuade them to do something or to buy something). Explain also the idea of headhunting (when a specialised recruitment agency contacts someone to persuade them to take a new job).

- Discuss points 1 and 2 quickly with the whole class.

B – **C** 🔊 CD2.7

- Get students to look at the questions and listen to the conversation.

- Discuss the answers to the exercises with the whole class.

Exercise B

1 To ask if Enid is interested in a position as Chief Negotiator at KB Financial Services.

2 No, because Enid is happy in her current job.

Exercise C

1 your name

2 I call; position; vacant

3 a bit more

4 any point

5 sound; out

6 I'd appreciate

D – **E** 🔊 CD2.8

- Explain the situation, get students to look at the two questions in D and play the recording.

- Elicit the answers with the whole class.

- Play the recording again, with students looking at the script on page 158 of the Course Book. Students underline the two types of expressions, as per the task in E.

- Explain any difficulties and elicit the answers.

Exercise D

She says that they are offering a six-figure salary (c. 150,000) and a great benefits package with an above-average annual bonus.

They agree to meet at three o'clock the following Wednesday at the Chamberlain Hotel.

Exercise E

a

KB are offering a top salary and great benefits package …

Well, it's over six figures … probably in the region of a hundred and fifty …

They give staff a substantial bonus at the end of the year – usually well above the industry average.

b

People often say that to me … but they change their mind when they hear more about the offer.

Would you like to know the salary range?

There's another thing you should bear in mind. It's a very attractive part of the package they offer.

Look, why don't we get together and I'll give you some more details?

F

- Consolidate work so far in this section by getting students to look at the Useful language box, working on intonation of the expressions. Tell them they will be using the language in the role play that follows.

- Explain the situation and allocate roles, ensuring that each member of each pair knows which role they are taking.

- Go round the class and assist where necessary with preparation.

- When students are ready, get them to start the role play. Circulate and monitor. Note language points for praise and correction.

- Bring the class to order. Do a round-up of language points for praise and those that need correction, getting individual students to say the right thing.

- Then get one of the pairs to do the role play again for the whole class, incorporating these corrections.

One-to-one

This role play can be done directly between teacher and student. Don't forget to note language points for praise and correction afterwards.

↪ Resource bank: Speaking (page 180)

CASE STUDY

Just good friends?

A chief executive is worried about close relationships between employees and their effect on the company. Students role-play members of the Human Resources department and suggest what action the company should take.

Background

● Get the students to read the Background section for themselves and meanwhile write the points on the left of the table below on the board. When the students have finished reading, elicit adjectives and expressions that describe the points on the left, and write them up.

Company/industry	Techno21/Information technology
CEO	Patrick McGuire (PMcG)
Nature of IT industry	Highly competitive
Working hours and their effect	Long – employees spend a lot of time with each other
Company culture	Relaxed, maybe too relaxed
Close relationships between members of staff	Increasingly frequent

● Get students to talk about the advantages and disadvantages of working in this kind of environment and report back to the whole class.

Relationships at work: three cases

● Get the students to read PMcG's assistant's notes in three groups, each group concentrating on one of the cases, ready to report on it for the rest of the class.

● While students are reading and discussing 'their' case, write the points on the left of the table below on the board.

● When the students have finished reading, elicit information about the points on the left, and write them up.

Subject	Policy on office relationships
Main point	PMcG's concern about relationships between members of staff
Case 1: Promotion application of Judith Fisher (JF)	JF had a relationship with CFO Peter Walters (PW) that ended. JF then applied for deputy job. Didn't get it – thinks it's PW's revenge. JF might now take legal action against company.
Case 2: Sales conference – possible transfer of Erica Stewart (ES) to Brad Johnson's (BJ) sales team	Sales manager BJ met and spent a lot of time with ES. Asked for her transfer to his sales team. ES wants to refuse but hears from Veronica Simpson (VS) that BJ is impressed and wants her to join his team. VS advises her to accept. ES doesn't know what to do.
Case 3: The loving couple – relationship between Lisa Davis (LD) and Steffan Olsen (SO)	LD and SO thought relationship was secret, but it wasn't. Other team members upset by their behaviour. A rep of the team talked to team leader to ask her to do something.

McGuire's proposal 🔊 CD2.9

● Prepare students for what they are going to hear, tell them they should take notes and then play the recording once or twice.

● Then get students to outline what the four options are: 1) insist that staff leave the company if a relationship develops, 2) ask staff in special relationships to sign a 'love contract', 3) staff to inform their team leader, or 4) do nothing.

Task

● Get students to read the discussion document e-mail. Divide the class into groups of about four.

● When the situation is clear to everyone, the meetings in parallel groups can start. Circulate and monitor, but do not intervene except if absolutely necessary. Note language points for later praise and correction.

● At the end of the activity, praise good language points that you heard while you were circulating and monitoring, and work on three or four points that need improvement, getting individual students to say the correct forms.

● Ask each group to summarise its recommendations. Compare those of different groups. Invite comments and encourage discussion.

One-to-one

The student can discuss the different cases directly with you and decide on appropriate action to take. Don't forget to note language points for praise and correction afterwards.

◎ Students can watch the case study commentary on the DVD-ROM.

Writing

● This writing exercise can be done as pair work in class or for homework. Point out that it must follow the structure of guidelines – bring students' attention to these in the Writing file on page 129 of the Course Book.

➡ Writing file, page 129

➡ Resource bank: Writing (page 208)

UNIT 6 Risk

AT A GLANCE

	Classwork – Course Book	Further work
Lesson 1 *Each lesson (excluding case studies) is about 45 to 60 minutes. This does not include administration and time spent going through homework.*	**Starting up** Students look at different types of risk. **Vocabulary: Describing risk** Verbs and adjectives used in the context of risk.	**Practice File** Vocabulary (page 24) **Practice exercises: Vocabulary 1&2** (DVD-ROM) **i-Glossary** (DVD-ROM)
Lesson 2	**Listening: Managing risks** Students listen to an expert on managing different types of risk. **Reading: Insuring trade risks** Students read an article about business insurance.	**Resource bank: Listening** (page 193) **Practice exercises: Listening** (DVD-ROM) **Text bank** (pages 134–137)
Lesson 3	**Language review: Adverbs of degree** Students look at adverbs such as *rather*, *slightly* and *extremely* and use them in a number of situations. **Skills: Reaching agreement** Students listen to the language of agreement in a company meeting then put this language into action in a role play.	**Practice File** Language review (page 25) **Practice exercises: Language review 1&2** (DVD-ROM) **ML Grammar and Usage** (Unit 10) **Resource bank: Speaking** (page 181) **Practice File** Survival Business English (page 65) **Practice exercises: Skills** (DVD-ROM)
Lesson 4 *Each case study is about 1½ to 2 hours.*	**Case study: Winton Carter Mining** A mining company decides whether to proceed with negotiations about a joint venture in Africa. Students assess different areas of risk involved and decide whether to proceed with the joint venture or not.	**Case study commentary** (DVD-ROM) **Resource bank: Writing** (page 209) **Practice File** Writing (page 26) **Test File: Progress test 2**

For a fast route through the unit focusing mainly on speaking skills, just use the underlined sections.

For one-to-one situations, most parts of the unit lend themselves, with minimal adaptation, to use with individual students. Where this is not the case, alternative procedures are given.

BUSINESS BRIEF

All business is built on risk. Operating in politically unstable countries is one of the most extreme examples of this. The dangers may range from **kidnapping** of managers through to **confiscation of assets** by the government. Company managers may have to face **fraud** and **corruption**. But the fact that companies want to work there at all shows that they think the **returns** could be very high. As always, there is a **trade-off** between risk and return: investing in very challenging conditions is a graphic, if extreme, illustration of this trade-off.

Companies do not have to go to unstable countries to be harmed by criminal activity. **Industrial espionage** has existed for as long as there have been industries to spy on, but this can now be carried out at a distance by gaining access to company computer networks. **IT security** specialists may try to protect their company's systems with **firewalls** (technical safeguards against such snooping by **hackers**, and against **computer viruses)**.

So far we have looked at some of the more extreme examples of risk, but even business as usual is inherently risky. For example, by putting money into a new venture, investors are taking serious financial risks. Most new businesses fail – some put the figure as high as nine out of ten. **Venture capitalists** who put money into such businesses **spread their risk** so that the **payback** from the one or two successful ventures will hopefully more than compensate for the money lost in the failures. For more on financial risk, see Unit 9 Raising finance.

There is also the risk that even **well-established companies**, which are seemingly in touch with their customers, can easily start to go wrong: we can all think of examples in soft drinks, clothing, cars and retailing, to name a few. Here, the risk is of losing sight of the magic ingredients that made for success. Some companies are able to reinvent themselves, in some cases several times over. Others don't understand what they need to do to survive and thrive again, or if they do understand, are unable to transform themselves in the necessary ways. The things about the company that were formerly strengths can now become sources of weakness and obstacles to change. The financial markets see this and the company's shares fall in value. Investors are increasingly quick to demand changes in top management if there are not immediate improvements. In some cases, companies that were the leaders in their industry can even go bankrupt: in airlines, think of PanAm.

And then there is the risk of management **complacency**. Take Toyota. A few production faults can put a car company at risk through **product liability claims** following accidents caused, for example, by stuck accelerator pedals. **Product recalls** are the worst possible publicity imaginable for companies, and in the worst cases their image is so damaged that they never recover. This is a case study in **reputational risk**: the trust that customers put in a company can be lost overnight. Another example of a company that destroyed the trust of its clients is the Internet service provider that announced free access at all times, and then immediately withdrew the offer. One commentator described this as **brand suicide**.

Read on

Chris Chapman, Stephen Ward: *Project Risk Management*, Wiley, 2003

Michel Crouhy et al: *The Essentials of Risk Management*, McGraw Hill, 2006

Andy Jones, Debi Ashenden: *Risk Management for Computer Security,* Butterworth-Heinemann, 2005

Tony Merna and Faisal Al Thani: *Corporate Risk Management*, Wiley, 2008

LESSON NOTES

Warmer

- Write the word *Risky* on the left of the board and dashes indicating the number of letters in the words that come after it, like this (the figures in brackets indicate the number of dashes to write up):

	_ _ _ _ _ _ _ _ (8)
	_ _ _ _ (4)
	_ _ _ _ _ _ _ _ _ _ (10)
Risky	_ _ _ _ _ _ _ (7)
	_ _ _ _ _ _ (7)
	_ _ _ _ _ _ _ _ (8)
	_ _ _ _ _ _ _ _ _ _ _ (11)

- Tell the students that all the missing words are or can be business-related. They have to guess what they are. Tell them to call out words they think of.

- If they have trouble, give them clues by showing particular letters, for example all the Es in the words, like this:

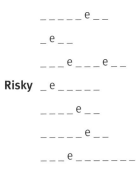

	_ _ _ _ _ e _ _
	_ e _ _
	_ _ _ e _ _ _ e _ _
Risky	_ e _ _ _ _ _
	_ _ _ _ e _ _
	_ _ _ _ _ e _ _
	_ _ e _ _ _ _ _ _

- For words that the students still don't get, start giving other letters, or clues to their meaning, for example, the third one means 'when you put money into a business activity, or the amount of money you put in'.

- Students should eventually end up with seven typical combinations, like this:

> business
>
> deal
>
> investment
>
> **Risky** lending
>
> project
>
> strategy
>
> undertaking

- Point out that the last one has nothing to do with funerals, and means 'project' or 'enterprise'.

Overview

- Tell the students that they will be looking at risk.

- Ask the students to look at the Overview section at the beginning of the unit. Tell them a little about the things on the list, using the table on page 51 of this book as a guide. Tell them which points you will be covering in the current lesson and which in later lessons.

Quotation

- Ask the students to look at the quotation and say what it means. You could ask them to 'translate' it into more normal English, e.g. 'If you never take risks, you'll never drink champagne.' Invite comments and encourage brief discussion.

Starting up

Students look at different types of risk.

 A

- Talk about the question with the whole class. Work on risk-related vocabulary relevant to the discussion that you have, e.g. *cautious, conservative, risk-averse, prudent* versus *daring, bold, adventurous,* etc.

B

- Get the students to work in pairs on the different types of risk and say which thing is the most and least risky in each group. Circulate and assist.

- Ask pairs for their findings. Invite comments and encourage discussion. (In the case of travel, don't get too bogged down in lugubrious statistics!)

- In discussing money, ask the students if anything is done in their country/countries to warn of the risks inherent in particular types of investment. You could mention health warnings on cigarettes and, on some investment products in the UK, this 'health warning': 'The value of your investment can go down as well as up, and you may not get back the money you invested.' Point out the use of 'health warning' in this financial context.

- Ask if the students think such warnings are a) effective and b) necessary. Also ask: 'Shouldn't people just be free to indulge in risky behaviour if they want to?'

C

- Get the students to work in pairs on the risks that businesses face. You could get them to suggest examples of risks that have actually materialised for particular companies. Circulate and monitor.

- With the whole class, ask pairs for what they came up with. Invite comments and encourage discussion.

LESSON NOTES

Vocabulary: Describing risk

Students look at verbs and adjectives used in conjunction with risk.

A

- Do as a whole-class activity. Write the four verbs *predict*, *meet*, *assess* and *manage* on the board and get the students to say which heading the other verbs should come under, explaining their meanings if necessary. Work on pronunciation, e.g. of *gauge*.

predict	meet	assess	manage
anticipate	encounter	calculate	eliminate
foresee	identify	estimate	minimise
		evaluate	prioritise
		gauge	reduce
		measure	spread
		weigh up	

B

- Ask the students to work in pairs on the matching exercise, pointing out clues. For example, if there is *impossible to* at the end of an item on the left, look for an infinitive verb at the beginning of the item on the right.

- Circulate, monitor and assist. (An *actuary* – item 6 – is a specialist who works for or advises a financial institution. For example, life insurance companies employ actuaries to calculate future mortality rates of policyholders, the payouts that will have to be made, and their timing.)

- Ask the students for their answers.

> **1** e **2** f **3** g **4** d **5** c **6** b **7** a

C – **D**

- Get students to work on Exercise C in pairs. Elicit the answers.

Exercise C

1 slight **2** great **3** minuscule **4** considerable
5 potential **6** immediate **7** huge **8** remote
9 serious **10** negligible **11** significant
12 imminent **13** substantial **14** terrible
15 tremendous

- Then group adjectives on the board under the two headings with the whole class.

Exercise D

1 High: great, considerable, huge, serious, significant, substantial, terrible, tremendous	**Low**: slight, minuscule, remote, negligible
2 Possible: potential	**Very near future**: immediate, imminent

Work on the stress of words like *sigNIFicant*, *subSTANtial*, *NEGligible* and *IMMinent*.

- Point out to students that *MINuscule* is quite an 'advanced' word at this level, and that it is *not* pronounced *mini-school*.

E

- Get the students to work in pairs on the four types of risk mentioned. Circulate, monitor and assist. Note language points for praise and correction, especially in relation to the verb and adjective combinations in Exercises A and C above.

- With the whole class, praise good language points from the discussion and work on three or four points that need improvement, getting individual students to say the correct forms.

◎ i-Glossary

Listening: Managing risks

Students listen to an expert talking about ways of managing different types of risk.

A ◀)) CD2.10

- Go through the instructions with the class so that they know what information they are listening for. (You could tell them they will hear two types of internal risk and three types of external risk altogether.)

- Play recording 2.10 once or twice.

- Check answers with the whole class. Explain any difficult words and work on pronunciation, for example, of *mechanism*.

> Internal risk: injuries to employees within a factory, fire in a warehouse
>
> External risk: earthquake, tsunami, change in exchange-rate mechanism

B ◀)) CD2.10

- Play the recording again and ask the students to find the terms missing from the diagram.

- Check answers with the whole class. Work on pronunciation of difficult words, e.g. *typhoon* and *liquidity*.

> **1** hurricanes **2** floods **3** employment
> **4** lack of liquidity* **5** competition
> **6** availability of new technology
>
> *Means that a company has little immediately available cash, even though it has other assets. Not to be confused with insolvency, where a business can no longer operate because it has run out of money and is unable to borrow more.

C ◀)) CD2.11

- Play recording and ask the students to take notes on the five key steps to risk management.

- Elicit the answers with the whole class.

1 Recognise strategic objectives for organisation and key processes

2 Identify risks affecting the organisation (top down and bottom up)

3 Assess and prioritise risks

4 Mitigate (explain this as *reduce*) the risk and deal with it by a) treating it, b) terminating it, c) tolerating it or d) transferring it.

5 Flow actions back to strategic objectives

- Check answers with the class and explain any difficult words.

D 🔊 CD2.12

- Play the recording and get students to listen out for the three examples of organisations that failed to manage risk.

- Elicit the answers with the whole class. Get pairs to report their responses to the whole class. Invite comments and encourage further discussion.

- Banking industry: *systematic and reckless risk-taking** with massive implications for the organisations, the banks, their shareholders and the world in general

- US-based clothing retailer: lost 45 million credit-card details, losses of $80m and impact on reputation

- Video-cassette industry: failed to anticipate changes in customer demand caused by new technologies

*Means making investments which will not only have implications for the parties involved, but also for the whole industry or market, and done so with a disregard for the possible negative consequences.

- Get students to give other examples of badly managed risk, perhaps ones involving oil companies, car companies, pharmaceutical companies or food companies.

E

- Get students to look at the script on page 158–159 of the Course Book in pairs, underlining the structuring language.

- Go round the class and assist where necessary.

- Bring the class to order and get students to call out the expressions they found. Do as a quick-fire whole-class activity.

Key words and phrases from audio script

CD2 TRACK 10

...there are two ways of looking at risk. One way of looking at risk is to divide risks ...

...some examples of internal risks include ...

Examples of external risks can include ...

The other way of looking at risk is to divide up risk into four categories ...

And finally, and most importantly ...

CD2 TRACK 11

There are five key steps to ...

The first step ...

Following on from step one, step two then goes on to ...

Point three: after identifying risk, the next stage is to ...

Point four ...

Firstly ...; Secondly ...; Thirdly ...; Finally ...

Two examples could be ...

CD2 TRACK 12

A great example involves ...

Moving to a lower level of risk, there's a great example of ...

A great example is ...

🔘 Students can watch the interview with Steve Fowler on the DVD-ROM.

➡️ Resource bank: Listening (page 193)

Reading: Insuring trade risks

Students read an article about business insurance.

A

- Have a discussion with the whole class on this question as a quick-fire whole-class activity.

B

- Ask students to read the article quickly and come up with the main point of the article.

Suggested answer

Risk is becoming more complex.

C – **D**

- Get students to look at the three questions and the instruction in D and get them to read the article individually or in pairs.

- Go round the class and assist where necessary.

- Bring the class to order and elicit the answers.

Exercise C

1 It started when fourteenth-century shipowners wanted to protect the increasing value of their ships and cargoes.

2 Reinsurers provide a secondary market where insurance companies can place risks.

3 Because the attack on the World Trade Center took place in a developed country, it was well covered by insurance. However, the tsunami of 2004 affected mainly underdeveloped countries who had little or no insurance, so the cost to individuals was much higher.

- With the whole class, get students to suggest their summaries.

- Check and compare answers with the whole class.

E – F

- Do these exercises as quick-fire whole-class activities.

- Work on pronunciation and stress, e.g. *caTAStrophe*.

Exercise E

1 liability   2 damages   3 portfolio
4 accumulation   5 catastrophe

Exercise F

1 damages   2 liability   3 catastrophe
4 portfolio   5 accumulation

G – H

- Encourage the students to find and underline the word partnerships in the article so that they can see them in context and quickly refer back to them.

- Give students time to do both exercises and then bring the class to order and elicit the answers.

Exercise G

1 b   2 c   3 e   4 a   5 d

Exercise H

1 spring to mind   2 pave the way
3 bear the brunt   4 spread the risks
5 meet a need

I

- Depending on time available, do as a quick-fire whole-class activity or get students to work in small groups and then report their findings to the whole class.

 Text bank (pages 134–137)

Language review: Adverbs of degree

Students look at adverbs such as *rather*, *slightly* and *extremely* and use them in a number of situations.

- Go through the explanations with the whole class.

A

- Get students to work on the exercise in pairs. Go round the class and assist where necessary.

- Bring the class to order and elicit the answers.

Strengthen: entirely, exceptionally, extremely, fully, highly, increasingly, totally, very

Soften: a bit, fairly, moderately, quite, rather, reasonably, slightly, somewhat

- Work on pronunciation and stress, for example *enTIRElly, exCEPTionally*.

B

- Get the students to complete the dialogues. Ask them which adverbs are possible in each sentence and which are not. For example, in question 1, *exceptionally*, *extremely* and *very* are possible, but the other adverbs from the same group would be very unlikely. Tell the students there are no 'rules' about this: it's a question of learning the typical combinations.

Suggested answers

1 Extremely/Exceptionally/Very   2 highly/very
3 increasingly/exceptionally/extremely
4 fully/very   5 Quite/Fairly/Reasonably

- In parallel pairs, get students to read the dialogues using correct intonation and stress.

- Then get individual pairs to give performances for the whole class.

C

- Get the students to work in pairs, each pair working on four or five phrases. (For example, half the pairs could work on situations for the first five phrases and the other half on situations for the last ten.) Each pair should make up mini-conversations like the ones in Exercise B above.

S1: *What did you think of the presentation?*

S2: *Fascinating. And the speaker was incredibly well-prepared. All the equipment worked first time and the handouts were very useful.*

- Circulate and monitor, but this time don't make notes of all language points. Concentrate on the intonation of the adverb expressions. Encourage the students to exaggerate slightly, but not to go too far over the top!

- Get pairs to give performances of the situations in front of the whole class. One performance for each situation will probably be enough. Work on intonation of adverb expressions as necessary.

Skills: Reaching agreement

Students listen to the language of agreement in a meeting called in order to organise a sales conference. They then put this language into action in a role play.

A 🔊 CD2.13

- Remind students of the context of the brainstorming meeting from Unit 2. Play recording 2.13 once right through and then once or twice more, pausing at convenient points.

- Elicit the answers with the whole class.

> **1** Florence **2** interactive quiz
> **3** banquet-style buffet in hotel **4** January

B

- Go through the expressions in the Useful language box. Get individual students to read them out, completing them as if they were contributing to the meeting they have just listened to, for example: *Does anyone have strong feelings about the location?* (They should not use exactly the same expressions as they heard on the recording.)

- Ask the students to work in pairs on expressions 1–13. Tell them they can look at the audio script on page 159 to check the context if necessary, and that some expressions go under more than one heading. Circulate and assist.

> Asking for opinions: 5, 6, 9
>
> Giving opinions: 2, 4, 11
>
> Agreeing: 3, 12, 13
>
> Disagreeing: 10
>
> Making suggestions: 7, 8, 11
>
> Summarising: 1, 3, 9

- Ask pairs for their answers, and to give their reasoning for them.

C

- Present the situation to the whole class and make sure they understand it.

- Put the students into threes or fours and start the discussion.

- Circulate and monitor, noting language points for praise and correction, especially in relation to discussion language.

- When the students have completed their meetings, call the class to order. Ask each three what they decided.

- Praise good language points from the discussion and work on three or four points that need improvement, getting individual students to say the correct forms, especially for discussion language. (Be especially strict with expressions with *agree*. For example, correct students who say *I am agree.)*

> **One-to-one**
>
> This role play can be done one-to-one. Don't forget to note language points for praise and correction afterwards.

➡ Resource bank: Speaking (page 181)

CASE STUDY

Winton Carter Mining

A mining company decides whether to proceed with negotiations about a joint venture in Africa.

Background

- Tell the students to read the Background section for themselves. While they are doing this, write the points on the left in the table below on the board. When the students have finished reading, elicit information to complete the table.

Company	Winton Carter Mining (WCM)
Based in	Canada
Value	C$85 million
Structure	Going public next year (=shares being made available to outside investors for the first time)
Activity	Mining copper, cobalt and bauxite
Areas where active	Politically stable African countries

- Ask students to talk about the discussion question in groups of four or five. (To pre-empt confusion, you could point out that the adjective _unstable_ relates to the noun _instability_.)

- Go round the class and assist where necessary.

- Bring the class to order. Ask a representative of each group to report its findings.

- Get students to read quickly through the article and check understanding by asking some comprehension questions.

A difficult decision

- Get students to read through the text and explain _joint venture_ to them if necessary: when two companies work together on a particular project.

- Ask students to talk about the discussion questions quickly in the same groups of four or five again.

- Bring the class to order and ask for their opinions. (Students might mention that WCM will probably run into trouble with the stock market authorities where they issue their shares if they don't mention the project in the prospectus, and then go ahead with it!)

🔊 CD2.14

- Get students to focus on the background to the recording and the two questions and then play it. (Point out that _CFO_ stands for _chief financial officer._)

- Elicit the answers: they decide to wait for the report from the New Business department. It's probably a good idea to have as much information as possible before making the decision.

Task

- Go through steps 1 and 2 in the task with the whole class.

- Allocate roles in each group of four or five, ensuring that each student knows which role they have.

- Start the activity. Go round the class and monitor the language they are using.

- When most groups have evaluated the risks, bring the class to order.

- Go through steps 3 and 4. Then appoint a strong student as chair of the meeting of the whole class.

- Get the chair to ask a representative of each group what their evaluations were and write the results on the board.

- The chair should then ask the whole class to vote on whether to continue negotiations with ATZ or not.

- Praise good language points from the group and whole-class discussions and work on three or four points that need improvement, asking individual students to say the correct forms. Refer especially to their use of language from the Skills section if they studied it earlier.

One-to-one

Stages 1 and 2 of the case study can be done one-to-one as a discussion between teacher and student. In the role play, take the part(s) of one or more of the directors and get your student to take one of the other parts. Then get them to take the decision in point 4 of the task. Don't forget to note language points for praise and correction after the activities. Praise and correct your student's use of language as appropriate, and highlight some of the language you chose to use as well.

◉ Students can watch the case study commentary on the DVD-ROM.

Writing

- Ask the students to do this collaboratively in class or individually as homework. Remind them that they should outline the risks and give the final recommendation as to whether to continue negotiating with ATZ or not. Also remind them that this writing task should follow the format of a report, as in the Writing file, page 131.

➡ Writing file, page 131

➡ Resource bank: Writing (page 209)

Working in new markets

This unit focuses on aspects of cultural awareness important for people in companies that would like to start selling in new markets abroad.

- Go through the introduction, checking students' understanding.

A

- Discuss the question with the whole class. (Before the class, check that you know where Kazakhstan is!) Answers could range from what clothes to take on a business trip at particular times of year to information about Kazakh tax law.

B 🔊 CD2.15

- Prepare students for what they are going to hear by going through the headings with them.

- Play the recording once or twice, getting students to complete the information.

- Go through the answers with the whole class.

General information

- Population: just under 15 million

- Land area: ninth largest country in world, same size as western Europe

- Ethnicity: mainly Kazakhs (51.8%) and Russians (31.4%), also Chechens, Ukrainians, Tatars, Germans and Koreans

- First contacts: don't immediately talk about business, but start with some small talk (teach this expression) about family

Verbal/Non-verbal communication

- Space between speakers: arm's length

- Eye contact: keep good eye contact

- Handshakes: definitely with a man; allow woman to take initiative

- Voice: they speak quietly and may give a lot of background information when answering a question

- If there is time, get students to compare the cultural information with that for their own country, e.g. *In Finland, we would tend to stand further apart than at arm's length when talking to someone. We would keep eye contact about half of the time.* etc.

C

- Explain the task and go through the questions.

- Then get students to read the extract in parallel pairs. Go round the class and assist where necessary.

- Bring the class to order and elicit the answers.

1 Men: black/dark trousers, white/light shirt
   Women: fashionable, latest designer clothes

2 More relaxed than other countries, e.g. can drop in and see an official during working hours without an appointment

3 Bosses, because of Soviet influence

4 Knowledgeable, showing leadership qualities, being approachable

5 **a)** Decisive, clear leadership
   b) People-oriented

6 Build trust by talking about things that matter to Kazakhstanis, e.g. family, children, health.

7 A lot of food, a variety of drinks and lots of toasts

- Again, if there is time, get students to compare Kazakhstan with their own countries, but don't preempt the following sections too much.

D

- Discuss these questions with the whole class. Treat cultural issues tactfully.

Task

- Explain the task. In larger classes, students could prepare the presentation in groups of three, not knowing in advance which one of them will have to give it. Preparation could be done as homework, and you could get students to do one or two presentations in each of the next few classes. (To maintain interest, it would probably best not to have more than about three one after the other in one class.)

- During the presentations, note language points for praise or correction later, especially ones in relation to cultural issues/vocabulary. After each presentation, go through these.

UNIT B Revision

This unit revises and reinforces some of the key language points from Units 4–6 and from Working across cultures 2, and links with those units are clearly shown. You can point out these links to your students.

4 Success

Vocabulary

● This exercise revisits prefixes used in front of particular verbs and adjectives. As always, get students to look at the complete context of each sentence before deciding on the answer.

> **1** ultra- **2** under **3** de **4** over **5** co-
> **6** re **7** mis **8** out **9** ex- **10** multi

Skills

● Students have another chance to put negotiating skills language into practice. Get them to look at the complete conversation before doing the exercise.

> **1** increase **2** give **3** repeat **4** deliver
> **5** have **6** lowered **7** saying **8** is **9** ask
> **10** planning **11** make **12** leave

Writing

● Point out the importance of a good opening in this type of e-mail. Emphasise that a friendly lead-in, before getting to the nitty-gritty (teach this expression) of the negotiation is very important.

> **Suggested answer**
>
> Dear Lo Chi,
>
> I was very pleased to have met you last week at your office. I found the discussions very interesting. I've been thinking further about how to resolve the order size and scheduling problem. I'd like to suggest that we break the order into three parts. If we order 150,000 today, can you deliver 50,000 on 3 April, 50,000 on 10 April and 50,000 on 17 April? That would allow you enough time to deliver and would keep the item price down.
>
> I look forward to hearing from you.
>
> Sincerely,
>
> Anton

5 Job satisfaction

Vocabulary

● Students work further on synonyms and the correct grammatical form of expressions.

> **Exercise 1**
>
> **1** e **2** d **3** c **4** h **5** b **6** g **7** a **8** f
>
> **Exercise 2**
>
> **1** frustration **2** satisfied **3** recognised
> **4** motivating, motivation(al)* **5** frustrating
> **6** recognition
>
> * Point out that the noun *motivation* can be used adjectivally here.

Passives

● This is to reinforce work on formation and use of passives.

> **1** The working week has been cut to 30 hours (by the management) since the downturn.
> **2** My team were/was given a new assignment (by me).
> **3** The employees are being listened to (by the management).
> **4** A lot of change was caused by the new regulations.
> **5** Customers should be encouraged to give feedback.
> **6** New e-mail addresses are always set up by Ben in IT.
> **7** Some important maintenance was carried out overnight.
> **8** The new workers will be expected to speak good English.

Writing

● Remind students that they can check the format of guidelines in the Writing file, Course Book page 127.

> **Suggested answer**
>
> **1** What should I do if I think someone is overworking and getting burnt out?
>
> Talk about their workload with them. Try to find out if they, too, think they're getting burnt out. If possible, take away some of their workload. Encourage them to work reasonable hours and keep in regular communication about possible problems.
>
> **2** How can I motivate staff who complain that they are underpaid?
>
> If you can't offer them a pay increase, try to motivate them with fringe benefits. Encourage them to take advantage of the flexitime system. Also remember to lead by example. Be cheerful at work, and be a good listener. Be approachable. Speak clearly and honestly with them.

> **3** What should I do if a worker arrives at work late every day?
>
> Try to deal positively with the situation. Remind them that flexitime is available. Encourage them to use it. If you feel that the employee may be suffering from depression, encourage them to speak with their doctor.

6 Risk

Vocabulary

- As ever, get students to look at the grammatical context of the gapped expressions, e.g. in Exercise 1, item 1, *We're* followed by *a downturn* suggests that the missing word will be a continuous form of a verb.

> **Exercise 1**
>
> **1** anticipating   **2** weighed up   **3** prioritise
> **4** identified   **5** spreading   **6** estimate
> **7** encounter   **8** eliminate
>
> **Exercise 2**
>
> **1** immediate   **2** remote   **3** potential
> **4** minimal

Adverbs of degree

- Again, get students to look at the overall sense of each item before completing them.

> **1** exceptionally   **2** increasingly   **3** totally
> **4** a bit   **5** fully   **6** highly

Skills

- More work on language for reaching agreement.

> **1** d   **2** a   **3** h   **4** g   **5** b   **6** f   **7** e   **8** c

Cultures 2: Working in new markets

- Students get more practice in cross-cultural vocabulary.

> **1** Dress   **2** punctuality   **3** formality
> **4** decision-making   **5** Socialising
> **6** leadership quality   **7** eye contact
> **8** Shaking hands

Management styles

	Classwork – Course Book	Further work
Lesson 1 *Each lesson (excluding case studies) is about 45 to 60 minutes. This does not include administration and time spent going through homework.*	**Starting up** Students comment on some statements about management style. **Vocabulary: Management qualities** Students look at vocabulary relating to management qualities and use it to discuss different management styles.	**Practice File** Vocabulary (page 28) **Practice exercises: Vocabulary 1&2** (DVD-ROM) **i-Glossary** (DVD-ROM)
Lesson 2	**Listening: Successful managers** Students listen to an expert talking about the qualities of good managers and the management style that gets the best results. **Reading: Management styles** Students read about people with two very different management styles and say which style they prefer.	**Resource bank: Listening** (page 194) **Practice exercises: Listening** (DVD-ROM) **Text bank** (pages 138–141)
Lesson 3	**Language review: Text reference** Students look at the ways texts are held together by words like *it*, *this* and *they*. **Skills: Presentations** Students study some presentations language and put it into practice.	**Practice File** Language review (page 29) **Practice exercises: Language review 1&2** (DVD-ROM) **Resource bank: Speaking** (page 182) **Practice File** Survival Business English (page 67) **Practice exercises: Skills** (DVD-ROM)
Lesson 4 *Each case study is about 1½ to 2 hours*	**Case study: Selig and Lind** A multinational company must choose a new manager with the right management style to lead an international project team. Students evaluate the suitability of four managerial candidates and try to reach a decision on who to appoint.	**Case study commentary** (DVD-ROM) **Resource bank: Writing** (page 210) **Practice file** Writing (page 30)

For a fast route through the unit focusing mainly on speaking skills, just use the underlined sections.

For one-to-one situations, most parts of the unit lend themselves, with minimal adaptation, to use with individual students. Where this is not the case, alternative procedures are given.

BUSINESS BRIEF

Traditionally, the model for **leadership** in business has been the army. Managers and army officers give orders and their **subordinates** carry them out. Managers, like army officers, may be sent on leadership courses to develop their **leadership skills**. But some would say that leaders are born, not made, and no amount of training can change this. The greatest leaders have **charisma**, a powerful attractive quality that makes other people admire them and want to follow them. A leader with this quality may be described as a **visionary**. Leaders are often described as having the **drive**, **dynamism** and **energy** to inspire the people under them, and we recognise these qualities in many famous business people and politicians. The leadership style of a company's boss can influence the management styles of all the managers in the organisation.

In some Asian cultures, there is management by **consensus**: decisions are not **imposed** from above in a **top-down approach**, but arrived at in a process of **consultation**, asking all employees to contribute to decision-making, and many western companies have tried to adopt these ideas. Some commentators say that women are becoming ever more important as managers, because they have the power to build consensus in a way that the traditional **authoritarian** male manager does not.

One recent development in consensual management has been **coaching** and **mentoring**. Future senior managers are 'groomed' by existing managers, in regular one-to-one sessions, where they discuss the skills and qualities required in their particular **organisational culture**.

Another recent trend has been to encourage employees to use their own **initiative**: the right to take decisions and act on their own without asking managers first. This is **empowerment**. **Decision-making** becomes more **decentralised** and less **bureaucratic**, less dependent on managers and complex formal management systems. This has often been necessary where the number of management levels is reduced. This is related to the ability of managers to **delegate**, to give other people responsibility for work rather than doing it all themselves. Of course, with empowerment and delegation, the problem is retaining control of your operations, and keeping those operations profitable and on course. This is one of the key issues of modern management style.

Empowerment is related to the wider issue of company **ownership**. Managers and employees increasingly have shares in the firms they work for. This of course makes them more **motivated** and **committed** to the firm, and encourages new patterns of more responsible behaviour.

Read on

John Adair, Neil Thomas: *The Best of Adair on Leadership and Management*, Thorogood, 2008

David Clutterbuck, David Megginson: *Techniques for Coaching and Mentoring*, Butterworth-Heinemann, 2004

Richard Mead, Tim Andrews: *International Management: Culture and Beyond*, Wiley Blackwell, 2008

LESSON NOTES

Warmer

- Write *management styles* in big letters on the board. Ask the students to brainstorm what they understand by this term.

- Ask them for their definition ('ways that managers relate to and deal with the people under them' or something similar, if your students are stuck). Invite comments and encourage brief discussion to arouse interest, without pre-empting the topics in the unit.

Overview

- Ask the students to look at the Overview section at the beginning of the unit. Tell them a little about the things on the list, using the table on page 62 of this book as a guide. Tell them which points you will be covering in the current lesson and in later lessons.

Quotation

- Read out the quotation and ask the students to comment. (This quotation should not be too controversial!)

- Write *Management is …* on the board, adding *tasks* and *discipline* one above the other on the right of the board. As a quick-fire whole-class activity, get the students to give you other words that could follow 'Management is …'. Students might say 'structure' and 'organisation' but also encourage more unexpected words like 'imagination', 'vision' and 'creativity'.

Starting up

Students comment on some statements about management style and talk about the role of manager.

A

- Ask the students to comment on the statements in pairs. Circulate and assist with any difficulties.

- With the whole class, discuss the pairs' findings. If there are students from more than one country, obviously be tactful and do not disparage any particular style. However, there should be some interesting material for cross-cultural comparisons, even if the students are from the same country, but thinking about different companies with different management styles.

Emphasise that there are no 'right' answers, but here are some ideas:

1 A good idea if the department is small enough (but be careful with people who dislike mixing their personal and professional lives).

2 This could seem intrusive, but was for a long time seen as a manager's prerogative, and may still be in some places.

3 Most people enjoy occasional praise. Criticism must be constructive and not degenerate into bullying.

4 Most employees would probably like managers to arbitrate in at least some disputes.

5 People with specific, hard-earned skills may be happy to be able to do things that their managers are unable to do.

6 Some companies have an 'open-door' policy, and encourage employees to take comments and pursue grievances to the highest level. Others would not encourage this. 'At all times' might mean being able to phone your manager at home until late in the evening, but in many places there is a strict division between home and work and you would not be able to do this.

7 There are probably two basic types of manager here: those who get involved in socialising with staff and those who find it easier to manage by staying clear. Again, this can be a cultural issue.

8 Probably a good idea in theory, but many organisations are known for profane language between employees when away from customers with, at times, highly-developed in-house slang. Racist or sexist comments should not be tolerated, of course.

9 True in many, if not most, cultures. But there are managers who pride themselves on finishing the day on time, for example by refusing to be distracted from the tasks at hand, and gain the admiration of their less organised employees for being able to do this.

10 Staff with customer contact would probably expect to be commented on if their appearance is not up to scratch. Others might find it more difficult to accept this. There are many employer–employee disputes in this area, of course.

B – C

- Ask the students to discuss both questions in pairs and then ask the pairs to report to the whole class. Invite comments and encourage discussion.

Vocabulary: Management qualities

Students look at related forms of words for management qualities and use it to discuss different management styles.

A

- Ask your students to work in pairs to look at the adjectives. You could get some pairs to look at adjectives 1–7 and other pairs 8–14. You could ask the students to use a dictionary such as the *Longman Dictionary of Contemporary English*. (If the question comes up, you could say that there are negative forms for some but not all of the nouns, but that some can be pretty rare – for example, *inconsiderateness* exists, but not *inconsideration* or *uncreativity*.)

Adjective	Opposite adjective	Noun form
considerate	inconsiderate	consideration/ considerateness *
competent	incompetent	competence/ competency *
creative	uncreative	creativity/ creativeness *
diplomatic	undiplomatic	diplomacy
efficient	inefficient	efficiency
flexible	inflexible	flexibility
inspiring	uninspiring	inspiration
logical	illogical	logic/logicality
loyal	disloyal	loyalty
organised	disorganised/ unorganised **	organisation
decisive	indecisive	decisiveness/ decision
responsible	irresponsible	responsibility
sociable	unsociable	sociability
supportive	unsupportive	support

Where there are alternative forms, say that:

* Here, they are more or less interchangeable when talking about people, though some forms (such as *creativity*) are more frequently used than the other.

** Here, there is a slight difference of meaning: *disorganised* – very bad at arranging or planning things; *unorganised* – having no organisation at all. Reassure students that most native speakers would find it hard to define this difference!

● Discuss the answers with the whole class, but don't get bogged down talking about the alternative forms.

B 🔊 CD2.16

● Start by pointing out the stress of *conSIDerate* versus *consideRAtion*. Say that students should listen out for the stress patterns in the words in the recording (or read them out yourself).

● Play the recording and get students to underline the stressed syllables.

● Go through the answers with the whole class.

1 considerate, consideration	**2** competent, competency
3 creative, creativity	**4** diplomatic, diplomacy
5 efficient, efficiency	**6** flexible, flexibility
7 inspiring, inspiration	**8** logical, logic
9 loyal, loyalty	**10** organised, organisation

11 decisive, decisiveness	**12** responsible, responsibility
13 sociable, sociability	**14** supportive, support

● You could then relate the stress patterns to the stress marks shown in the dictionary for these words.

C – **D**

● Get students to rank the qualities quickly in pairs.

● Bring the class to order and ask different pairs for their rankings. Compare and discuss.

● Then, with the whole class, get them to add other management qualities or weaknesses, again being tactful about students' own organisations.

As an additional activity, you could get students to match these pairs of contrasting management styles. Write them up quickly on the board (or prepare a PowerPoint or overhead projector slide before the lesson).

1 autocratic	**a)** collaborative
2 centralising	**b)** controlling
3 directive	**c)** delegating
4 empowering	**d)** democratic
5 hands-on	**e)** people-orientated
6 task-orientated	**f)** laissez-faire

● With the whole class, elicit the answers and discuss the expressions. (You could make a joke about French not having an expression for *laissez-faire*! Also spelled *laisser-faire*, by the way.)

2 a **3** f **4** b **5** c **6** e

E

● Rather than discussing this topic in the abstract, get the students to talk in pairs or threes about particular work tasks and situations in their organisation and the appropriate style for each situation.

● With the whole class, ask the pairs and threes for their comments and encourage discussion. (If your students are pre-work, they may find it difficult to talk about this. If so, move on to the next section.)

 i-Glossary

Listening: Successful managers

Students listen to an expert talking about the qualities of good managers.

A 🔊 CD2.17

● Before you play the recording, get students to guess what the factors mentioned in the question might be. (This could be difficult for students, especially if they are pre-work, but it will get them to concentrate on what they are about to hear.)

● Play the recording and elicit the answers.

1 The ability to manage in an increasingly competitive, volatile, changing business environment; concern for recognition of the individual within the organisation.

Example: the growth of the BRICK* nations (Brazil, Russia, India, China, [South] Korea)

2 Managing with an increasing rate of technological change, allied to the competitive and challenging business environment.

Example: ICT, e.g. used in managing remote teams

* BRIC is the original term, coined in 2001 by Jim O'Neill, head of global economic research at Goldman Sachs. Korea is not really in the same category as the others. Some even add Mexico, to give 'BRIMCK', a rather unwieldy acronym. For more information, see http://en.wikipedia.org/wiki/BRICs

B 🔊 CD2.18

- As ever, get students to focus on the question before you play the recording.

- Play the recording once or twice. You may need to pause it at key points to allow the students to make notes.

- Check the answers with the class.

1 Consideration, respect and trust
2 Recognition and credit
3 Involvement and availability
4 A sense of justice
5 Positive action on an individual basis
6 Emphasis on end results

C 🔊 CD2.19

- Get students to read through the text before you play the recording. Ask them to say what they think might go in the gaps.

- Play the recording once or twice, stopping at convenient points and elicit the answers.

1 direction   2 organised   3 structure
4 routine   5 individual   6 organisational
7 committed   8 direction   9 control

D

- Put the students in pairs and ask them to think of five ways in which managers can get the best out of people. Then ask the pairs to join another pair, making a group of four, and pool their ideas.

- Get a representative of each group to report their ideas to the class.

◎ Students can watch the interview with Laurie Mullins on the DVD-ROM.

➡ Resource bank: Listening (page 194)

Reading: Management styles

Students read an article about the management styles of two very different people, and compare them.

A

- Discuss the questions with the whole class. Be tactful in dealing with question 1, especially if you are teaching in-company and there are managers present!

B

- Get students to look through the statements 1–6. Allocate the articles to students and get them to read them, deciding which statements are true. Go round the class and assist where necessary.

- Bring the class to order and elicit the answers from the different readers of each article.

Anna Wintour: 2, 3, 5
Jim Buckmaster: 1, 4, 5, 6

C

- Get students to read their respective articles in more detail.

- Then get them to compare and contrast Anna Wintour and Jim Buckmaster, using expressions such as: *On the one hand …, on the other …; whereas; however,* etc. Get students to use more interesting expressions than *but.*

D

- Ask the students who have read the Anna Wintour article to answer the question.

demanding, perfectionist, ruthless

E – F

- The students can do this activity individually or in pairs.

- With the whole class, elicit the answers.

- Work on stress and pronunciation, e.g. *perFECTionist.* (You could point out to that *ruthless* has no positive form 'ruthful'!)

Exercise E

1 ruthless   2 perfectionist   3 talented
4 self-motivated   5 anti-authoritarian
6 approachable 7 demanding   8 volatile

- Then get students to complete the text as a quick-fire whole-class activity.

Exercise F

1 approachable   2 volatile   3 perfectionist
4 anti-authoritarian   5 talented   6 self-motivated

G

- Get students to discuss the questions in pairs. Go round the class and assist where necessary.

- Bring the class to order and get representatives of pairs to report their 'findings' and encourage discussion.

- Work on any remaining difficulties, especially ones related to management styles vocabulary.

Text bank (pages 138–141)

Language review: Text reference
Students look at the ways texts are held together by words like *it*, *this* and *they*.

- Go through the points in the Language review box with the whole class, explaining any difficulties. (Point out that a lot of these features occur in spoken English as well, of course.)

A – E

- Get students to look through the articles individually or in pairs, going through all the exercises A–E.

- With the whole class, elicit the answers, discuss them and clarify any difficulties.

Exercise A

We: the people who work in the office
that sort of thing: arcade games, fussball, ping-pong tables
it: the atmosphere in the office
it: being in the office
I: Jim Buckmaster
we: the people who worked for the organisations Jim used to work for
thing: management action
those things: the management style of his previous employers
our: the workforce of Craigslist's
it: what they're supposed to do
they: Craigslist employees
we: Craigslist managers
they: deadlines
They: artificial deadlines
it: stress
We: the management of Craigslist
my: Jim Buckmaster's
it: 'empty' subject
that: being in a position of authority
you: Jim Buckmaster
there: at Craigslist
it: the philosophy at Craigslist
We: the management of Craigslist
we: the management of Craigslist
it: 'empty' subject
their: the people who work at Craigslist's
you: the company
them: meetings
I: Jim Buckmaster
they: closed-door meetings

Exercise B

It should also be said (line 6)

Exercises C/D

She: Wintour
she: Wintour
Her: Wintour's
It: empty subject
she: Wintour
your: Wintour's
She: Wintour
I: Wintour
I: Wintour
I: Wintour
I: Wintour
they: people
that: liking people who are representative of what they do
you: people
I: Wintour
She: Wintour
I: Wintour
you: staff
It: a magazine
I: Wintour
I: Wintour
mine: Wintour's
We: staff
we: staff
our: staff's
one: a person
it: empty subject
I: Wintour
It: empty subject
We: staff
she: Wintour
I: Talley
that: intimidation
her: Wintour's
she: Wintour
She: Wintour
you: people
her: Wintour's
She: Wintour
she: Wintour
your: staff's
it: looking at your work
I: Coddington
she: Wintour
you: people
her: Wintour's
You: staff
you: staff
her: Wintour's
I: Coddington
it: having to walk a mile before getting to her desk

Exercise E

The former: Wintour's critics

F

- Ask the students to write the article in pairs, or individually for homework. If they are writing it in class, circulate, monitor and assist. Note any strong points and any problems in writing, perhaps ones common to more than one pair.

- Praise good language used in the writing and work on three or four points that need improvement, getting individual students to say the correct forms.

- Get one or two pairs to read out their articles for the whole class (choose at least one agreeing with the statement and one disagreeing with it). If they do the exercise for homework, they can read them out in the next lesson.

- Encourage further discussion generated by the students' articles.

Skills: Presentations

Students look at some of the language typically used in presentations. (Presentations language is also dealt with in Unit 12.)

A ◀))) CD2.20, 2.21

- Before going any further, get students to look at the expressions in the Useful language box to get an idea of what presentations language involves. Work on stress of difficult words, for example *unDOUBTedly*.

- Then get students to look at the instruction for Exercise A and questions 1–4. Play the recording and elicit the answers.

> 1 Quench Iced Tea
> 2 early next March
> 3 available in several flavours (lemon, green, strawberry, grape) and in three different varieties (sweetened, unsweetened, diet); contains a high percentage of vitamins, especially C and E; two different sizes; eye-catching, appealing design
> 4 information pack including a web link

B ◀))) CD2.20

- Get students to look at items 1–5. Play the first part of the recording again

- Elicit the answers and discuss any difficulties.

> 1 launched   2 unique features
> 3 different versions; edge
> 4 stress; wide appeal
> 5 health-conscious customers; selling point

C ◀))) CD2.21

- Follow the same procedure as for Exercise B above.

> 1 **a** Turning now to **b** high-quality
> 2 slide
> 3 **a** mean **b** means **c** choice
> 4 **a** beautifully designed **b** eye-catching
>   **c** appealing **d** stand out
> 5 **a** summarise **b** appeal
>   **c** outstanding design
>   **d** comprehensive marketing programme

D

- Do as a quick-fire whole-class activity and work again on stress and intonation of the expressions. Get students to read the expressions in a slightly over-the-top way (but not too much!), for example: *It has MAny outSTANding FEAtures*.

> **Exercise B**
> 1 Stating the purpose
> 2 Involving the audience
> 3 Discussing implications
> 4 Emphasising/Exemplifying
> 5 Persuading
> **Exercise C**
> 1 Changing the subject
> 2 Referring to visuals
> 3 Involving the audience
> 4 Referring to visuals
> 5 Persuading

E

- Get students to prepare a short presentation in pairs or for homework. (Where appropriate, they could make this more like a salesperson's product demo – it would be good if they could have the product with them to demonstrate, for example a camera, iPad, etc.)

- If students prepare it in class, circulate, monitor and assist.

- Then get one member of the pair to give their presentation demo. Note any strong points and any problems, perhaps ones common to more than one presentation.

- After each presentation, praise strong language points and correct ones that need work, getting individual students to say the right thing.

➡ Resource bank: Speaking (page 182)

CASE STUDY

Selig and Lind

A multinational company must choose a new manager with the right management style to lead an international project team.

Background

- Ask the students to read the background information about Selig and Lind (S&L). Meanwhile, write the points in the first column of the table on the board.

- With the whole class, elicit the information to complete the table.

Products	Top-of-the-range electronics products for affluent people
	Classical look, innovative design
History	Founded 1985, international expansion, 500 stores now
Research team	Project team – 16 members carrying out research into customer service to retail outlets in 6 countries
Structure of team	16 members from different countries
Current problems	Report deadlines missed
	Morale low
	Project manager, Paul Johnstone, not up to it (teach this expression) because of wrong management style
Solution	Replace Paul Johnstone with someone more suitable

Paul Johnstone's management style

🔊 CD2.22, 2.23, 2.24

- Go through the instructions with the class before you play the recording. Ensure that everyone understands that they are directors of S&L who have interviewed three members of the project team. Go through the six headings with the students and encourage them to use these headings to structure their notes when they hear the recording.

- Play recordings 2.22, 2.23, and 2.24. You may need to play it more than once and pause it at appropriate points to allow the students to complete their notes. Explain any difficulties.

- When the students have finished, ask them to compare their notes in pairs or small groups.

- Have a whole-class feedback session on the strengths and weaknesses of Paul Johnstone's management style.

Replacing the project manager

- Ask the students to read the description that each of the candidates to replace Paul Johnstone has written about their own particular management style. Circulate, monitor and assist.

- With the whole class, get different students to sum up the management style of each candidate.

Task

- Divide the class into groups of four and go through the instructions with the whole class. Get each group to appoint someone to take notes about who says what. These notes must be particularly clear if you are going to ask the students to do the follow-up writing task.

- When the students are clear what they have to do, the first part of the meeting, during which they discuss the four candidates and analyse their strengths and weaknesses, can begin.

- When they have finished, ask the students to go back to working in their groups and to rank, individually, the four candidates in terms of their suitability for the position of project manager. Make sure that they use the numbering system suggested in the Course Book and ensure that clear notes are taken in each group about their discussion and their decision.

- Then get students in each group to come to a consensus on the order of the candidates, for example, by voting for each one.

- Bring the whole class together again and ask one representative from each group to report back to the class, in the form of a short presentation, on what they discussed and how the group ranked the candidates. Write the recommendation of each group on the board.

One-to-one

This case study can be done one-to-one, with the student analysing the information and then discussing the candidates and choosing one of them for the position. Don't forget to note language points for praise and correction afterwards. Highlight some of the language you chose to use as well.

◎ Students can watch the case study commentary on the DVD-ROM.

Writing

- Ask the students to base their writing on the notes taken in their group during the simulated meeting. The writing can be done collaboratively in class or as homework.

- If your students are doing the writing task individually for homework, you may want to photocopy the notes made by the notetaker in each group so that each student has a record of what was said and decided in their group.

➡ Writing file, page 131

➡ Resource bank: Writing (page 210)

Team building

AT A GLANCE

	Classwork – Course Book	Further work
Lesson 1 *Each lesson (excluding case studies) is about 45 to 60 minutes. This does not include administration and time spent going through homework.*	**Starting up** Students talk about their experiences of teams they have been in and do a quiz about different types of team members.	
	Vocabulary: Prefixes Students look at a number of prefixes and use them in context to talk about people they have worked with and teams they have been in.	**Practice File** Vocabulary (page 32) **Practice exercises: Vocabulary 1&2** (DVD-ROM) **i-Glossary** (DVD-ROM)
	Listening: Building successful teams A specialist in team building talks about the key success factors.	**Resource bank: Listening** (page 195) **Practice exercises: Listening** (DVD-ROM)
Lesson 2	**Reading: New ways of team building** Students read about the use of cookery courses for team building.	**Text bank** (pages 142–145)
	Language review: Modal perfect Students look at how modal perfect verbs such as *needn't have*, *may have*, *might have*, *must have*, *could have*, *should have* and *would have* are used.	**Practice File** Language review (page 33) **Practice exercises: Language review 1&2** (DVD-ROM) **ML Grammar and Usage** (Unit 8)
Lesson 3	**Skills: Resolving conflict** Techniques for dealing with disagreements: students apply the language for this to a role play in which one member of a team is causing problems.	**Resource bank: Speaking** (page 183) **Practice File** Survival Business English (page 69) **Practice exercises: Skills** (DVD-ROM)
Lesson 4 *Each case study is about 1½ to 2 hours*	**Case study: Motivating the sales team** There are problems when a new manager takes over the sales team of a kitchenware company. Students role-play the directors of the company and attempt to resolve these problems.	**Case study commentary** (DVD-ROM) **Resource bank: Writing** (page 211) **Practice File** Writing (page 34)

For a fast route through the unit focusing mainly on speaking skills, just use the underlined sections.

For one-to-one situations, most parts of the unit lend themselves, with minimal adaptation, to use with individual students. Where this is not the case, alternative procedures are given.

BUSINESS BRIEF

In constructing teams, it's important not just to get talented people, but the right combination of talents. In the famous phrase, it's important to have a great team of minds, rather than a team of great minds. Meredith Belbin sees these types as necessary in teams, whether in business or elsewhere:

- The **Implementer**, who converts the team's plan into something achievable
- The **Co-ordinator**, who sets agendas, defines team-members' roles and keeps the objectives in view
- The **Shaper**, who defines issues, shapes ideas and leads the action
- The **Plant**, who provides the original ideas and finds new approaches when the team is stuck
- The **Resource Investigator**, who communicates with the outside world and finds new ways to get things done
- The **Monitor Evaluator**, who evaluates information objectively and draws accurate conclusions from it
- The **Team Worker**, who builds the team, supports others, and reduces conflict
- The **Completer/Finisher**, who meets deadlines, gets the detail right and makes sure nothing is forgotten.

This model lends itself better to some business situations than others, but the idea of roles and competencies in a team is important, whatever form these take in particular situations. Some organisations are more **hierarchical** and less **democratic** than others, and team members are obviously expected to behave more deferentially in the former. Senior managers there have the traditional leader's role: what they say goes. In other organisations, power is more **devolved** and managers talk about, or at least pay lip-service to, the **empowerment** of those under them: the idea that decision-making should be decentralised to members of their teams.

In addition to the traditional organisation, we increasingly find **virtual organisations** and virtual teams. People are brought together for a particular project and then disbanded. Here, in addition to Belbin's types above, the role of the **Selector/Facilitator** is crucial. Finding the right talents and co-ordinating them takes on new importance, especially when the team members may never actually meet face-to-face, but work by e-mail and phone.

Stages of team life

The typical team is said to go through a number of stages during its existence.

1 **Forming:** The group is anxious and feels dependent on a leader. The group will be attempting to discover how it is going to operate, what the 'normal' behaviours will be: how supportive, how critical, how serious and how humorous the group will be.

2 **Storming:** The atmosphere may be one of conflict, with rebellion against the leader, conflict between sub-groups and resistance to control. There is likely to be resistance to the task, and even the sense that the task is impossible.

3 **Norming:** At this stage, members of the group feel closer together and the conflicts are settled, or at least forgotten. Members of the group will start to support each other. There is increasingly the feeling that the task is possible to achieve.

4 **Performing:** The group is carrying out the task for which it was formed. Roles within the group are flexible, with people willing to do the work normally done by others. Members feel safe enough to express differences of opinion in relation to others.

5 **Mourning:** The group is disbanded, its members begin to feel nostalgic about its activities and achievements. Perhaps they go for a drink or a meal to celebrate.

All this may be familiar from the groups we encounter, and play our role in managing, in language training!

Read on

John Adair: *Effective Teambuilding*, Pan, 2009

Meredith Belbin: *Team Roles at Work*, Butterworth Heinemann, 2010

Brian Cole Miller: *Quick Team-Building Activities for Busy Managers*, Amacom, 2003

The first four stages of team life above were suggested by B W Tuckman, as quoted in Michael Argyle: *Social Interaction*, Tavistock, 1969

LESSON NOTES

Warmer

- Write the word *teams* in big letters on the board. Ask students in pairs or threes to brainstorm all the types of team they can think of, in the business world and outside. (Point out that you are not looking particularly for words that come in front of *team*.) Circulate and monitor.

- After a few minutes, ask pairs and threes to say what they came up with. Invite comments and encourage discussion.

Examples:

sports teams, project development teams, sales teams, medical teams doing operations, management teams, teams of ministers with their political advisers and civil servants

Overview

- Tell students that in this unit they will be looking at team building.

- Ask students to look at the Overview section at the beginning of the unit. Tell them a little about the things on the list, using the table on page 70 of this book as a guide. Tell them which points you will be covering in the current lesson and in later lessons.

Quotation

- Ask the whole class what they understand by the quotation and if they agree with it.

Starting up

Students talk about their experiences of the teams they have been in and do a quiz about different types of team members to see what profile they themselves have.

A

- Ask students to discuss in pairs. Circulate, monitor and assist.

- Get pairs to report their findings to the whole class.

Possible issues

Advantages	Disadvantages
Things can be achieved by a team that can't be achieved by individuals working separately – some things can only be achieved by teams.	Explaining and organising the task can take so much time that it's easier and quicker to do it yourself.
Some people prefer working with others rather than on their own.	Communication breakdowns can lead to severe problems in achieving the task.

Teamworking allows everyone to feel they have something to contribute.	Conflict between team members can be very destructive.

B – C

- Go through the quiz with the whole class and explain any difficulties.

- Divide the class into threes or fours. Appoint someone in each group who will record members' responses but also do the quiz themselves.

- Tell the notetakers that after the activity, they will be giving a mini-presentation about the group members' profiles as team players. Read out the text in the box below to give them the idea.

Anita is a creative type who values original ideas over detailed planning. Bertil, on the other hand, is more interested in clear thinking. Catherine found that the quiz told her that she is more interested in details and clear planning, and she was a bit surprised by this. The quiz told me I'm more of a creative person, which I tend to agree with.

- Students in each group do the quiz individually, finding what sort of team player they are by looking at the key on page 136 of the Course Book. Students then tell the other members of the group what sort of team player they are and the notetaker records this. Notetakers should also record if the other students agree with what the quiz tells them.

- Circulate, monitor and assist. Note language points for praise and correction.

- When students have finished the quiz, the notetaker summarises the profile of each group member as you did in the example above.

- Praise good language points from the discussion and work on three or four points that need improvement, getting individual students to say the correct forms.

- Ask your students to work on the questions in Exercise C in threes or fours. Circulate and monitor.

- Ask the groups for their answers. Invite comments and encourage discussion.

Vocabulary: Prefixes

Students look at a number of prefixes and use them in context to talk about people they have worked with and teams they have been in.

A

- Go through the prefixes quickly with the whole class. Get students to read the words with the correct stress patterns, e.g. *PRO-EuroPEan, DISconNECT*. Point out the pronunciation of *bi-* as in *buy*, not as in *bee*.

- Get students, in pairs, to match the prefixes to their meanings.

- With the whole class, quickly go through the answers.

> **1** b **2** b **3** c **4** a **5** c **6** b* **7** c **8** a
> **9** b **10** b
>
> *You could point out that some words beginning *ex* do not relate to the meaning 'former'. For example, a common error among native speakers is to spell *expatriate* with a hyphen, making it look as though it means someone who was, but is no longer, patriotic! The prefix *ex* here means 'outside', of course – someone living outside their own country.

- With the whole class, get students to give typical combinations containing the words with prefixes. Give them one or two possible combinations from the list below as examples. Do as a quick-fire activity.

> - mismatch a person with a particular job
> - pro-European voters, politicians
> - predict events, the future
> - pre-event arrangements
> - post-activity reports
> - disconnect a machine, etc. (You could also point out the increasing use of *disconnect* as a noun: e.g. 'the disconnect between voters and politicians'.)
> - ex-military security personnel
> - bilateral trade agreements
> - remotivate demoralised staff
> - multicultural society, teams

B – C

- Point out the correct pronunciation of *Esprit de corps* – nothing to do with dead bodies! Get students to work in pairs on the text. Circulate and assist.

- Check the answers with the whole class.

> **Exercise B**
> **1** mismatched **2** disconnected
> **3** remotivate **4** multicultural **5** ex-military
> **6** pre-event **7** post-activity **8** hyperlink
>
> **Exercise C**
> **2** maximise **3** break down **4** stimulate
> **5** inspire **6** build **7** reduce

D

- Add the prefixes as a quick-fire activity with the whole class.

> **1** uncommunicative **2** indecisive
> **3** inefficient **4** unenthusiastic **5** inflexible
> **6** unfocused **7** unimaginative **8** disloyal
> **9** disorganised **10** impractical
> **11** unsociable **12** unstable **13** intolerant
> **14** impatient

- Get students to work, in pairs, on the questions. Circulate, monitor and assist. Treat question 1 tactfully. Tell students they don't have to name the people involved.

- When reporting back to the class, each member of the pair talks about the other member's colleagues in relation to question 1. For question 2, one member of the pair talks about their general findings.

◉ i-Glossary

Listening: Building successful teams

A specialist in team building talks about the key factors for success.

A 🔊 CD2.25

- Tell students they are going to listen to Dan Collins, who runs a team-building consultancy. Ask students to listen out for the answer to the specific questions.

- Play the recording once or twice, explaining anything that is unclear.

- Elicit the answers.

> **1** A team is a group of people working towards a common goal.
> **2** A leader's role is to make sure that goal is well understood and is clear, and then to encourage people along the way as they work towards that objective.

B 🔊 CD2.26

- Play recording 2.26 once or twice, helping with any difficulties.

- Elicit the answer.

> They do not have the chance to have conversations without a 'subject heading' – i.e. informally – about what they want to achieve as a team.

C 🔊 CD2.27

- Play the recording and ask the students to answer and discuss the questions in pairs or small groups. Circulate, monitor and assist, noting language points for praise and correction.

- Get pairs or groups to report their responses to the whole class. Invite comments and encourage further discussion.

- Praise good language use from the discussion and work on three or four points that need improvement, getting individual students to say the correct forms.

> Leaders: either appointed to the position or natural leaders
>
> Creators: solve problems either by having random ideas or by using analysis and research
>
> 'Gluers': pull the team together, motivated by relationships, pastoral* needs of team, e.g. arranging a Christmas party or birthday cards

Doers: look at process and project management, so that things are done on time, accurately and to a high quality

*Explain that this means looking after the emotional or 'spiritual' needs of people.

D 🔊 CD2.28

- Get students to focus on the question. Play the recording and elicit the answers.

a) Empowered form of leadership, where someone is given an instruction and left to do it how they want to

b) Command-and-control approach, with specific instructions and people working to those instructions

- If any students have worked or are working in Asia, ask tactfully whether they agree with the description of teamworking given by Dan Collins.

E

- Get students to provide ideas about the tasks that a team would be used for in their organisation, or one they would like to work for, and write them up on the board quickly.

- Allocate a task to each small group of students and get them to choose four people that they know for it, giving their reasons in terms of what they contribute to the team. (Try to go beyond the idea that they 'would be nice to work with'.)

- Each group then talks about which people they have chosen with the whole class, and why, again concentrating on the skills/qualities that they could bring to the team.

  ◎ Students can watch the interview with Dan Collins on the DVD-ROM.

  ➡ Resource bank: Listening (page 195)

Reading: New ways of team building

Students read about why it is important for people in business to be team players.

A

- Ask the whole class what they think of the idea of cookery classes to encourage team building. (Don't be surprised at some would find the idea strange!) Point out the pronunciation of *recipes*.

B

- Ask the students to read the article quickly. Go round the class and assist where necessary.

- Ask if their earlier ideas were confirmed and what other advantages there are. Check the answers with the whole class.

Foster team spirit; relax; entertain clients; bring people together; therapeutic; help break down barriers; cut across ages, backgrounds and cultures; choice of level of participation; meal at the end; feel natural, not contrived; opportunity to see how teams work under different circumstances

C – D

- Get students to scan the article for the information. Get individual students to volunteer the answers as soon as they find them.

Exercise C

1 cookery schools	2 clients	3 location
Venturi's Table	Abbott Mead Vickers, Merrill Lynch, eBay, Cereal Products Worldwide, Mars	Wandsworth
The Cookery School	Investec, BP, Iron Mountain	Little Portland Street, London
Mosimann's Academy		
Lavender House		Norfolk
The Food and Wine Academy		

1 a) Anna Venturi is the founder of Venturi's Table. She says cooking appeals because it brings people together; it's relaxing, not competitive; wide range of people; can build teams

b) Masele Siatu'u is Human Resources Vice-President at CPW. He says cooking brings together employees from different parts of the world.

c) Christi Strauss is Chief Executive of CPW. She says cooking bridges backgrounds and cultures. Anyone can take part and participate as much as they like.

d) Richard Pash is Marketing Manager at Mars. He says cookery feels natural and not contrived compared to some team-building activities, which seem pointless.

e) Rosalind Rathouse is the Principal of The Cookery School. She says corporate clients make up about 33% of her business.

f) Letizia Tufari is the daughter of Anna Venturi. She says that client hospitality is becoming a bigger part of the business.

2 They offer client entertaining. This is successful because just eating out has become boring; cooking a meal for yourself is more unusual.

E

● With the whole class, get students to volunteer the answers.

> **1** foster   **2** barriers   **3** venture   **4** hospitality
> **5** stream

F

● Get students to work on these questions in pairs.

● Get representatives of each pair to give their 'findings'.

● In relation to question 4, for homework, you could get them to research the websites of organisations that offer team-building courses and report back in the next lesson. What do your students think of 'paintball battle'-type team-building courses, for example? Be prepared for very different attitudes from some male and female students to the more 'military' type of activities!

G

● Preferably, get students to do this for homework. Don't forget to ask them for it (for example, by e-mail), check it and give feedback.

➡ Text bank (pages 142–145)

Language review: Modal perfect

Students look at how modal perfect verbs such as *needn't have, may have, might have, must have, could have, should have* and *would have* are used and what they mean.

● Go through the points in the Language review box with the whole class, inviting and answering queries.

A

● Ask individual students to read out the sentences in italics, without doing the exercise. Concentrate on stress and the correct pronunciation of contractions like *needn't* and *couldn't*.

● Do the exercise as a whole-class activity, elaborating where necessary.

> **1** no
> **2** yes
> **3** no
> **4** no
> **5** not sure
> **6** yes
> **7** no
> **8** not sure

B

● Ask students to work on the questions in pairs. Circulate, monitor and assist.

● Go through the answers with the whole class, pointing out the subtleties mentioned below, but don't make it too complicated in relation to the students' level.

> **1** It's too late to sign the contract. You **should** have done it last week. (But you didn't and now it's too late.)
>
> **2** I'm a bit angry. You **could** have told me you had invited the entire team for dinner. (But you didn't.)
>
> **3** Correct. Point out to students that it means the same as 'might have ruined'. (But it didn't.) And if you say 'may have ruined', you don't know yet whether the team spirit was ruined or not, a) because you haven't found out yet if it was ruined or not, or b) because you're not sure if this was the cause of it being ruined.
>
> **4** They bought the shares when they were cheap and sold them at their peak, so they **must** have made a lot of money. (We don't know for sure, but we think this is very likely.)
>
> **5** Correct. (We don't know for sure what the reason was. 'She must have been delayed' would show more certainty.)
>
> **6** Correct.
>
> **7** She's made a lot of mistakes. She **must** have been very careless. (We're assuming that her carelessness was the cause of the mistakes.)
>
> **8** Abi was inspirational and a motivator. We **should** have made her team leader. (But we didn't.)

C

● Go through the situation quickly with the whole class.

● Divide the class into pairs, appointing a sales rep and Finance Director in each pair.

● To show the class what to do, take the part of the Finance Director and ask one of the students to be the sales rep. Say: 'You shouldn't have stayed in a five-star hotel', to which the sales rep should reply something like: 'There was no alternative. There was a big conference on and it was the only place I could get a room.'

● Continue with one or two of the other points, emphasising that the sales rep should find convincing excuses each time and vary the formula, so they don't say, 'There was no alternative' every time, but use sentences like 'I had no choice', and 'There was nothing else I could do.'

● When the whole class has understood the idea, ask them to role play the situation. Circulate, monitor and assist, especially with the modal perfect. Note language points for praise and correction.

● Praise good language points from the discussion and work on three or four points that need improvement, especially with the modal perfect, getting individual students to say the correct forms.

● Ask for one or two public performances of the situation for the whole class.

One-to-one

This role play can be done one-to-one. Ask your student to be the sales rep and you take the role of Financial Director. Then change roles. Encourage imagination. Don't forget to note language points for praise and correction, especially in relation to the modal perfect.

Skills: Resolving conflict

Students look at techniques for dealing with disagreements in teams. They work on the language for this and apply it to a role-play situation in which one member of a team is causing problems.

A

- Go through the suggestions with the whole class.

Suggested answers

Do: 3, 4, 5, 7, 9, 10

Don't: 1, 2, 6, 8

- Ask students to categorise the statements with a show of hands for each one.

- Invite comments and encourage discussion. The above division is for illustration only – there may be disagreements. For example, there are those who say that there is no point in trying to win over impossible people, and that energy is best expended elsewhere. Some may say that anger also has its place.

B CD2.29

- Play recording 2.29 and ask the students to put a tick next to the suggestions in Exercise A that Karen uses. You will probably have to play the recording several times.

- Allow the students to compare answers in pairs before checking with the class.

1, 5, 10

C 🔊 CD2.29

- Go through the expressions already in the Useful language box and ask students, in pairs, to add one more expression under each heading when you play the recording again.

Making suggestions

I think there's one thing you could all do ...

... maybe you should talk to her, tell her how you feel ...

Why don't we wait for a while?

Showing sympathy

OK, Larissa, I think I understand now.

OK, I've got the picture. I understand your feelings, Larissa ...

Resolving the conflict

What do you want me to do?

Reviewing the situation

Let's talk about this in a few weeks' time.

We can review the situation then.

D

- Divide the class into pairs, appointing the team leader and team member in each pair.

- Tell students to turn to their particular role description. Get them to read it silently. Circulate, monitor and assist.

- If you think it's necessary, do a demonstration in front of the whole class of the beginning of the situation, with you as the team member and an outgoing student as team leader.

- When all the students are clear about their roles and about the situation, start the activity.

- Circulate and monitor but do not intervene except if absolutely necessary. Note language points for praise and correction, especially in the area of conflict-resolving language.

- When students have finished, call the whole class to order. Praise good language points and work on three or four points that need improvement, getting individual students to say the correct forms.

- Ask one of the pairs to give a public performance in front of the whole group.

➡ Resource bank: Speaking (page 183)

CASE STUDY

Motivating the sales team

There are problems when a new manager takes over a sales team. Students role-play the directors of the company in their efforts to resolve them.

Background

● Get students to read the Background section and the notes on David Seymour and the members of the sales team. Meanwhile, write the points in the first column of the table below on the board.

● Elicit information from students to complete the table.

Company and location	Designer Kitchen Products (DKP), Leicester, England
Products	Range of high-quality kitchenware
Sales Manager	David Seymour (DS)
Appointed	1 year ago
His task	Improve sales revenue, create high-performing sales team
Problems	Sales below target (20% increase had been the objective)
	Low morale
	Asian expansion in doubt
	Launch of new products next year in doubt

David Seymour's plans 🔊 CD2.30

● Focus students' attention on the question. Tell them they should listen to the meeting, taking notes on David Seymour's training plans and the team members' reactions to them. Play the recording, stopping and convenient points. Afterwards, ask students to describe DS's plans.

● More training: Two courses a year to update knowledge – compulsory. DS and staff members to suggest subjects

● Max (top salesman): Not a good idea. Doesn't like courses, doesn't need more training. Wants to concentrate on customers.

● Hank: Thinks Max has an easy sales area (W. London). Training a good idea, for some of the others at least – Natalya, for example.

● Laura: More training needed but not for everyone. Clients should not be neglected.

● Natalya: Agrees training not needed for everyone (for example Max), but thinks she would benefit if not more than once a year.

● Sonia: Thinks training is a waste of time.

● Chang: Thinks things need to be addressed on an individual basis.

● Get students to discuss in pairs whether or not they think the plans will be helpful to the team's performance.

Task preparation

● Divide the class into groups of four and allocate roles. Establish that the four members of each group are all directors of DKP and that they are going to have a meeting to discuss the situation and decide what to do. Director A leads the meetings.

● Tell them that each of the directors has thought about the company's problems and has different opinions and suggestions about what they should do. The students should read their role cards carefully (without showing them to other members of the group) and prepare to represent their views at the meeting. If their role cards mention any of the members of the sales team specifically, they should read the descriptions of those people carefully. Circulate, monitor and assist with anything the students don't understand.

● Go through the three points (points 2, 3 and 4) that will form the basis of the discussion with the whole class and answer any queries.

Task

● When the situation is clear, the discussions can begin. Circulate and monitor. Note language points for praise and correction, especially in the area of team building.

● When the groups have finished, with the whole class praise good language points from the discussion and work on three or four points that need improvement, getting individual students to say the correct forms.

● Ask the groups for the conclusions they have come to and the action they have decided to take. Note them on the board under the respective headings.

● Invite comments and encourage discussion, comparing the findings of the different groups.

> **One-to-one**
>
> This discussion can be done one-to-one. Give the student plenty of time to read and absorb the background information, the profiles of the different salespeople and the points for discussion. Discuss the issues with your student as if you are both directors of DKP.

 Students can watch the case study commentary on the DVD-ROM.

Writing

● For the first task, say that the letter should come in the form of a report to the chief executive of DKP, who was not present at the discussion.

● For the second task, say that this should be a personal letter from the sales manager to a member of the sales team.

➡ Writing file, page 126

➡ Resource bank: Writing (page 211)

Raising finance

AT A GLANCE

	Classwork – Course Book	Further work
Lesson 1 *Each lesson (excluding case studies) is about 45 to 60 minutes. This does not include administration and time spent going through homework.*	<u>**Starting up**</u> Students compare sources of borrowing and discuss some common sayings about money. **Vocabulary: Financial terms** Students look at some key financial vocabulary. **Listening: Ways to raise money** A finance specialist talks about different ways of raising finance.	**Practice File** Vocabulary (page 36) **Practice exercises: Vocabulary 1&2** (DVD-ROM) **i-Glossary** (DVD-ROM) **Resource bank: Listening** (page 196) **Practice exercises: Listening** (DVD-ROM)
Lesson 2	**Reading: Finding finance** Students read about different ways of obtaining new business finance. **Language review: Dependent prepositions** Students look at the prepositions that follow certain verbs, adjectives and nouns and use them in context.	**Text bank** (pages 146–149) **Practice File** Language review (page 37) **Practice exercises: Language review 1&2** (DVD-ROM)
Lesson 3	<u>**Skills: Negotiating**</u> Students discuss negotiating tips, look at different techniques used in negotiations and put them into action in a role play.	**Resource bank: Speaking** (page 184) **Practice File** Survival Business English (page 71) **Practice exercises: Skills** (DVD-ROM)
Lesson 4 *Each case study is about 1½ to 2 hours*	<u>**Case study: Last throw of the dice**</u> Two young filmmakers negotiate for finance to make a feature film. Students role-play the filmmakers and distributors and try to negotiate a deal.	**Case study commentary** (DVD-ROM) **Resource bank: Writing** (page 212) **Practice File** Writing (page 38) **Test File: Progress test 3**

For a fast route through the unit focusing mainly on speaking skills, just use the underlined sections.
For one-to-one situations, most parts of the unit lend themselves, with minimal adaptation, to use with individual students. Where this is not the case, alternative procedures are given.

BUSINESS BRIEF

You have a brilliant but unusual business idea. You could put all your life savings into it, and ask friends and family to invest in it as well. But this may not be enough. Or your friends may, perhaps wisely, refuse to lend you money. You go to your local bank, but they don't understand your idea and suggest you look elsewhere.

You go to a **venture capitalist**. Venture capitalists are used to looking at new ideas, especially in hi-tech industries, and they see the potential in your brilliant idea. The venture capitalist also recommends it to some **business angels**, private investors looking for new **start-ups** to invest in. They provide you with **seed capital** to set up your business.

You launch your business and it's a great success. But the amount of money it generates from sales is not enough to invest in it further: it's not **self-financing**, so you decide to raise more capital in an **initial public offering** or **IPO**: your company is **floated** and you issue shares on a stockmarket for the first time, perhaps a market or a section of one that specialises in shares in hi-tech companies.

You wait anxiously for the day of the **issue** or **float**. Interest from investors is high and all the shares are sold. Over the next few weeks, there is a stream of favourable news from your company about its sales, new products and the brilliant new people it has managed to recruit. The shares increase steadily in value.

Now look at this process from the point of view of investors. The venture capitalists and business angels, for example, know that most new businesses will fail, but that a few will do reasonably well and one or two will, with luck, hit the jackpot, paying back all the money they lost on unprofitable projects and much more. This exemplifies the classic trade-off between **risk and return**, the idea that the riskier an investment is, the more profit you require from it.

In your IPO, there may be investors who think that your company might be a future IBM or Microsoft, and they want to get in on the ground floor, holding on to the shares as they increase inexorably in value. They make large **capital gains** that can be **realised** when they sell the shares. Or they may anticipate selling quickly and making a quick profit.

Other investors may prefer to avoid the unpredictable world of **tech stocks** altogether and go for steady but unspectacular returns from established, well-known companies. These are the **blue chips** that form the basis of many conservative investment **portfolios**. One day in a few years' time, when your company is **mature** and growing at five or 10 per cent a year, rather than doubling in size every six months, your brilliant business idea may have become a blue chip company itself.

Governments increasingly depend on investment from the private sector for their public projects. These **public-private partnerships** are financed by a combination of commercial investment and public money from taxation and government borrowing.

Read on

Mark Blaney: *Raising Finance for your Business*, How To books, 2006

Stephen Bloomfield: *Venture Capital Funding: A Practical Guide to Raising Finance*, Kogan Page, 2008

Modwenna Rees-Mogg: *Dragons or Angels? What investors in business are really like*, Crimson, 2008

LESSON NOTES

Warmer

- Introduce the unit to students by saying that you can talk about *raising finance*, *raising capital* or *raising money* for a project. They are all used to talk about obtaining money through borrowing of different kinds. (Even issuing shares in your company is a form of borrowing: the company is in effect borrowing money from shareholders even if it is not referred to as such.)

- Write the word *money* in big letters on the right side of the board, with the word *raise* on the left.

- Ask students to brainstorm in small groups the different verbs that can come in front of money. Each group should think of as many verbs as possible.

- With the whole class, ask how many verbs each group has found. Get students to call them out and write them on the left.

Possible verbs include:

borrow, donate, earn, invest, lend, lose, make, obtain, provide, save, spend, transfer, waste, win

Overview

- Tell students that in this unit they will be looking specifically at borrowing, especially by businesses raising finance in order to develop.

- Ask students to look at the Overview section at the beginning of the unit. Tell them a little about the things on the list, using the table on page 78 of this book as a guide. Tell them which points you will be covering in the current lesson, and which in later lessons.

Quotation

- Ask the whole class for their reactions to the quotation.

Starting up

Students compare sources of borrowing and talk about and discuss some common sayings about money.

- Explain *loan shark* (someone who lends money at very high rates of interest to people who aren't able to borrow from banks, and may threaten violence if it is not repaid) and *pawnbroker* (a 'shop' where you can leave something valuable such as jewellery and borrow money against it for a time. If you repay the money, you can get the article back).

- Get students to discuss the advantages and disadvantages of the different sources in pairs. Circulate and monitor. Note language points for praise and correction.

- When pairs have finished their discussion, call the class to order and praise good language points from the discussion and work on three or four points that need improvement, especially in relation to this topic, getting individual students to say the correct forms.

- Ask pairs what they came up with. Invite comments and encourage whole-class discussion.

Possible issues:

1 Bank: Advantages include: It's a business transaction that doesn't involve friends. Disadvantages include: High rates of interest, which mean it can be expensive; all sorts of problems if you can't repay the loan (your credit rating [explain] will be affected and it might be difficult to get loans in future).

2 Friend or colleague: Advantages include: Unlikely that interest will be charged. Disadvantages include: Possible damage to the relationship, particularly if the loan is not repaid promptly.

3 Member of family: Families are the main source of borrowing for many business start-ups but they might be less willing to lend for other purposes. Can lead to family tensions if the money is not repaid, of course.

4 Loan shark: Advantage: People with no credit history (because they have never had bank accounts or credit cards) can borrow money.

   Disadvantage: Interest rates are extortionate (teach this word); borrowers might be harmed if they don't repay.

5 Pawnbroker: Advantage: You can get back the article against which you borrowed money.

   Disadvantage: The amount lent will only be a proportion of the real value of the object.

   Credit card company: Advantage: Easy to do (explain *cash advance*).

   Disadvantage: Interest rates are very high; a bank loan would be cheaper.

- Ask students if they can think of other sources of borrowing. They might begin to anticipate some of the areas covered in this unit: raising money through shares and bonds.

B

- Ask the students to discuss the items and the sources of finance they would use in pairs or threes.

- Circulate and monitor.

- Ask the pairs or threes to present their findings to the whole class. Invite comments and encourage further discussion.

- Praise good language use from the discussion and work on three or four points that need improvement, getting individual students to say the correct forms.

C

- Do this with the whole class, inviting individual students to give their explanations of the sayings.

LESSON NOTES

1 Money is very persuasive.

2 Don't put all your money in the same investment. If your only investment fails, you'll be in trouble.

3 If you want to make money, you have to invest. (*Speculate* here is being used unpejoratively.)

4 If you see that what you are investing in is not working, stop investing in it.

5 Don't lend to friends.

6 This expresses the 'old' attitude to borrowing: the idea that it's to be avoided. Ask your students what attitudes are like in their own countries in relation to borrowing for different purposes, e.g. borrowing to buy a house versus borrowing to buy consumer goods.

7 The person who lends decides how the money is spent.

8 People without money can't choose, but have to make do with what they are given.

- Discuss the sayings one by one. Encourage counter-arguments and alternative viewpoints!

D

- You could do this as a fantasy exercise, encouraging students individually or in pairs to come up with some exciting (if perhaps unrealistic) business ideas!

Vocabulary: Financial terms

Students look at some financial expressions and learn how to use them.

A – **B**

- Get students to work on these in pairs. Go round the class and assist where necessary.

- Call the class to order. Elicit the answers and discuss any remaining difficulties.

Exercise A

1 a   2 b   3 c   4 a   5 c   6 a   7 b   8 c   9 b   10 b

Exercise B

2 grant   3 debtor   4 A dividend   5 Liabilities
6 A return   7 liquidation   8 Collateral*

* Explain the words *collateral* and *security* (something of value belonging to the person seeking the loan, that will pass to the lender if the loan is not repaid). The term *collateral* is used more in the US.

- Practise stress and intonation of, for example, *liaBILities, coLLATeral.*

C

- Do this as a whole-class activity or as pair work, depending on the general level of financial knowledge among your students.

The answer to most of these questions is 'It depends'. Here are some ideas.

1 Leasing is where a company pays to use machines and equipment without buying and owning them. The equipment, etc. does not appear on the company's balance sheet, which can be an advantage.

2 During the post-credit crunch recession of 2009 onwards, banks were criticised for not being willing to lend to companies and for putting *too many* controls on access to credit.

3 This is often true: a fast-growing company sells more and more, but it has to pay its employees, suppliers, etc. It will usually have to borrow money to do this, to bridge the period between the time when it pays them and the time when it receives payment from customers.

4 In some cultures, this is more than acceptable and feasible than in others, even for private individuals. Ask students about attitudes to bankruptcy in their own countries.

5 This can lead to a lot of problems for suppliers, especially ones that are small businesses – see point 3 above. In some countries such as the UK, the government is encouraging big companies to pay their small suppliers faster.

6 It depends what the business is. Opening a small restaurant will require less finance than building airliners!

 i-Glossary

Listening: Ways to raise money

A finance specialist talks about different ways of raising finance.

A 🔊 CD3.1

- Prepare students for what they are about to hear and get them to look through the two questions.

- Play the recording once or twice, depending on their level and prior financial knowledge.

- Elicit the answers.

1 equity shares, borrowing, hybrid (convertible bonds: starts out as borrowing but converts to equity)

2 **a)** confidentiality, remains 'below the radar screen' (teach this expression)

   b) more funds available

   c) more funds available

B 🔊 CD3.2

- Go through the questions and play the recording once or twice.

- Elicit the answers.

a) significant capital cost; investors expect a return that reflects the risk

b) interest burden required to be paid over time, reducing cash the company has available for investment

c) no private relationship with investors; dispersed (i.e. widely-spread) shareholder base

d) possible lack of capital available; investors want a significant return and some control over the management of the business

C 🔊 CD3.3

● Again, go through the questions and play the recording once or twice, stopping at convenient points if necessary.

● Elicit the answers. Explain any difficulties.

1 Breadth of opportunity gives investors a range of investment choices.

2 The speed and quality of information makes it easier to make a decision.

3 Banks are less relationship-driven for financing; loans are a more tradable feature. (Explain that loans are sold on by the original lender and then traded [= bought and sold] between financial institutions that have nothing to do with the original lending).

4 Easy to buy and sell shares, so the 'churn' (or turnover) of shares is high.

D

● Discuss this question with the whole class.

The idea of investing for the long term (waiting for an increase in the value of the investments, rather than taking a cut in the profits) is attractive, but many people and financial institutions want a quicker return on their money!

◎ Students can watch the interview with Simon Davies on the DVD-ROM.

➡ Resource bank: Listening (page 196)

Reading: Finding finance

Students read about different ways of raising new business finance.

A

● Discuss the question with the whole class.

Students might mention some of the ways in Starting up above, e.g. asking family members, using a credit card, etc. or in Listening, e.g. raising money through bank borrowing, shares or bonds. However, you should point out that companies issuing shares or bonds are usually pretty well established already. Most brand-new businesses will probably have to go to banks for money.

B

● Ask the students to work on the exercise in pairs. They can use a dictionary, preferably a specialised one such as the *Longman Business English Dictionary*. Circulate, monitor and assist.

● With the whole class, elicit answers from the pairs.

1 Business angels are wealthy investors, often people who have made a lot of money from a business that they themselves founded, and are now looking for new companies in which to invest.

2 Borrowing money from a bank or banks in the form of loans

3 Raising money in the form of shares (*equity capital* and *share capital* are exactly the same thing)

4 Borrowing money in the form of bonds, i.e. bondholders lend money to borrowers in the form of bonds

5 Venture capital funds look for new(ish) businesses to invest in. They know that most will fail or produce disappointing results, but that with luck they will hit the jackpot with a very successful one from time to time.

C

● Divide the class into pairs and be clear who is Student A and Student B in each pair.

● Get students to read their part of the article. Circulate, monitor and assist.

● When students are ready, get them to ask and answer questions about the other half of the article.

● Call the class to order. Clarify any difficulties. Then get some of the pairs to give 'performances' of their questions and answers for the whole class.

D

● Get students to read the entire text. Circulate, monitor and assist.

● With the whole class, elicit the answers.

1 They cost a lot to join.

2 Sanchita could pitch to roughly 100 business angels.

3 She went on the g2i four-day programme.

4 Two Finnish investors and five individuals from London Business Angels

5 The costs are high.

6 Despite reports to the contrary (teach this expression), it is still quite difficult to get funding.

7 It is taking twice as long to get funding as before the recession.

E – F

● Get students to do both exercises in pairs. Circulate, monitor and assist.

Exercise E

1 go the distance **2** a lucky break
3 hedge your bets **4** keep your ears to the ground*

* The answer is in the plural ('ears') here (leading to the alarming image of someone trying to put both ears to the ground at once!), but the idiom is more common in singular: 'keep your ear to the ground'. Tell students to use this form.

Exercise F

1 go the distance **2** lucky break
3 hedge your bets **4** Keep your ear to the ground

G

- You could do this as a role play in pairs, with one of the students playing Saha and the other the investor. Circulate, monitor and assist. Work especially on investment vocabulary.

- Call the class to order and ask one of the pairs to do a performance for the whole class.

- Do this with the whole class. This is a good opportunity to compare and contrast approaches in different parts of the world.

➡ Text bank (pages 146–149)

Language review: Dependent prepositions

Students look at the prepositions that follow certain verbs, adjectives and nouns and use them in context.

Tell students that they are going to look at prepositions following verbs, adjectives and nouns – this is what is meant by 'dependent'. Read out and comment on the examples in the Language review box. These patterns are often shown in dictionaries. For example, in the *Longman Business English Dictionary*, the pattern *invest in* is shown by (*in*) in front of the example. Get students to refer to their dictionaries if they have one.

A

- Get students to read the text and do the exercise in pairs. Circulate, monitor and assist.

- Check and discuss the answers with the whole class.

1 looked into **2** access to **3** investing in
4 turned down **5** settled on **6** pitch to

B

- Get students to look at the Grammar reference on page 150 of the Course Book.

- Prepare students for this exercise by saying that they should try to anticipate the preposition that will occur at the beginning of the second half of each sentence. For example, in question 1 they should be looking for *to*, thereby eliminating everything except parts b) and c). The sense tells you that part c) must be the right answer.

- Get students to do the exercise in pairs. Circulate, monitor and assist.

- Check and discuss the answers with the whole class, asking pairs how they came to their conclusions.

1 c **2** a **3** f **4** b **5** h **6** d **7** e **8** g
9 j **10** i

Skills: Negotiating

Students discuss negotiating tips, look at different techniques used in negotiations and put them into action to role-play a situation.

A

- Tell students they are going to look at a number of negotiating tips, which they will discuss in pairs or threes. Tell them there are no right or wrong answers, and that the statements are designed to encourage thought and discussion.

- Circulate and monitor. Intervene only if necessary. Note language points for praise and correction, especially in relation to the subject of negotiation.

- With the whole class, praise good language points from the discussion and work on three or four points that need improvement, getting individual students to say the correct forms.

- Ask the students for their findings. Invite comments and encourage whole-class discussion.

1 May depend on the complexity of the negotiation. Above all, you must listen carefully to the answers.

2 Presumably there will be a point where the other side becomes irritated if they are interrupted too much.

3 This one comes up in a lot of textbooks on negotiating. Some people think that giving something away can produce a good atmosphere. Others say that it shows weakness.

4 This is really two separate points. Simple language is probably a good idea, but some might say that it's important to underplay one's high-priority objectives and over-emphasise low-priority ones.

5 Again, there will come a point where too much of this becomes irritating.

6 On the whole, negotiators probably do not do this enough, so it's worth emphasising.

7 Some might argue that this is true in an ideal world, but in practice assertiveness (as opposed to aggressiveness) can have its place. But ideas about what is assertive rather than aggressive vary between individuals, even within the same culture. With people from different cultures, there could easily be misunderstandings.

8 Some people will be more comfortable with this than others. Some negotiators are good at exploiting the feelings of the other side. Showing emotions is more acceptable in some cultures than others.

B

- Ask students to look at expressions in the Useful language box. Go through the expressions and ask students to match the headings with the definitions given.

- Point out that open questions often begin with *wh-* words like *what*, *why*, *when*, etc. *How* is also an honorary member of this group. Closed questions can often be answered *yes* or *no*. Point out that *seems to be* is a good softening phrase.

1 d	**2** e	**3** b	**4** a	**5** c

C CD3.4

- Explain what students have to do, and then get them to work in pairs. Play recording 3.4 and pause it after each expression.

a) 2	**b)** 3	**c)** 5	**d)** 1	**e)** 4

D CD3.5

- As ever, get students to look through the exercise before they do it.

- Play the recording, giving students time to write in the answers.

All the expressions use softening phrases. In addition:
1 providing finance (*open question*)
2 approached (*closed question*)
3 make a suggestion (*signalling phrase*)
4 repayment terms (*open question*)
5 Let me clarify (*summarising*)
6 sum up (*summarising*)

E

- Explain the situation. Divide the class into threes: each three contains a business owner, a business angel and an observer. The job of the observer will be to note how the negotiation progresses and the techniques and language used by each side.

- Make sure everyone knows which role they are taking.

- Give time for students to absorb the information needed for their role. Get the observer to skim the information for both roles. Circulate, monitor and assist.

- When all students are clear about their role and what they have to do, the activity can begin. Circulate and monitor, but do not intervene unless it's necessary. Make sure that the observer in each three is taking notes.

- Note language points for praise and correction, especially ones relating to the language of negotiation.

- When students have finished their negotiation, praise good language points from the discussion and work on three or four points that need improvement, getting individual students to say the correct forms.

- Ask the observer from each three to recap the different stages and point out the techniques and language used by each side in the situation they were observing. Ask the students playing the roles in each three to say if this is a good summary of what happened.

- Recap the key negotiating phrases again, and relate them, if appropriate, to those in the Useful language box.

One-to-one

This negotiation can be done one-to-one. Ask your student which side they would prefer to represent. You represent the other side. Don't forget to note language points for praise and correction. Afterwards, ask the student about their negotiating plan, the tactics they were using, etc.

➡ Resource bank: Speaking (page 184)

CASE STUDY

Last throw of the dice

Two young filmmakers negotiate for finance to make a feature film.

Background

- With the whole class, get students to read the Background section including the Executive summary. Meanwhile write the points in the first column of the table below on the board. When students have finished reading, elicit information to complete the table.

Film makers	Charles Williams, Gunnar Larsson
Career so far	Met on film-studies course, Paris. Formed company. Made shorts (teach this expression) for TV
Project	To make a low-budget feature film
... in the form of	a business plan

- Get individual students to recap the information in complete sentences in their own words for the whole class.

Financing the film

- Apply the same steps as above to these sections.

Medium for film	Digital video
Running time	110 mins
Budget required	€1.2 million
Amount already raised	€200,000
Film's title	*All for One*
Story	Three women of different nationalities in Paris
	They become friends
	Their experiences and advice to each other
	Difficulties with French culture
	Complex relationships with men
	Bitter-sweet ending underlining strength of friendship
Potential distributor	Concordia (but Charles's father offers other possibilities)

- Get students to read quickly through the information panel on page 89 and check their understanding with some quick questions. Get them to use the points to talk about the film in complete sentences of their own.

Task

- Divide the class into fours. In each four, there are the two filmmakers and two directors from Concordia.

- Get students to turn to the correct page and give them time to read and absorb their respective information. Circulate and assist.

- Before the negotiation begins, get the two members of each side to confer with each other about their negotiation objectives and tactics: what would they be willing to compromise on?

- When everyone is clear about their information, objectives and tactics, the negotiations can begin. Circulate and assist but do not intervene unless necessary.

 CD3.6

- When you judge that both sides in each role play have come to some sort of initial agreement, call the class to order and play the recording.

- Tell students that they must decide whether they want to revise the terms of their agreement in the light of what they have just heard, and then get them to continue the negotiation in parallel groups.

- From the beginning of the negotiation, note language points for praise and correction, especially in relation to negotiation language.

- When the negotiations are complete, bring the class to order, praise good language points from the discussion and work on three or four points that need improvement, getting individual students to say the correct forms.

- Ask a member of each group to summarise briefly what happened and what was decided. Invite comments and encourage discussion.

One-to-one

This negotiation can be done one-to-one. Ask your student which side they would prefer to represent. You represent the other side. While doing the negotiation, note language points for praise and correction. Afterwards, ask the student about their negotiating plan and the tactics they were using.

Students can watch the case study commentary on the DVD-ROM.

Writing

- Students can do the writing task collaboratively in class, or for homework.

▸ Writing file page, 129

▸ Resource bank: Writing (page 212)

Managing international teams

This unit focuses on aspects of cultural awareness important for successful international teams.

A

- Get students to work in pairs on the questions and report back to the whole class. If the class is multinational, it is, by nature, a multicultural 'team', so get students to talk (tactfully) about their experiences working with people from other cultures. In monocultural groups with no experience of team working, discuss the questions quickly with the whole class.

B

- Again, get students to work in pairs on the questions. Circulate, monitor and assist. Help with the pronunciation of *charismatic* if necessary.

- Call the class to order and get representatives of each pair to report their findings. Insist on correct use of cultural vocabulary.

- Get students to draw some general conclusions about different cultural attitudes to leadership, but don't pre-empt the next section too much.

C

- Get pairs to discuss the points – you could allocate the first four points to half the class and the last four to the other half. Circulate, monitor and assist.

- Call the class to order and discuss the pairs' findings.

D – **G** 🔊 CD3.7, 3.8, 3.9

- Prepare students for what they are about to hear and read the questions. Tell them to make notes while they listen.

- Go through the various exercises and elicit the answers after each one.

Exercise D

1 motivation and rewards, problem-solving, sharing knowledge, the purpose/role of meetings, social behaviour

2 sharing of knowledge

Exercise E

1 mixed nationalities in same location, virtual teams

2 Whether they set out the tasks for the team or expect team members to use their own initiative; whether praise should be given to individuals or to the whole team

3 Because it may be felt that the whole team should either be praised or take the blame

Exercise F

a) Knowledge shared on a 'need-to-know' basis – favours the individual expert

b) Knowledge shared for the common good, built up through group discussion and trust, not felt to be the 'property' of an individual, so no 'copyright'

c) Knowledge exchanged – 'I'll scratch your back if you scratch mine'

(Here you could ask students if they agree with the statements that 'Knowledge is power' and 'Knowledge is valuable – we don't just give it away!')

Exercise G

1 If purpose isn't clear (e.g. for planning, for keeping track of progress, for talking about problems); scheduling across different time zones

2 Body language, dress, manners (e.g. handshaking), eye contact

3 It can mean different things in different cultures, and can set the tone for a business relationship

- Round off by asking the final question. In a multicultural class, be tactful about the varying opinions.

Task

- Read through the instructions with the students and clarify any problems.

- Read through the agenda for the meeting.

- Divide the class into groups of four and allocate the roles, ensuring that each student turns to the correct page.

- When the students are ready, the role plays can begin. Circulate, monitor and assist where necessary.

- Note down good use of language, especially in relation to the subject of the unit, and areas where students need further work.

- When most groups have decided on a list of recommendations and tips, call the class to order and ask representatives of each group to say what they are. Compare and contrast the recommendations from each group.

- Praise good use of language that you heard and select three or four points that need work, getting individual students to say the right thing in context.

7 Management styles

Vocabulary

This section practises vocabulary from Unit 7 Management styles.

- Get students to complete the table and the sentences in pairs. Circulate, monitor and assist where necessary.

- Call the class to order and elicit the answers.

Exercise 1

1 inconsiderate   2 consideration
3 competent   4 competence/competency
5 creative   6 uncreative   7 undiplomatic
8 diplomacy   9 decisive
10 decision/decisiveness   11 flexible
12 inflexible   13 uninspiring   14 inspiration
15 logical   16 logic   17 loyal   18 disloyal
19 disorganised   20 organisation   21 efficient
22 efficiency   23 responsible
24 irresponsible   25 unsociable
26 sociability/(society)   27 supportive
28 support

Exercise 2

1 collaborative   2 people-orientated
3 centralising   4 task-orientated
5 hands-on   6 democratic

- Get students to look through the completed table and practise stress of any words that are still causing difficulty.

Text reference

- Go back to the Language review section of Unit 7 (page 70) if necessary to recap the idea of text reference.

- Do the exercise with the whole class, getting individual students to explain the answers.

---

1 It   2 he   3 them   4 they   5 the one   6 we

Skills

- Get students to complete the exercise in pairs. When they have finished, they can go back to Unit 7 and check their answers in the Useful language box of the Skills section on page 71.

- Go through the answers, getting individual students to say each sentence. Work on stress and intonation where necessary.

---

1 b   2 e   3 a   4 f   5 g   6 d   7 h   8 c

---

8 Team building

Vocabulary

- Get students to give the meanings of the prefixes before doing the exercise in pairs or with the whole class.

- Elicit the answers.

---

1 dis   2 pre-   3 pro-   4 mis   5 post-   6 bi
7 multi   8 hyper

Skills

- Work on the stress and intonation of sentences a) to f).

- Get students to work in pairs on the exercise.

- Check the answers.

---

1 c   2 a   3 f   4 b   5 e   6 d

- Call the class to order and check the answers, then get one of the pairs to do a public performance for the whole class.

Writing

Get students to do this in class or for homework. If you give it for homework, ask students to e-mail their answers to you and work on points that are causing difficulty in the next class.

Suggested answer

Nick

I hope everything's going well. I'm sure you don't need reminding, but the sales conference is next week. I've just realised that the rest of the team have given practice presentations and shared their PowerPoint shows, but we haven't seen anything from you yet. Practice presentations are a great opportunity to improve your performance. How is your preparation going? Do you need any help with anything? I'd be happy to look at it with you any time, and I'm sure everyone else on the team would like to see what you're working on.

Please let me know if I can do anything, and let's schedule your practice presentation as soon as possible!

Ana

---

9 Raising finance

Vocabulary

- Run through the key vocabulary in the main course unit again, page 83.

- Do the exercises as quick-fire whole-class activities, working on any difficulties, e.g. pronunciation of *debtors*.

Exercise 1

1 h   **2** c   **3** f   **4** b   **5** e   **6** g   **7** a   **8** d

Exercise 2

1 assets   **2** a debtor   **3** collateral
4 a creditor

Dependent prepositions

- Before doing the exercise, get students to close their books and 'test' the students by reading out some of the words from the Language review section of Unit 9 and asking students for the prepositions that follow them.

- Then get them to do the exercise.

1 to   **2** to   **3** for   **4** about   **5** of   **6** of
7 to   **8** about   **9** to   **10** in

- Work on any remaining difficulties.

Skills

- Get students to refresh their memories by looking at the Skills section on page 87 of the Course Book.

- Get students to look through the whole exercise before doing it.

- Check the answers with the whole class.

1 softening   **2** aggressive   **3** Open
4 closed   **5** signalling   **6** summarising

Cultures 3: Managing international teams

- Get students to look through the exercises before doing them.

- With the whole class, elicit the answers and discuss the reasoning behind them.

Exercise 1

1 individual   **2** collective
3 individual, mutual debt   **4** collective
5 mutual debt   **6** individual, mutual debt
7 collective   **8** collective

Exercise 2

1 initiative   **2** expectations   **3** scheduling
4 face to face   **5** connotations   **6** cultures

Customer service

AT A GLANCE

	Classwork – Course Book	Further work
Lesson 1 *Each lesson (excluding case studies) is about 45 to 60 minutes.* *This does not include administration and time spent going through homework.*	**Starting up** Students talk about what irritates them about customer service and about the place of customer care in a company's success. **Vocabulary: Complaints** Students look at words related to customer service and some common idioms, using them in context.	**Practice File** Vocabulary (page 40) **Practice exercises: Vocabulary 1&2** (DVD-ROM) **i-Glossary** (DVD-ROM)
Lesson 2	**Listening: Customer service** A hotel/restaurant manager talks about key customer service issues. **Reading: Changing customer service** Students read about modern customer service and its place in a company's overall strategy.	**Resource bank: Listening** (page 197) **Practice exercises: Listening** (DVD-ROM) **Text bank** (pages 150–153)
Lesson 3	**Language review: Gerunds** Students study gerund formation and the way that gerunds are used. **Skills: Active listening** Students study listening skills in the context of customer service. They listen to interviews with satisfied and angry customers and learn some key expressions.	**Practice File** Language review (page 41) **Practice exercises: Language review 1&2** (DVD-ROM) **ML Grammar and Usage** (Unit 6) **Resource bank: Speaking** (page 185) **Practice File** Survival Business English (page 73) **Practice exercises: Skills** (DVD-ROM)
Lesson 4 *Each case study is about 1½ to 2 hours*	**Case study: Hurrah Airlines** A US budget airline receives a lot of communication from its passengers. Students work on prioritising different types of communication and discuss how to deal with customer complaints and how to improve customer service in the future.	**Case study commentary** (DVD-ROM) **Resource bank: Writing** (page 213) **Practice File** Writing (page 42)

For a fast route through the unit focusing mainly on speaking skills, just use the underlined sections.

For one-to-one situations, most parts of the unit lend themselves, with minimal adaptation, to use with individual students. Where this is not the case, alternative procedures are given.

BUSINESS BRIEF

Philip Kotler defines **customer service** as 'all the activities involved in making it easy for customers to reach the right parties within the company and receive quick and satisfactory service, answers, and resolutions of problems'.

Customers have **expectations** and when these are met, there is **customer satisfaction**. When they are exceeded, there may be **delight**, but this depends on the degree of **involvement** in the purchase. There is a scale between the chore of the weekly shop at the supermarket and the purchase of something expensive such as a car, that for many people only takes place once every few years. The scope for delight and, conversely, **dissatisfaction** is greater in the latter situation.

Telephone and the Internet can be used to sell some services such as banking or insurance, entirely replacing face-to-face contact. The **customer helpline** can be a channel of communication to complement face-to-face contact. Or it can be used before or after buying goods as a source of information or channel of complaint.

The figures are familiar: ninety-five per cent of dissatisfied customers don't complain, but just change suppliers. As the article in the main course unit relates, customers receiving good service create new business by telling up to 12 other people. Those treated badly will tell up to 20 people. Eighty per cent of those who feel their complaints are handled fairly will stay **loyal** and **customer allegiance** will be built.

Customer retention is key: studies show that getting **repeat business** is five times cheaper than finding new customers. **Customer defection** must of course be reduced as much as possible, but a company can learn a lot from the ones who do leave through **lost customer analysis**: getting customers to give the reasons why they have defected, and changing the way it does things.

Service providers such as mobile phone or cable TV companies have to deal with **churn**, the number of customers who go to another provider or stop using the service altogether each year.

In many services, satisfaction is hard to achieve because the **customer interaction** is difficult to control, which is why service organisations like airlines, banks and legal firms create high levels of dissatisfaction. If a product or service breaks down, fixing the problem may build **customer loyalty**, but it will also eat into the **profit margin**. Customers must be satisfied or delighted, but **at a profit**. If salespeople or call centre staff or hotel receptionists are over-zealous, there may be lots of satisfied customers, but the business may be operating at a loss.

Kotler says that it is not companies that compete, but **marketing networks,** comprising a number of companies. For example, a PC is assembled from components made by several manufacturers, sold through a call centre which may be a subcontractor, delivered by a transport company and perhaps **serviced** by yet another organisation as part of the manufacturer's **product support**. It is the customer's total experience that counts. Making the computer is just one part of this. The **logistics** of selling and organising the services needed by each customer becomes key. All this is part of **customer relationship management (CRM)**.

Read on

Francis Buttle: *Customer Relationship Management*, Butterworth Heinemann, 2008

Leonardo Inghilleri et al: *Exceptional Service, Exceptional Profit,* Amacom, 2010

Philip Kotler et al: *Marketing Management*, Prentice Hall, 2009 edition, part 3: "Connecting with Customers"

Paul R Timm: *Customer Service: Career Success through Customer Loyalty,* Prentice Hall, 2010

LESSON NOTES

Warmer

- Write *Customer service* in big letters on the board. Ask the students, in threes, to brainstorm briefly:

    - what they understand by this term.

    - what their own organisation or educational institution does in this area.

There is this definition of customer service quoted at the beginning of the Business brief on the previous page: 'all the activities involved in making it easy for customers to reach the right parties within the company and receive quick and satisfactory service, answers, and resolution of problems'. This relates mainly to situations where things have gone wrong.

Customer service is also used in a neutral sense to talk about normal dealings when customers are buying products or services. Students may refer to both these senses in their brainstorming sessions.

Students working in business will have something to say about customer service, whoever their customers are, whether business-to-business or business-to-consumer. It could be interesting to see how those working for government organisations view their 'customers' and what they understand by customer service. In the case of educational institutions, do they view their students as 'customers'? How are 'customer complaints' dealt with?

Overview

- Tell the students that in this unit they will be looking particularly at customer service.

- Ask the students to look at the Overview section at the beginning of the unit. Tell them a little about the things on the list, using the table on page 89 of this book. Tell them which points you will be covering in the current lesson and in later lessons.

Quotation

- Ask the students to look at the quotation. Ask them if they know it in its other form: 'The customer is always right.' Do they agree? Why? / Why not?

Starting up

Students talk about what irritates them about customer service and about the place of customer care in a company's success.

A – B

- Get the students to discuss the different points in both exercises in pairs. Say that there is some overlap between the items, e.g. service personnel who are 'disinterested' or 'unhelpful'. (Tell them that *disinterested* is being used here in the sense of *uninterested*. Many native speakers would consider that this is wrong – get students to look at the dictionary definitions of the two words.) The main idea is to encourage students to think of specific incidents they have encountered, even ones of too much

customer care, for example, the waiter who asks three times during the meal if everything is alright.

- Pairs report back to the whole class. Invite comments and encourage discussion.

Vocabulary: Complaints

Students look at words related to customer service and some common idioms, using them in context.

A – C

- Get students to work through exercises A–C in pairs. Circulate, monitor and assist when necessary.

- Check the answers with the whole class, looking at the *process* of how students find the answers, and work on any remaining difficulties.

Exercise A

1 d complaints   2 c rapport*   3 g guarantee
4 b standards   5 f refunds   6 e payment
7 a compensation

*Point out the pronunciation of *rapport* – the *t* is silent.

Exercise B

1 c   2 d   3 e   4 a   5 b   6 g   7 f

Exercise C

1 get to the bottom of the problem   2 pass the buck
3 ripped off   4 slipped my mind
5 talking at cross purposes   6 the last straw
7 go the extra mile

D

- Tell the students that they will be drawing up a shortlist of suggestions for dealing with customer complaints, and then compiling a list of the most useful ones.

- Divide the class into As and Bs. The As discuss the list of ways of dealing with customer complaints for Group A and the Bs those for Group B. Say that each group has to decide on the five most useful suggestions in its particular list.

- Circulate and monitor. Do not intervene unless necessary. Note language points for praise and correction.

- When the groups have made their shortlists, praise good language points from the discussion and work on three or four points that need improvement, getting individual students to say the correct forms.

- Match half the As with half the Bs, getting the students to change places if necessary. Tell them that each group (a mixture of As and Bs) has to negotiate a final list of six suggestions from the ten suggestions that they have chosen between them.

- Circulate and monitor again. Do not intervene unless necessary. Note language points for praise and correction.

- When the groups have made their final list, praise good language points from the discussion and work on three or four points that need improvement, getting individual students to say the correct forms.

- Ask each group for its final list. Compare the lists from different groups, invite comments and encourage discussion, perhaps comparing the customer service suggestions that are suitable in different contexts and with different cultures. (For example, putting things in writing might be seen as essential in some cultures, but just an extra burden on the already irritated customer in others.)

One-to-one

This discussion can be done one-to-one. Ask the student to look at and discuss each list separately, choosing five points from each list. Ask them to explain the reasons for their choice. Then ask them to choose the six most important ones from the ten they have selected and, again, to explain their reasons.

 i-Glossary

Listening: Customer service

A hotel/restaurant manager talks about key customer service issues.

A

- Establish with students that Raymond Blanc's Le Manoir aux Quat'Saisons is considered one of the best restaurants in the UK. It is also a hotel.

- Do the discussion point in small groups or as a quick-fire whole-class activity. Write up a list of areas for complaint on the board.

B ◀)) CD3.10

- Play the recording and elicit students' answers to the question, with reasons. (It will make a change for them not to have answer comprehension questions!)

C ◀)) CD3.11

- Get students to anticipate what might go in the gaps.

- Play the recording and elicit the answers.

1 customers' expectations   2 empathy   3 client
4 individually   5 looking   6 provide
7 consistent standards   8 standards   9 get

D – E ◀)) CD3.12, 3.13

- Get students to look at the questions.

- Play the recording and elicit the answers.

Exercise D

1 They all stay in the house overnight. It helps them understand what it is like for a guest and what guests might expect.

2 Expectations are very high. Philip says it's very 'high-end', meaning it's expensive, and therefore customers expect the best standards.

Exercise E

Customers are questioning what they receive for their money. They are complaining more; this can be useful because it gives feedback.

- Ask students if they think that it is true that people are complaining more than they used to. Explain that until recently in the UK, people were reluctant to complain. Ask students about their own countries. (This will lead nicely into the Reading section that comes next.)

- Students can watch the interview with Philip Newman-Hall on the DVD-ROM.

➡ Resource bank: Listening (page 197)

Reading: Changing customer service

Students read about modern customer service and its place in a company's overall strategy.

A

- Get students to look at the questions and to scan through the article individually for the answers.

1 Yes   2 No

B

- Ask students to read the article again in pairs to find the answers to the four questions.

1 It is less personal and is dealt with by customer service experts and technology.

2 They didn't like speaking to customer service representatives based in other parts of the world or mechanical systems.

3 They can collate and analyse it to build profiles of customers.

4 Because companies rely on canned, scripted responses, poorly trained agents and clunky systems.

C

- Get students to work together in pairs on the summary.

- Circulate, monitor and assist where necessary. (It will probably be necessary to explain *recoil from*, *pre-empt* and *intuitively*.)

- Then get some of the students to read out their summaries for the whole class.

D – E

- Get students to do the exercises in pairs. Circulate, monitor and assist again.

- Call the class to order and elicit the answers.

Exercise D

1 pay lip service   2 face to face   3 word of mouth

Exercise E

1 face to face   2 Word of mouth   3 pay lip service

F

- Discuss the questions with the whole class. Get students to talk about the industries that they work in or would like to work in.

⟶ Text bank (pages 150–153)

Language review: Gerunds

Students study gerund formation and the way that gerunds are used. The students then use them in drawing up guidelines for customer service.

- Go through the gerunds in the Language review box with the whole class.

A

- Refer back to the article on the previous page, and, with the whole class, get students to identify gerunds used in it.

> **Suggested answers**
>
> **1** using analytics (line 81), maintaining (line 97), acquiring (line 98), outsourcing (line 104)
>
> **2** dealing (line 10), missing (line 109)
>
> **3** by using (line 7), on dealing (line 10), by refocusing (line 12), to speaking (line 19), as searching (line 95), between maintaining … and being (lines 100–103), of missing (line 109) by keeping (line 116)

B – **C**

- Students can work on these exercises in pairs. Circulate and assist.

- With the whole class, elicit the answers.

> **Exercise B**
>
> **1** b **2** a **3** d **4** c **5** f **6** e
>
> **Exercise C (suggested answers)**
>
> **2** carrying out **3** introducing **4** dealing
> **5** ensuring **6** learning **7** establishing*
> **8** finding out **9** giving/offering **10** reassuring
>
> * Remind students that the *t* in *rapport* is not pronounced.

Skills: Active listening

Students look at listening skills in the context of customer service. They listen to interviews with satisfied and angry customers and learn some key expressions.

A

- With the whole class, ask about the points here. Invite comments and encourage discussion.

B

- Divide the class into pairs or threes to discuss these points in relation to a) the English-speaking world and b) their own cultures. Circulate, monitor and assist.

- Ask the students for their responses. Invite

comments and encourage discussion. Some interesting cultural issues should emerge here.

> - *Look people directly in the eye at all times* but don't overdo it. It will make them feel uncomfortable. How much eye contact is appropriate in your students' culture(s) a) between people of the same status and b) between people of differing status?
>
> - *Nod your head often to show interest.* Again, don't overdo it. Ask your students about nodding in general: in their culture(s) does it indicate interest, agreement, something else or nothing at all?
>
> - *Repeat what the speaker has said in your own words.* Can be useful as a way of checking key points. Another useful technique is to repeat *exactly* some of the expressions the speaker has used.
>
> - *Be aware of the speaker's body language.* People will be aware of this whether they try to be or not.
>
> - *Interrupt the speaker often to show you are listening.* It's good to make some 'phatic' noises such as *aha, mmm, I see, right*. Ask your students how much it's normal to do this in their own language, and what the equivalent of *aha* is in their own language(s).
>
> - *Think about what you are going to say while the speaker is talking.* Yes, but pay attention to what they are saying as well. Some cultures, such as Japan and Finland, allow the other person time for reflecting on what the first person has said before they are expected to respond. Ask the students if this is the case in their culture(s).
>
> - *Use body language to show you are attentive.* Again, don't overdo it. It can be intimidating.
>
> - *Try to predict what they are going to say next.* But don't jump to conclusions.
>
> - *Ask questions if you do not understand.* Yes, but try to avoid questions that result from not having listened properly. If someone has to answer too many questions about what they said earlier, it will undermine rapport.
>
> - *Say nothing until you are absolutely sure that the speaker has finished.* Butting in is the usual habit in some places. Ask your students what they think about this.

C ◀)) CD3.14, 3.15, 3.16

- Tell the students that they are going to hear three customers talking about their experiences. Ask your students to look at the questions.

- Play the recording once right through, and then once again, stopping at the end of each conversation to allow the students to take notes.

- With the whole class, ask individual students to summarise each incident. Use this as an opportunity to practise summarising skills. Say they should not get sidetracked by details such as what exactly was wrong with the wine, etc.

	a) the product or service involved	b) reasons why the service was good or bad
1	Bottles of wine	Bad: customer thought the wine was too sweet, but nothing was done about the complaint
2	Airline	Good: staff were friendly and helpful, brought games for children, plane was on time, some free food
3	Printer	Bad: broken printer wasn't replaced, despite several promises to do so

D ◀)) CD3.14, 3.15, 3.16

- Go through the expressions in the Useful language box with the students first. Get them to practise stress and intonation.

- Play the recording again and get them to identify the key expressions.

Expressions heard in the recording are underlined. Conversations are shown in brackets (1,2, 3). One other expression is suggested for each heading in italics, but your students may have thought of others.

Showing interest

Really? How can I help? (1)

Right (2)

OK (3) / *I see.*

Showing empathy

How awful! (3)

That must have been terrible!

Asking for details

What did you do? (1)

What else impressed you? (2)

What happened? (3)

Tell me more!

Clarifying

What exactly do you mean by ...? (1)

When you say ..., what are you thinking of?

Summarising

(So) you're saying ... (1)

(So) if I understand you correctly ...

Repetition / Question tags

30 per cent off if you bought two bottles, wasn't it? (1)

A *Customer satisfaction levels are increasing.*

B *Increasing? / Are they?*

E

- Ask your students to talk about excellent and poor experiences in pairs. You can show the whole class the sort of thing you are looking for by asking an individual student for one of their experiences, and using some of the expressions in the Useful language box to ask them about it.

- When the class understands the idea, start the discussions.

- Circulate, monitor and assist if necessary. Note language points for praise and correction, especially in relation to the language in this section.

- With the whole class, praise good language points from the discussion and work on three or four points that need improvement, getting individual students to say the correct forms.

- Ask for one or two public performances of the situations that the students just talked about so that the whole class can listen.

- Invite comments and encourage discussion about the situations.

⟹ Resource bank: Speaking (page 185)

CASE STUDY

Hurrah Airlines

Students work on prioritising different types of customer communication at an airline.

Background

- Get students to read the Background section. Meanwhile, write the points in the first column of the table below on the board. When the students have finished reading, elicit the information from them to complete this table.

Company	Hurrah Airlines
Positioning	Low-cost, budget airline – limited services before, during and after flights
HQ	JFK Airport, New York
Complaints	Frequently received by letter, phone calls, voicemail messages
Problem	Callers forget that Hurrah is a low-cost, no-frills (teach this expression) airline
	Complaints must be dealt with and solutions found.

Complaints

- Get different groups of students to look at different complaints on the spread. Go round the class and assist where necessary.

- A representative from each group reports back to the whole class. You could get each representative to come up to the front of the class and make a mini-presentation and write notes on the board about the complaint that their group looked at. Leave these notes on the board for the task below.

- If there is time, you could then get students to work in pairs on follow-up phone conversations for the complaints. Do the beginning of one conversation with an individual student to give them the idea, for example:

> Martha Gómez: *Hello, I'm phoning about an e-mail I sent a couple of days ago. It was about a suitcase that was lost when I flew from New York to London last week. I haven't received any reply or anything, and I'm phoning to check the situation.*
>
> Customer service agent: *What did you say your name was? How do you spell that?* etc.

- Then allocate the situations to different pairs and get students to enact the corresponding phone call, sitting back-to-back. Circulate, monitor and assist.

- When pairs have finished, get two or three pairs to do a public performance for the whole class. Ask the other pairs to summarise what happened in their conversations.

Task 🔊 CD3.17, 3.18

- Play the first recording and get students to make notes on this complaint.

- Elicit the main points of the complaint and write them quickly on the board.

- Students will now see all the complaints on the board including those they heard in the recording.

- Play the second recording. Tell the students that this is not, in fact, a complaint, but a message about a *positive* experience someone has had with Hurrah Airlines. Get students to make notes.

- Elicit the main points and write them on a different part of the board.

- Divide students into pairs (Customer Service Manager and Assistant) and ask them to decide which complaints are top-priority and which ones less urgent, bearing in mind that Hurrah is a low-cost airline. They should number them 1 to 6, with 1 as top priority and 6 as not urgent. Ask them to discuss the ones that they have judged to be top priority and to decide how they are going to deal with them.

- Circulate, monitor and assist if necessary.

- When the pairs have finished, get them to report back to the whole class on their discussions and decisions. Then ask the whole class to discuss ways in which customer service could be improved in the company, using the notes from the positive experience to help them do so.

One-to-one

These activities can be done one-to-one, with the student analysing the information and then discussing it with you. Don't forget to note language points for praise and correction afterwards. Highlight some of the language you chose to use as well.

⊙ Students can watch the case study commentary on the DVD-ROM.

Writing

- Students can do the writing task collaboratively in class, or for homework. Tell them they can look at the format of reports on page 000 of the Writing file in the Course Book.

⇨ Writing file, page 131

⇨ Resource bank: Writing (page 213)

UNIT 11 Crisis management

AT A GLANCE

	Classwork – Course Book	Further work
Lesson 1 *Each lesson (excluding case studies) is about 45 to 60 minutes. This does not include administration and time spent going through homework.*	**Starting up** Students look at the steps to take in crisis situations. **Vocabulary: Handling crises** Students look at noun phrases with and without *of* and use them in context.	**Practice File** Vocabulary (page 44) **Practice exercises: Vocabulary 1&2** (DVD-ROM) **i-Glossary** (DVD-ROM)
Lesson 2	**Listening: Dealing with crises** An expert talks about how to deal with crisis situations, and gives some examples. **Reading: Dealing with crises** Students read two articles about two company crises and how each one was handled.	**Resource bank: Listening** (page 198) **Practice exercises: Listening** (DVD-ROM) **Text bank** (pages 154–157)
Lesson 3	**Language review: Conditionals** Students revisit the different types of conditionals. **Skills: Asking and answering difficult questions** A chief executive answers difficult questions on a TV consumer protection programme. Students listen to the language used, and apply it themselves in a similar situation.	**Practice File** Language review (page 45) **Practice exercises: Language review 1&2** (DVD-ROM) **ML Grammar and Usage** (Unit 5) **Resource bank: Speaking** (page 186) **Practice File** Survival Business English (page 75) **Practice exercises: Skills** (DVD-ROM)
Lesson 4 *Each case study is about 1½ to 2 hours*	**Case study: *In Range*** A video-games company is accused of encouraging violence in users of its products. Students analyse the related information and role-play the company's directors and media representatives at a press conference.	**Case study commentary** (DVD-ROM) **Resource bank: Writing** (page 214) **Practice File** Writing (page 46)

For a fast route through the unit focusing mainly on speaking skills, just use the underlined sections.

For one-to-one situations, most parts of the unit lend themselves, with minimal adaptation, to use with individual students. Where this is not the case, alternative procedures are given.

BUSINESS BRIEF

'Never let a crisis go to waste,' says one of Barack Obama's aides. A crisis may well be an opportunity to test a company's capabilities, but it is an opportunity that most companies would prefer to do without. Some businesses never recover from disasters involving loss of life, such as these:

● PanAm and the Lockerbie bomb terrorist attack

● Townsend Thoresen and its capsized ferry off Zeebrugge, Belgium

● Union Carbide and the Bhopal disaster: plant explosion.

Presumably, no amount of **crisis management** or **damage limitation** would have saved these organisations.

There are entire industries that live under a permanent cloud of crisis. For example, accidents and incidents around the world, small and large, have **discredited** the nuclear power industry and given it a permanently negative image. People perceive it as **secretive** and **defensive**.

Even in disasters where there is no loss of life, the results can be dire, because there are situations that everyone can understand and relate to.

Food and drink is a very sensitive area. The mineral water and soft drinks companies that distribute **contaminated products** because of mistakes in their bottling plants know this all too well. Perrier struggled to recover from the contamination of its source more than 20 years ago. Despite repeated **reassurances** about the purity of its product, it never regained full **credibility** in the eyes of some consumers.

The way that Toyota seemed slow to react to problems with its accelerator pedals and other mechanical issues left it with a severe **image problem**. It will be interesting to see if it fully recovers its reputation for quality over time.

The new cruise ship that breaks down on its maiden voyage, or the liner that leaves on a cruise with workmen still on board because refurbishment is not finished, with passengers filming the chaos on their video cameras, scenes then shown on television, are **public relations nightmares**.

All the examples so far relate to the effect of crises on companies' external audience: customers and potential customers. But businesses are also increasingly being judged on how well they treat their internal audience in crisis situations: their staff. Companies may offer **employee assistance programmes** to help them through difficult situations or **traumatic incidents**. For example, bank staff may be offered counselling after a bank robbery. This is part of the wider picture of how companies treat their people in general. A reputation for **caring** in this area can reduce **staff turnover** and enhance a company's overall **image** in society as a whole. This makes commercial sense too: high staff turnover is costly, and an image as a caring employer may have a positive effect on sales.

Read on

Crisis Management: *Master the Skills to Prevent Disasters*, Harvard Business Essentials, 2009

Robert Heath and H Dan O'Hair: *Handbook of Risk and Crisis Communication*, Routledge, 2008

Mike Seymour, Simon Moore: *Global Technology and Corporate Crisis*, Routledge, 2005

Warmer

- Write the word *Crisis* in big letters on the right of the board. Ask the students what the plural is, and write up *crises* in big letters. Practise the pronunciation of both words.

- Then draw seven lines to the left of *Crisis* to represent words that can come in front of it, with the first letter of each word.

- Tell the students that some of the words relate to people, some to countries, and others to both. Say that you are going to give examples of each type of crisis situation, and the students must guess the related word.

- Read example 1 below and ask the students to guess the word.

- Continue with the other examples in the same way. If the students have trouble guessing the word, give the next letter and, if they still don't get it, one letter at a time until they do.

1 **Domestic:** A child is ill and its parents are very worried and unable to go to work.
2 **Currency:** A country's money is fast losing its value in relation to the money of other countries, and the government wants to stop this.
3 **Economic:** A country has high unemployment, falling production and so on.
4 **Financial:** A country has problems in its banking system.
5 **International**: There is a border dispute between two countries, and they may go to war with each other.
6 **Mid-life:** Someone in their late 40s has feelings of uncertainty about their life and career.
7 **Political:** A government cannot win votes in the country's parliament, and there may have to be an election.

Overview

- Tell the students that in this unit they will be looking particularly at crisis management.

- Ask the students to look at the Overview section at the beginning of the unit. Tell them a little about the things on the list, using the table on page 96 of this book as a guide. Tell them which points you will be covering in the current lesson and in later lessons.

Quotation

- Ask the students to look at the quotation. Discuss it with the whole class.

- Ask the students the questions:

  - What does it mean to say that a crisis can be an opportunity?

  - Is every crisis an opportunity?

- Invite quick comments and encourage brief discussion.

Starting up

Students discuss crises they have experienced and the steps involved in resolving them.

A – D

- With the whole class, ask students the first question to get the discussion going. You could refer back to some of the types of crisis that students mentioned in the Warmer section above.

- Then ask the students to do exercises B–D in pairs.

Exercise B

5 predict 6 Set up 7 Inform 8 Disclose
9 Analyse 10 Practise

Exercise C

before the crisis: 2, 4, 5, 6, 10; during the crisis: 7, 8; after the crisis: 1, 3, 9

- Circulate, monitor and assist if necessary. In Exercise D, note language points for praise and correction, especially ones relating to the pronunciation of *crisis* and *crises* and crisis language in general.

- With the whole class, ask pairs for their answers. Invite comments and encourage discussion.

- Praise good language points from the discussion in Exercise D and work on three or four points that need improvement, getting individual students to say the correct forms.

- For homework, you could ask students to research on the Internet the current state of a) the Gulf of Mexico and b) the company BP following the oil spill of 2010, and report back in the next lesson.

Vocabulary: Handling crises

Students look at noun phrases with and without *of* and use them in context.

A – B

- Talk through the two types of noun phrases with the whole class. Look at the nouns and, where necessary, their pronunciation (e.g. *contingency*). Get students to do the two exercises in pairs.

- Circulate, monitor and assist.

- With the whole class, ask for the answers and discuss any difficulties.

Exercise A

Noun phrases with *of*	Noun phrases without *of*
admission of liability	action plan
flow of information	contingency plan
loss of confidence	damage limitation
speed of response	legal action
	press conference
	press release

Exercise B

1 speed of response
2 press conference
3 press release
4 flow of information
5 action plan
6 contingency plan
7 legal action
8 admission of liability
9 loss of confidence
10 damage limitation

C

- Ask the students to work in pairs to categorise the word partnerships according to their timing in a crisis.

2 a press release   3 legal action*
4 a press conference   5 a loss of confidence
6 a contingency plan   7 the flow of information

*Point out that you say *to take legal action*, not *to take a legal action*

D

- Get students to categorise and exemplify in small groups. Circulate, monitor and assist. Opinions may differ.

- Call the class to order and discuss pairs' findings.

- i-Glossary

Listening: Dealing with crises

A crisis management expert talks about how to deal with crisis situations, and gives some examples.

A

- Get students to discuss this in small groups.

- With the whole class, ask individual students what the points they mentioned were.

B ◀)) CD3.19

- Play the recording and ask students if any of the points that they mentioned in Exercise A above came up. If so, which ones?

C ◀)) CD3.19

- Get students to try and remember what was in the gaps from the first playing of the recording.

- Play the recording and check answers with the whole class. Work on any difficulties – for example, the pronunciation of *acknowledge*.

1 slow to acknowledge   2 slow to respond
3 problem   4 recall   5 unclear   6 confused
7 tell it all   8 tell it quickly   9 get out there
10 doing something

D – **E** ◀)) CD3.20, 3.21

- Go through the questions to both exercises and play the recordings, stopping to give students time to take notes.

- Elicit the answers.

Exercise D

1 Before, during and after the crisis

2 1 Carry out an audit (what could go wrong)
   2 Take steps to avoid the avoidable or insure against it
   3 Prepare a contingency plan

Exercise E

1 Identify the crisis   2 Contain the crisis
3 Resolve the crisis

F ◀)) CD3.22

- Get students to anticipate what the questions might be.

- Then play the recording and elicit the questions.

1 How do you reintroduce the product? How do you recover from the storm that has damaged your stores and caused employees to lose their homes?

2 What can be learnt as a result of seeing what worked, what didn't work?

3 How does the organisation rebuild its reputation externally? How does it restore the confidence of its customers, other stakeholders and its employees?

- Students can watch the interview with Craig Smith on the DVD-ROM.

→ Resource bank: Listening (page 198)

Reading: Dealing with crises

Students read two articles about two company crises and how each one was handled.

A

- Have a whole-class brainstorming session on this question and write the students' suggestions on the board. (As well as *buggy*, some students may use the word *stroller* to refer to what is known as a *pushchair* in British English.)

B

- Go through the headlines and allocate the articles to the students.

- Circulate, monitor and assist where necessary.

- Call the class to order and work on any remaining difficulties. Elicit the answers.

Article A: 2   Article B: 1

C – **D**

- Get students to read 'their' articles again in order to find the answers to the questions. Circulate, monitor and assist.

- When students are ready, get them to explain their articles to their partners, using points 1–3.

- Do this as a quick-fire whole-class activity.

> **Suggested answers**
> **1** b, c, d, e, f, g **2** a, e **3** b, c, d, e, f
> **4** d, e **5** b, c, d, e, f **6** b, c, d, e, f, g **7** f

- You could get students to mention different crises and then research them further for homework. Don't forget to check this in the next lesson.

➡ Text bank (pages 154–157)

Language review: Conditionals

Students revisit the different types of conditionals.

- Go through the conditionals in the Language review box and make the link with the Grammar reference section, page 151.

A

- Get students to work on the exercise in pairs. Circulate, monitor and assist.

- Elicit the answers.

> **1** d **2** f **3** b **4** e, f **5** d **6** a **7** e, f
> **8** c **9** b **10** f **11** d **12** c

B

- Get students to discuss the situations in pairs. Circulate, monitor and assist, concentrating on correct forms of conditionals.

- With the whole class, get members of particular pairs to report what their partners said about themselves.

C

- Ask students to work on this situation in pairs. Circulate, monitor and assist, as before concentrating on correct use of conditionals.

- With the whole class, get individual students to repeat the sentences that they came up with. Work on any remaining difficulties.

Skills: Asking and answering difficult questions

A chief executive answers difficult questions from a journalist. Students listen to the language used, and apply it themselves in a similar situation.

A – **B** 🔊 CD2.23, 2.24

- Present the situation described, and tell your students that they are going to listen to a consumer protection programme. Read through the questions with the whole class, explaining any difficulties. Ask if anything in the written questions strikes them as being a) neutral/polite or b) forceful/aggressive?

- Emphasise that it may be difficult to judge until they hear the recording: words like *please* and *sorry* can be used quite aggressively, as in *I'm sorry but … .*

- Write students' ideas on the board in note form to refer to later.

Exercise A
1 Stuffed toys (grey rabbits, dogs, penguins, reindeer, elephants)
2 50,000
3 The problem is very serious because:
- the toys are their best-selling product. It would therefore have an impact on the company's profits if the products were withdrawn from the market.
- if they are indeed dangerous and injure children, they would have to pay compensation or face court action.
- they hold large stocks of the toys. They could not sell these if the toys which are already in the market were withdrawn.

Exercise B
1 a **2** a **3** a **4** b **5** b
6 a *or* b (*depends on tone*)
7 b **8** b **9** b **10** b

C

- Give the students the general background to the situation. Divide the class into pairs, each pair containing a Sales Manager from the furniture company and a journalist.

- Ask the journalists to read their information on page 138 of the Course Book, and the Sales Managers theirs on page 144.

- Circulate and assist in the preparation of roles. Explain any difficulties.

- When the students have absorbed the information, the role play can begin.

- Note language points for praise and correction, especially in relation to the question-and-answer types above. Only intervene if the questioning falters.

- When the interviews run out of steam, get students to bring them to a close.

- Praise good language points from the programmes and work on three or four points that need improvement, getting individual students to say the correct forms.

- Ask the Sales managers and the journalists about their relative strategies and methods. Invite comments and encourage discussion.

- To round off the section, recap the language in the Useful language box, getting students to read and repeat the expressions.

> **One-to-one**
>
> This programme can be done on-to-one as above, of course. Ask your student which side they would prefer to represent. You represent the other side. Give the student plenty of time to prepare and absorb the information. Afterwards, ask the student about their strategy for asking or answering the questions and the tactics they were using.

➡ Resource bank: Speaking (page 186)

CASE STUDY

In Range

A video-games company is accused of encouraging violence in users of its products. Students analyse the related information and role-play the company's directors and media representatives at a press conference.

Background

- Ask the students to read the *Business Today* article about *In Range*. Meanwhile, write the points in the first column of the table below on the board.

- With the whole class, elicit the information to complete the table.

Company	ExtremAction (EA)
Game to be launched	*In Range*
Accusation made by Prof. Davis	Violent games increase levels of aggression in young people and desensitise them.
Risk for EA	Disruption of imminent product launch – loss of potentially enormous sales
Other critics	Politicians, academics, community leaders, police, media

🔊 CD3.25

- Prepare students by saying who the speakers are and getting them to look in the panel at the points they should listen out for in the conversation.

- Check the information with the whole class.

Plans for launch	Extracts from game will show in *Universal* movie theatre with an invited audience (famous people with influence)
	After party at the *All Seasons Hotel*
	Hotel staff dressed in combat gear – good publicity stunt (teach this expression)
Sales projections	7 million copies in the US generating $350m in revenue (first month only)
	4 million copies in the UK generating $200m in revenue (first month only)
Why Chief Executive is worried	Because of the criticism from the competition

Sample reactions

- Get individual students to speak in the first person, as if they are the people quoted, but using their own words, and elaborating on the information given. For example, you could give this example for the Senator to give students the idea:

> *I really think we need a new law to protect young people from the effects of these horrible games. I'm going to introduce this new law next week in Washington, and I'm pretty certain there'll be a lot of support for it.*

- Then call on different students to 'speak for' each of the other people in a similar way.

Task

- Tell students that EA is holding a press conference in an attempt to defend the company and defuse (teach this word) the crisis.

- Divide the class into two groups: EA managers and Journalists.

- Get students to turn to the correct page.

- Circulate, monitor and assist with both groups as necessary. Tell EA's Chief Executive that he/she will make a brief opening statement about why the press conference has been called and then invite questions from the journalists.

- When the students are ready, the press conference can begin. The Chief Executive makes the opening statement and then invites questions.

- Note language points for praise and correction.

- Do not intervene unless necessary, but make sure that journalists are asking follow-up questions if the answers to their original questions are not satisfactory.

- Give yourself enough time to discuss the language and other points arising at the end of the session, and ask EA's Chief Executive to wind up the press conference.

- Praise good language points from the role play and work on three or four points that need improvement, getting individual students to say the correct forms.

- Ask EA's management team and the journalists how they thought the press conference went.

One-to-one

This case study can be done one-to-one. Instead of the press conference, you can be a journalist interviewing EA's CEO. Don't forget to note language points for praise and correction afterwards. Highlight some of the language you chose to use as well.

◉ Students can watch the case study commentary on the DVD-ROM.

Writing

- Go through the information with the students, making clear that they can choose whether to write a journalist's article or a director's report; whatever role they had in the role play.

- Ask the students to write their report collaboratively in class or as homework.

⇨ Writing file, page 131

⇨ Resource bank: Writing (page 214)

Mergers and acquisitions

AT A GLANCE

	Classwork – Course Book	Further work
Lesson 1 *Each lesson (excluding case studies) is about 45 to 60 minutes. This does not include administration and time spent going through homework.*	**Starting up** Students talk about takeovers and mergers, the reasons for them and examples that they know of. **Vocabulary: Describing mergers and acquisitions** Students study words and expressions related to this area and learn how to use them. **Listening: Making acquisitions** Students listen to a business professor who specialises in the study of mergers and acquisitions.	Practice File Vocabulary (page 48) **Practice exercises: Vocabulary 1&2** (DVD-ROM) **i-Glossary** (DVD-ROM) **Resource bank: Listening** (page 199) **Practice exercises: Listening** (DVD-ROM)
Lesson 2	**Reading: Acquiring a green business** Students read an article on multinationals that take over small, environmentally-friendly companies. **Language review: Prediction and probability** Students look at the language features associated with this area.	Text bank (pages 158–161) Practice File Language review (page 49) **Practice exercises: Language review 1&2** (DVD-ROM) **ML Grammar and Usage** (Unit 8)
Lesson 3	**Skills: Making a presentation** Students look at and practise key presentations language.	Resource bank: Speaking (page 187) Practice File Survival Business English (page 77) **Practice exercises: Skills** (DVD-ROM)
Lesson 4 *Each case study is about 1½ to 2 hours*	**Case study: Rinnovar International** The management of an American cosmetics company wants to expand by making an acquisition. Students analyse three possible target companies and make a recommendation as to which company should be chosen.	Case study commentary (DVD-ROM) Resource bank: Writing (page 215) Practice File Writing (page 50) Test File: Progress test 4 Exit test

For a fast route through the unit focusing mainly on speaking skills, just use the underlined sections.

For one-to-one situations, most parts of the unit lend themselves, with minimal adaptation, to use with individual students. Where this is not the case, alternative procedures are given.

BUSINESS BRIEF

Magnetic's board rejected TT's bid as 'derisory, unsolicited, unwelcome and totally inadequate'. This is a familiar refrain from the board of a company that is the **target** of a **hostile bid**, one that it does not want, for example, because it thinks that the **bidder** is **undervaluing** its shares: offering less for the shares than the target company thinks they are worth in terms of its future profitability. A bid that a target company welcomes, on the other hand, may be described as **friendly**.

Bidders often already have a **minority stake** or **interest** in the target company: they already own some shares. The bid is to gain a **majority stake** so that it owns more shares than any other shareholder and enough shares to be able to decide how it is run.

A company that often takes over or **acquires** others is said to be **acquisitive**. The companies it buys are **acquisitions**. It may be referred to, especially by journalists, as a **predator**, and the companies it buys, or would like to buy, as its **prey**.

When a company buys others over a period of time, a **group**, **conglomerate** or **combine** forms, containing a **parent company** with a number of **subsidiaries**, perhaps including many different types of business activity. A group like this is **diversified**. Related companies in a group can have **synergy**, sharing production and other costs, and benefitting from cross-marketing of each other's products. Synergy is sometimes expressed as the idea that two plus two equals five, the notion that companies offer more **shareholder value** together than they would separately.

But the current trend is for groups to **sell off, spin off** or **dispose of** their **non-core assets** and activities, in a process of **divestment** and **restructuring**, allowing them to **focus on** their **core activities**, the ones they are best at doing and make the most profit from. Compare an old-style conglomerate like Hanson in the UK, with a wide variety of sometimes unrelated activities, and a group like Pearson, which has decided to concentrate on media, in broadcasting, publishing and now Internet ventures.

Companies may work together in a particular area by forming an **alliance** or **joint venture**, perhaps forming a new company in which both have a stake. Two companies working together like this may later decide to go for a **merger**, combining as equals. But as the Course Book unit points out, mergers (like takeovers) are fraught with difficulty and for a variety of reasons often fail, even where the merger involves two companies in the same country. One of the companies will always behave as the dominant partner.

Take the scenario where one company's base is used as the headquarters for the merged company. The other company's office closes, and many managers in both companies lose their jobs. Those remaining feel beleaguered and under threat of losing theirs later. They may dislike the way the managers from the other company work. In **cross-border mergers**, these difficulties are compounded by cross-cultural misunderstandings and tensions. Problems such as these explain why merged companies so often fail to live up to the promise of the day of the press conference, when the two CEOs vaunted the merger's merits.

Read on

Chris Brady, Scott Moeller: *Intelligent M & A*, Wiley, 2007

John Child, David Faulkner: *Strategies of Co-operation: Managing Alliances, Networks and Joint Ventures*, OUP, 2005

Timothy Galpin, Mark Herndon: *The Complete Guide to Mergers and Acquisitions*, Jossey Bass, 2007

Gunter Stahl, Mark Mendenhall: *Mergers and Acquisitions: Managing Culture and Human Resources*, Stanford University Press, 2005

LESSON NOTES

Special note

Teaching this unit will be much easier if you read it right through from beginning to end before the first lesson, as familiarity with later parts of the unit will be of great help in teaching the earlier parts.

Warmer

- Write *merge – merge* and *acquisition – acquire* in big letters on the board. Ask the students to say what the difference is between a merger and an acquisition. Ask them what *merge* and *acquire* mean in a non-business context, e.g. roads can merge, and you can acquire an accent. Get students to look in general dictionaries for more examples.

- Work on stress of *acQUIRE* and *ACQuisITion*.

Overview

- Ask the students to look at the Overview section at the beginning of the unit. Tell them a little about the things on the list, using the table on page 102 of this book as a guide. Tell them which points you will be covering in the current lesson and in later lessons.

Quotation

- Read out the quotation and ask the students to comment. What does Rivers mean exactly?

When someone says there's going to be an equal partnership, this often does not turn out to be the case.

Starting up

Students talk about takeovers and mergers, the reasons for them and examples that they know of.

A – **B** 🔊 CD3.26

- Ask students to discuss this question in pairs or threes. Circulate and assist.

- Ask pair representatives for their ideas.

- Play the recording to see if these ideas are confirmed, and discuss them with students.

1 A **takeover** or **acquisition** refers to one firm gaining control of another by buying over 50% of its shares. It may be friendly or hostile, which is when the company being targeted doesn't want or agree to the takeover. If a company acquires a part of another company's shares, which may be less than 50%, this gives them an interest, holding or stake. Over 50% is a controlling interest.

2 A **merger** involves two companies or organisations coming together to form a larger one. Some mergers can be like two companies coming together on equal terms, but others are more like takeovers for one of the businesses involved, as usually there is a dominant partner.

3 A **joint venture** involves two quite separate companies co-operating for a limited time, or in a particular geographical area on a particular project, but maintaining their own identities. Examples are building a plant (quite common in the oil and gas industry) or developing a new technology, which would benefit both companies.

C – **D**

- Get students to discuss these questions in pairs, or, if you think they will find them difficult, with the whole class.

The answers to these questions depend on how far the companies involved will continue to operate as separate entities under the same ownership, or whether they will be fully combined.

1 Some employees may find new career paths in the combined company, but in the short term, many will be worried about their jobs, as management tries to eliminate any duplication of posts.

2 Customers may be reassured or worried. When the Indian company Tata took over Land Rover and Jaguar, some were worried about loss of British 'heritage' values, while others saw the investment that Tata brought as a good thing.

3 Each company involved in the merger or acquisition may have had different suppliers, so some suppliers may be worried that they will be eliminated. Those that remain, however, can expect more work from the bigger business.

4 Shareholders in both companies will probably have been promised 'enhanced shareholder value' or words to that effect. Whether this happens or not is a different matter.

5 Again, this will be depend partly on whether the two companies continue to operate separately or not. In a fully merged operation, some products and services will be rebranded or disappear altogether. Others will benefit from increased resources, including wider marketing.

Vocabulary: Describing mergers and acquisitions

Students study words and expressions related to this area, and learn how to use them.

A – **C**

- Tell your students they are going to look at the language of mergers and acquisitions, and to work in pairs on matching the exercises. Circulate and assist if necessary.

- With the whole class, ask for the answers and explain anything that is unclear.

Exercise A

1 e **2** d **3** b **4** f **5** c **6** a

Exercise B

1 a stake **2** a bid **3** a bid **4** a company
5 a joint venture **6** an acquisition **7** a bid
8 a stake

Exercise C

1 merger **2** joint venture; acquisition
3 takeover bid **4** stake

D

● Discuss with the whole class. It might be more interesting to get students to research this on the Internet and report back in the next lesson.

> At the time of writing, relatively recent mergers/ acquisitions have included:
>
> ● Land Rover and Jaguar acquired by Tata (see above)
>
> ● Cadbury taken over by Kraft
>
> ● Volvo taken over from Ford by Geely, a Chinese company.
>
> ● Merger between United Airlines and Continental Airlines
>
> Point out that *taken over* and *acquired* mean exactly the same thing.

 i-Glossary

Listening: Making acquisitions

Students listen to a business professor who specialises in the study of mergers and acquisitions.

A 🔊 CD3.27

● Get students to look at the question and then play the recording.

● With the whole class, elicit the answers.

> **1** inadequate planning
> **2** due diligence done too quickly
> **3** lack of planning for post-merger integration period

● Students will probably have difficulty understanding *due diligence*. At another point in the interview, not included in the recording, Prof. Moeller said this:

> ● Due diligence is the process by which you look at what a company is doing to determine what it is that really makes that company tick. It includes looking at management. It looks at suppliers. It looks at clients. It looks at all employees.
>
> ● It looks at the product line, the intellectual property – that is, the patents, the new business plans, and the brands that the company has – to see whether in fact all of these are robust.

● Read this slowly to your students, paraphrasing and explaining any difficulties (for example *patent* and *robust*) where necessary.

B – **C** 🔊 CD3.28, 3.29

● Get students to look through the questions to both exercises so they know what information they are listening for. For Exercise B, you could ask them to predict what they think the speaker will say.

● Play the recording, stopping at appropriate points.

> **Exercise B**
>
> **1** **a)** To understand the company better or if you want it to operate as a separate subsidiary
>
> **b)** So as not to lose customers or employees, or if there is a time-critical element
>
> **2** Whether you want to impose your own culture and way of operations on that company, or keep that company's own culture separate
>
> **3** Are you going to appoint somebody from the company itself to run that division, or do you want to bring in new management, either from the acquirer's own management, or from the outside?
>
> **Exercise C**
>
> They met early before deal became public; determined the 'showstoppers' (what could stop the deal from being successful – you could point out that this means the same thing as *dealbreakers*); made sure the approach was friendly; put together a team of senior people from both sides; identified who was going to be running the firm; everyone knew what was happening; CEO and Chairman deeply engaged in deal strategy.

D

● Do this in pairs or, if your students do not have much knowledge/experience of mergers and acquisitions, with the whole class.

> From what Prof. Moeller says, the key things are information and open communication, rather than welcome parties, celebratory back-slapping, etc.

◎ Students can watch the interview with Scott Moeller on the DVD-ROM.

➡ Resource bank: Listening (page 199)

Reading: Acquiring a green business

Students read an article on multinationals that take over small companies with environmentally-friendly reputations.

A

● Do as a quick-fire whole-class activity. For question 3, get students to say what they know about the companies that they have heard of. (Some will be obscure to some people, even if they are familiar to British consumers, such as Cadbury Schweppes. Point out that chocolate company Cadbury was itself acquired by Kraft recently, as mentioned above.)

1 Danone: producer of dairy products; L'Oréal: producer of beauty products; Colgate-Palmolive: producer of toiletries; Unilever: producer of household cleaning agents; Cadbury Schweppes: producer of soft drinks and confectionery; Estée Lauder: producer of cosmetics and perfumes

2 Danone – Stonyfield Yogurt; L'Oréal – Body Shop; Colgate-Palmolive – Tom's of Maine; Unilever – Ben and Jerry's; Cadbury Schweppes – Green and Black's; Estée Lauder – Aveda

3 They are all smaller players, mostly in the same fields as the larger corporations that took them over. They had a 'green' image, priding themselves on the quality or source of their products.

B

- Ask the students to read the article by themselves and check the answers to Exercise A.

- With the whole class, ask where the answer to each question above can be found in the article.

C – **F**

- Get students to look at the questions for all three exercises. Circulate, monitor and assist.

Exercise C

1 true   2 true   3 false   4 false   5 true

Exercise D

1 Better distribution, access to more markets, more cash

2 Factory closings, job losses, management changes

Exercise E

Three from: swallowed up, in partnership with, owned by, acquired by

Exercise F

1 conglomerate   2 corporations
3 multinational   4 partnership   5 subsidiary

- Check the answers with the whole class.

G

- Get students to discuss the questions in pairs. Circulate, monitor and assist. Note especially how students are using mergers and acquisitions vocabulary.

- Call the class to order and get representatives of pairs to say what their conclusions were.

- Praise good language use that you heard, and work on any remaining difficulties especially in relation to mergers and acquisitions language.

➡ Text bank (pages 158–161)

Language review: Prediction and probability

Students look at the language features associated with this area.

- Go through the points in the Language review box with the whole class. (Point out how prediction and probability can be expressed through particular verb tenses, modals or vocabulary.)

A

- Do as a whole class activity, getting students to explain their reasoning for choosing answers. (Some of these are quite tricky – concentrate on the ideas of prediction and probability.)

1 will have paid   2 will have been
3 will be working   4 will be holding
5 be working   6 will be offering
7 will have launched   8 will be enjoying

B – **C**

- Get students to work on these in pairs. Circulate, assist and monitor the correct use of prediction and probability language.

- Call the class to order and get students to repeat some of the predictions for the whole class. Work on the idea of being able to express the same idea in different ways, for example: *There's almost no chance of Microsoft merging with Apple* has the same meaning as *It's highly unlikely that Microsoft will merge with Apple.*

Skills: Making a presentation

Students look at and practise key presentations language.

A ◀)) CD3.30

- Recap any work on presentations that you have already done with your students, for example in Unit 7, getting them to summarise any key ideas you have looked at in earlier lessons.

- Get students to focus on the situation and the two questions.

- Play the recording and elicit the answers.

1 The gap in the market, the market conditions and the opportunity for growth

2 They plan to expand in the UK and become the market leader in the budget hotel sector.

B ◀)) CD3.30

- Ask students to look at the Useful language box, explain any difficulties (for example *portfolio*) and ask individual students to read out the utterances, with convincing stress and intonation. Explain what a rhetorical question is.

- Play the recording again and get the students to identify the utterances that they hear. (For the Repetition category, you could make the joke that, for a recent UK prime minister, the top social priority was 'Education, education, education, but not necessarily in that order.')

> Right, as I mentioned earlier …
>
> I'll outline these later in my presentation.
>
> Right, why did we (buy) …
>
> The gap in the market …
>
> Right, I've told you why we've …
>
> We have a clear, realistic and ambitious strategy for the Highview brand.
>
> By that time, we'll have developed a portfolio …
>
> Highview will be the future …

C – D

- Get students, in pairs, to turn to the script on page 167 of the Course Book and work on reading it with feeling. Circulate, monitor and assist.

- When students are ready, get public performances from two or three students, who could come to the front of the class and do a stand-up presentation, based on the script but also gesturing appropriately. (Tell students to stick to fairly subdued, English-speaking world levels of body language!) Work on any remaining difficulties.

- Then get them to look at Exercise D and prepare a presentation in pairs or, in large classes, groups of three or four. Students map out and rehearse the presentation together but they do not know at this point which member of their group will have to give the presentation for the whole class. Circulate, monitor and assist.

- Call the class to order and get one member from each group to give the presentation, or, with a large group, part of their presentation. Concentrate on correct use of expressions from the Useful language box. You could get students to do their presentations in later lesson(s) if there is not enough time.

➡ Resource bank: Speaking (page 187)

CASE STUDY

Rinnovar International

The management of an American cosmetics company wants to expand by making an acquisition. Students analyse four possible target companies and make a recommendation.

Background

- Ask the students to read the background information about Rinnovar. Meanwhile, write the points in the first column of the table on the board.

- With the whole class, elicit the information to complete the table.

Company	Rinnovar International Inc. (RI)
Revenues (=sales)	$14 bn
Products	Cosmetics, fragrance and skincare
Markets	US and overseas
Market share	6%
Expansion so far	Has been through acquisitions rather than internal/*organic* growth (see Background text below)
Mission (=strategic objective)	To compete with the likes of Revlon, L'Oréal and Procter & Gamble
Survey results	Products: need to be more innovative and varied Markets: Expand in S. Asia and S. America Distribution: only exclusive agents overseas Production: in US, therefore high-cost

- Get individual students to expand on these notes by talking about the points in their own words, with complete sentences.

- Get students in pairs to look at the questions on expansion through acquisitions versus organic growth, and those on RI's ideal takeover target. Circulate, monitor and assist.

- With the whole class, elicit their ideas.

Making acquisitions can bring 'ready-made' growth, for example in markets where RI is not yet present. However, integrating new acquisitions has its problems (for example, cross-cultural ones). Organic growth can be a 'hard slog' (teach this expression), but RI would have more control of its activities.

The selection criteria are open to discussion.

For example, it's not clear:

- that a well-established position is essential. It might be preferable to buy a small, cheap company that provides entry into a particular market.

- what the advantage of a wide range of suppliers would be – the current trend is to reduce the number of suppliers.

- that it's good to have an experienced management team – RI might prefer to bring in its own managers.

Get students to justify their choices.

🔊)) CD3.31

- Explain that RI is looking at four target companies – put their names up on the board:

- Mumbai Herbal Products

- Good Earth

- Hondo Beauty Products

- Sheen Hair Products

- Play the recording and get students to answer the questions about the companies' financial performance last year and in the three previous years. Write the information up on the board next to the companies' names.

- Then play the recording again, stopping after each company to ask more comprehension questions about them – nationality, products, etc. Write this information on the board, too.

- Get individual students to recap the information in complete sentences and in their own words.

- Finally, get students to read the texts about each company on the opposite page in small groups. Different groups could 'specialise' in different companies, paraphrasing the information for the whole class when they have finished.

Task

- Divide the class into small groups. Tell them they are corporate strategists for RI. They will discuss and analyse the information they have read and heard about all four target companies. Circulate, monitor and assist.

- When the discussion has finished, praise good language use and work on three or four points that need improvement, especially in the area of mergers and acquisitions, getting individual students to say the correct forms.

- Call the class to order and explain the next step. Each group has to prepare a presentation, making a recommendation about which company RI should go for. Circulate, monitor and assist as the students prepare their presentations. (You could hand out overhead transparencies and marker pens if there is an overhead projector, or even get students to prepare PowerPoint slides if there is a data projector, but don't let the slide-making become the dominant activity!)

- When the students are ready, ask each group in turn to give its presentation. Remind the class that they need to listen carefully to the other groups' presentations and make notes about them because they will need the information in the next stage of the task when they discuss which company to choose as one group.

- Have a class discussion about which company to choose and try to reach a consensus. Note down good language use and points that need further work, especially in relation to the presentations language that students saw in the Skills section.

One-to-one

This case study can be done one-to-one, with your student analysing the information on the three target companies and then discussing which one would be best to choose. Don't forget to note language points for praise and correction afterwards. Highlight some of the language you chose to use as well.

 Students can watch the case study commentary on the DVD-ROM.

Writing

- Ask the students to base their writing on the final decision made by the class on which company to recommend as an acquisition target. If no consensus was reached, they could base it on the decision made in their small groups.

- The writing can be done collaboratively in class or as homework.

Writing file, page 131

Resource bank: Writing (page 215)

CASE STUDY

International negotiations

This unit looks at negotiations in a cross-cultural context. How you deal with this will depend largely on your students' level of experience, if any, of cross-cultural negotiations.

A

- With the whole class, get students to talk about negotiations at work or at home. This could be about anything from negotiating with employers for a pay rise to negotiating with children about their bedtime.

- Treat the activity light-heartedly where appropriate – there's no need to rigorously apply the four discussion points if they are not suitable for the particular type of negotiation under discussion.

B

- Get students to work on these questions in pairs. Circulate, monitor and assist.

- Call the class to order and elicit the answers when most students have finished, discussing the possible answers rather than just ploughing through them. Get students to check the meanings of all the items a)–c) for each question, perhaps using dictionaries.

1 a 2 b 3 c 4 b 5 c 6 a 7 a 8 c 9 b

C

- Get students to work on these ideas in pairs. They should look at the issues raised by each question. For example, in question 2, they could talk about when it's appropriate to compromise. Circulate, monitor and assist.

- Call the class to order and ask representatives of pairs to give their ideas about each point.

D

- Again, get students to work on these ideas in pairs, reporting back to the whole class at the end. With experienced negotiators, ask if they have had experiences like the ones here.

E ◀)) CD3.32

- Read through the questions with students before you play the recording. (Explain *misconceptions* if necessary – a polite way of saying *misunderstandings*!)

- Go through the answers with the whole class.

1 That international negotiations are no different to domestic ones (*domestic* here means within a particular country, rather than negotiations that you have at home); that everyone likes to get down to business straight away and focus on the result; that regional generalisations are often inaccurate.

2 a) perception of the business relationship, b) the nature of the contract, c) the way negotiations are conducted

F ◀)) CD3.32

- As ever, read through the questions with students before you play the recording again. Get students to anticipate what they think the answers will be.

- Play the recording and elicit the answers.

1 T 2 F 3 F 4 T 5 T 6 F

Task

- Explain the situation to students: they are going to discuss the negotiation issues in groups of four, i.e. two pairs, following the procedure here.

- Get students to turn to the pages they need to refer to.

- When they are ready, the discussion can begin. Circulate and monitor.

- Note the language that students are using well, especially in relation to negotiations language, but also note those points that are causing difficulty and that need work.

- When the discussion has ended with most groups of four, call the class to order and get a representative of each group to say what their five chosen points were, and why.

- The writing task can be done collaboratively in class, or as homework. If you ask students to do it as homework, you could get them to e-mail it to you and comment on any problems in the next class. (In appropriate circumstances, it would be good to circulate the tips given for different cultures so that students can compare and contrast them.)

UNIT D Revision

10 Customer service

Vocabulary

This section revisits some key customer service vocabulary.

- Students do this in pairs or as a whole class activity.

1 complaints **2** rapport **3** the point
4 clients **5** service **6** purposes
7 guarantee **8** products **9** refunds
10 mile **11** payment **12** compensation
13 the buck **14** the bottom

Gerunds

- Ask students what they remember about these. If necessary, go through the Language review box on page 100 of the main unit in order to refresh students' memories.

1 to tell **2** to tell **3** to break **4** talking
5 Working **6** dealing **7** speaking
8 to tell **9** stealing **10** to send
11 at making **12** Writing **13** applying
14 to send

Skills

- Go through the expressions before doing the exercise, asking students to read them with feeling.

1 e **2** d **3** a **4** f **5** b **6** c

11 Crisis management

Vocabulary

Before doing the exercise, remind students about the importance of looking at the 'logic' of what can follow the first parts of the sentences.

1 j **2** d **3** e **4** b **5** a **6** c **7** h **8** g
9 i **10** f

Conditionals

- Recap with students the different types of conditional before doing the exercise.

1 act **2** had done **3** would have been
4 are **5** would be **6** Ignore **7** 'll have
8 contact **9** Given

Writing

- Remind students about the format of press releases by referring them to page 128 of the Writing file in the Course Book.

Whirlblend

Press release

Blender recalled as safety precaution

Whirlblend is recalling its model WB-110 after a man reported being injured using one of the blenders.

The injury, which wasn't serious, was an isolated incident, and the man has been successfully treated and has not been hospitalised. However, we take the safety of our products and the quality and clarity of our instructions very seriously. We believe that if you follow the instructions for using any of our products, including the WB-110 blender, you will be completely safe. We are investigating the situation and will provide regular updates as we gather more information.

For additional information, visit our website (www.whirlblend.com) or contact the office of Steven Biggs on 0554-987-9983.

12 Mergers and acquisitions

Vocabulary

This exercise should remind students about the importance of word partnerships.

1 launched **2** made **3** make **4** rejected
5 sell **6** set up **7** taken **8** target

Prediction and probability

- Recap the different ways of expressing these by getting students to look again at the Language review box on page 116 of the Course Book.

1 e **2** b **3** d **4** a **5** c

Skills

- Make the link with the expressions in the Useful language box on page 117 of the Course Book.

1 As I mentioned earlier, the outlook is good.
2 I'll talk about the details of the acquisition later.
3 OK, what were our reasons for the merger?
4 The merger will make us stronger, more competitive and more profitable.
5 Right, I've told you what we're doing next.
6 We're absolutely delighted that our bid has been accepted.
7 By 2018, we'll have become market leader.
8 We have a great brand, we have great managers and we have great workers.
9 Would anyone like to ask any questions?

Cultures 4: International negotiations

- Get students to recap some of the key points they saw in the unit before doing the exercise.

1 b **2** g **3** a **4** i **5** d **6** f **7** e **8** c **9** h

Text bank

Introduction

The Text bank contains articles relating to the units in the Course Book. These articles extend and develop the themes in those units. You can choose the articles that are of most interest to your students. They can be done in class or as homework. You have permission to make photocopies of these articles for your students.

Before you read

Before each article, there is an exercise to use as a warmer that helps students to focus on the vocabulary of the article and prepares them for it. This can be done in pairs or small groups, with each group then reporting its answers to the whole class.

Reading

If using the articles in class, it is a good idea to treat different sections in different ways, for example reading the first paragraph with the whole class, and then getting students to work in pairs on the following paragraphs. If you're short of time, get different pairs to read different sections of the article simultaneously. You can circulate, monitor and give help where necessary. Students then report back to the whole group with a succinct summary and/or their answers to the questions for that section. A full answer key follows the articles.

Discussion

In the Over to you sections following each article, there are discussion points. These can be dealt with by the whole class, or the class can be divided, with different groups discussing different points. During discussion, circulate, monitor and give help where necessary. Students then report back to the whole class. Praise good language production and work on areas for improvement in the usual way.

Writing

The discussion points can also form the basis for short pieces of written work. Students will find this easier if they have already discussed the points in class, but you can ask students to read the article and write about the discussion points as homework.

TEXT BANK

CORPORATE COMMUNICATION

Before you read

Think about the biggest company in your country. What is its reputation?

Reading

Read the article from the *Financial Times* by Paul Argenti and do the exercises that follow.

FT

LEVEL OF DIFFICULTY ● ● ○

Time for communication to move towards centre stage

Paul Argenti

The last few years have seen the biggest collapse in confidence in business in almost a century – to the point where probably the least
5 trusted spokespeople on the planet today are corporate executives. When intense mistrust prevails, whatever a company does says something about it, everything com-
10 municates, and communication affects everything.

This is changing the definition of communication. Communication today is more of a two-way dialogue
15 and this has been aided by the rise of social media like Facebook and Twitter and the explosion of information-sharing online. Today's best-in-class companies, such as
20 Dell in the US and Philips in Europe, do not just engage in dialogue. They use the latest technology as a source of ideas, opinions and competitive intelligence, for product develop-
25 ment, employee engagement and media monitoring.

In addition to rethinking the definition of communication, the best companies are rethinking its struc-
30 ture. There is a greater need for integration, collaboration and partnership among corporate leadership, human capital, finance, sales and legal teams.
35 Another change in communication by leading companies is the rethinking of key themes. This was the main finding of research by the Tuck School of Business at Dart-
40 mouth, conducted with Doremus, a business-to-business communications agency. It found that the best-in-class companies have been guided by six themes:

45 **a Focus on value and values** Stakeholders demand value for money when buying goods and services, but they also expect to see a strong set of corporate values in the
50 companies with which they do business. Walmart, Hyundai and BMW have used this theme in their advertising and communications.

b Evolve a sense of responsibil-
55 **ity** Corporate responsibility today is not just about philanthropy or being green. It is about companies being responsible across all business practices. NGOs, consumers, employees
60 and investors are ready to punish companies that ignore evolving social values. JPMorgan Chase has done a fabulous job reflecting its corporate responsibility initiatives
65 on its website and in advertising.

c Strategy must drive communication As Jon Iwata, IBM's senior vice-president for marketing and communications, puts it: "Lincoln
70 said, 'Character is the tree; reputation is the shadow.' I'm afraid too many people in PR, marketing and advertising spend more time manipulating the shadow than tending to
75 the tree."

d Shifting from the problem to the solution Stakeholders are most receptive to realistic and optimistic plans, and are often ready to pay
80 less attention to problems of the past year.

e Not communicating is a communication in itself You either tell your story or have it told for you.
85 **f Re-evaluate positioning** The crisis has led to disruption in how companies are thought of by constituencies, which provides a tremendous opportunity to reposi-
90 tion, rebrand and redevelop.

1 Find words from the article (lines 1–44), and related words, to complete the table.

Verb	Noun
collaborate	
	collapse
define	
engage	
explode	
find	
	prevalence
research	

2 True or false? (lines 1–44).

a) There is great mistrust of companies at the moment.

b) When there is mistrust, everything that companies do is misunderstood.

c) Corporate communication is seen as increasingly two-way.

d) The best companies have just continued to use their traditional public relations departments in order to communicate.

e) In their new approach to communication, companies have been paying attention to five things in particular.

3 Find expressions (lines 45–65) that refer to the following:

a) a subject that can be used in different forms of communication (5 letters))

b) what people expect when they buy a company's products (5 letters)

c) what they expect to see as guiding a company's behaviour (6 letters)

d) employees, shareholders, suppliers and, above all in this context, customers (12 letters)

e) giving money to charity (12 letters)

f) having good environmental policies (5 letters, 5 letters)

g) things that society as a whole thinks are important (6 letters, 6 letters)

h) actions that have not been taken before (11 letters)

4 Imagine company board meetings where directors say these things (1–6). Which point a–f (lines 45–90) is each director most closely referring to?

1 'We have to have a press conference and be open about our quality problems – if we don't talk about it and journalists get on to the story, we're in big trouble!'

2 'Our customers are getting real value for money when they buy our products, and they also have the reassurance of knowing they are dealing with a socially responsible organisation!'

3 'We mustn't let this crisis go to waste! It gives us the chance to reposition ourselves as the most environmentally aware energy company in the world.'

4 'Corporate social responsibility isn't something we can just leave to the CSR people – it involves all of us!'

5 'Let's not keep talking about our past problems. Instead, let's look forward to the exciting new possibilities that exist for the future!'

6 'There's too much emphasis here on public relations and slick advertising. If we behave responsibly, our corporate image will take care of itself.'

5 Choose the best summary for the whole article.

a) Corporate communication is a speciality that is best left to the PR department and advertising agencies.

b) Everything a company does communicates something about it, and executives are becoming increasingly aware of this.

c) Whatever a company does, people will always misinterpret its actions, and companies just have to try to limit the damage.

Over to you 1

"Lincoln said, 'Character is the tree; reputation is the shadow.' I'm afraid too many people in PR, marketing and advertising spend more time manipulating the shadow than tending to the tree." How far is it possible to 'manipulate' the truth about an organisation's character?

Over to you 2

Think about your organisation or one you would like to work for. In what ways can each department show that it is responsible? How can this be communicated?

TEXT BANK

TWITTER

Before you read
Do you tweet? Why? / Why not?

Reading
Read the article from the *Financial Times* by Jonathan Moules and do the exercises that follow.

FT

LEVEL OF DIFFICULTY ● ● ○

To tweet or not to tweet is a business question

Jonathan Moules

Is there a commercial use for social networking sites such as Twitter and Facebook? This is an important question for many company owners,
5 who have found themselves devoting precious resources to keeping online followers updated through Twitter tweets, while wondering if there is a bottom-line benefit to their
10 businesses.

David Carruthers, user experience manager at Glasses Direct, the online spectacles retailer, claims that using Twitter is one of the most
15 enjoyable elements of his working day as it puts him in direct contact with customers. "I use it as an engaging way of talking to customers," he says. "We're extremely
20 proud of our customer service here, and this is another way of making sure customers are happy."

Twitter is an excellent way to provide immediate feedback to cus-
25 tomers, according to Carruthers. He cites a recent example where he came across someone using Twitter to complain about not being able to get his glasses fixed before an
30 important business trip. He had not

protested to Glasses Direct but had used the phrase "glassesdirect" in his tweet, which Carruthers tracked down through a search. "I found that
35 tweet, saw he was a director of photography, so probably needed some specs, and tried to figure out what we could do," Carruthers says. Within a couple of hours, Glasses Direct had
40 made a basic pair of replacement frames and had them in the Twitter-er's hands the following day.

But while such heroic tales of customer service can only help with
45 Glasses Direct's profile online, Carruthers admits that Twitter is not a financially important area for the business. Alan Stevens, who advises company owners on social media
50 use through his business, Media Coach, says: "I have a lot of examples of people who are using Twitter incredibly well and thousands more that are using it badly."
55 Even the founders of Twitter are famous for failing to come up with a way to monetise their ingenious and addictive network. However, many companies use the technology to
60 solve business challenges, such as

finding personnel, improving staff productivity and finding new customers. Vena Ramphal claims she would never have created her busi-
65 ness venture, Divining Femininity, without Twitter – because it was through chatting on the network that she hooked up with her co-founders.

Her success is all the more sur-
70 prising since, as a relationship coach, she had avoided social networking sites, believing that they were inferior to face-to-face communication. "I have been very
75 pleasantly surprised," she says. Her new business will run weekend workshops for women to explore different aspects of femininity. The founders marked the launch with a
80 tweet, and were surprised to have more than 300 people view their posting in the first few hours.

1 Match words from each column to make expressions from lines 1–22.

1	social	line	benefit
2	bottom-	spectacles	manager
3	user	networking	retailer
4	online	experience	sites

2 Now match the expressions above to the people and things mentioned in the article that relate to them.

a) an increase in profit for businesses in general

b) David Carruthers

c) Glasses Direct

d) Facebook or Twitter

3 Use appropriate forms of expressions from lines 1–42 to complete these statements.

If …

a) you spend a lot of time and money on something that you could use for something else, you .... to it.

b) something allows you to communicate with people, it .... you .... with them.

c) something is an interesting method for doing something, it is an .... of doing it.

d) you are very happy with your achievements, you are .... of them.

e) you reply straightaway to someone in relation to what they have told you, you .... them with ....

f) you find something after a lot of looking, you .... it ....

g) you find an answer about the correct thing to do in a particular situation, you .... out .... to do.

4 True or false? (lines 43–68)

Twitter …

a) is the direct cause of greatly increased profits at Glasses Direct.

b) is used wisely by many people, but not all.

c) has made a lot of money for its founders.

d) is used to solve four particular business challenges.

e) was used by Vena Ramphal to find partners for her new business.

f) allowed her to found her business but she could have done it in other ways as well.

5 Find an expression (lines 68–82) that:

a) refers to making contact with people and doing things together: to .... someone. (3 words)

b) refers to something that is not just surprising, but especially so because of a particular reason. (4 words)

c) is used to describe something that is less good than something else. (1 word)

d) is used to describe communication between people who are in the same room, rather than over the Internet. (3 words)

e) refers to a training course with active participants. (1 word)

f) refers to an occasion when something is seen or available to buy for the first time. (1 word)

g) means a message sent on Twitter. (1 word)

Over to you 1

In what ways could Twitter be of use in your line of business, or a business that you are interested in?

Over to you 2

Will social networking eventually replace face-to-face socialising completely? Why? / Why not?

GLOBAL BRANDS 1

Before you read

Which do you think are the top ten brands in the world at the moment, in terms of their value? Make a list.

Reading

Read this article from the *Financial Times* by John Gapper and do the exercises that follow.

FT

LEVEL OF DIFFICULTY ● ● ●

TEXT BANK

Big names prove worth in crisis

John Gapper

For companies whose financial value depends heavily on the health of their brands, the severity and abruptness of the recession was a
5 challenge. The abruptness with which many consumers stopped spending, and large companies reduced capital investment, caused a shock to the system. Many compa-
10 nies experienced not only the financial crisis, but also a crisis of confidence.

Marketers and advertising agencies preach the gospel that the
15 companies that emerge best out of recessions are those that maintain their marketing budget and protect brands when the going gets tough. In practice, few companies were cer-
20 tain enough of the future to comply. Yet some of the Doomsday scenarios about the value of brands in the post-recession world have not come to pass. Emerging from the recession,
25 luxury goods companies and many other consumer brand companies are enjoying a rebound.

The underlying value of any brand – the premium commanded by prod-
30 ucts and services with strong reputations and identities – has not been eliminated by the crisis. Even those companies that did not invest heavily in their brands in the worst
35 times are regaining some confidence. "Brands outperform in good times and when there is a recession they do go down, but they come out the other side with a sustainable
40 advantage," says Joanna Seddon, chief executive of MBO, the organisation that compiles the ranking.

The nature of brands continues to evolve. Technology rather than
45 marketing is now the defining characteristic of seven of the top 10 brands, with Coca-Cola, McDonald's and Marlboro making up the other three. Google remains the
50 world's most valuable brand, but edging up close behind it are two other technology companies, IBM and Apple. Both of these outrank Microsoft, whose brand value was
55 stable during the year. The resurgence in Apple under Steve Jobs, through the iPod, the iPhone and now the iPad, continues unabated and, on present trends, it could be
60 pressing Google for first place within a year or two. That is a tribute to a company that inspires devotion among customers.

It may also be a reflection of the
65 value of inspirational leadership, and the way in which consumers identify some of the world's most valuable brands, such as Oracle and Starbucks, with founders who
70 embody their qualities. Larry Ellison of Oracle and Howard Schultz of Starbucks are not only the founders but keepers of the flame. The social media boom led by companies such
75 as Facebook and Twitter – as well as the rise in smartphones led by Apple – has had a broader impact on the top 100. It has boosted mobile operators such as Verizon and
80 AT&T, despite the complaints of iPhone users about AT&T's 3G coverage.

1 Complete this table with words and grammatically related words from lines 1–12.

noun	adjective
	abrupt
	confident
	healthy
finance	
	severe
	valuable

2 Now match the adjectives above to their meanings.
   a) in good condition
   b) very difficult
   c) worth a lot of money
   d) feeling good about the future
   e) very sudden
   f) relating to money

3 Use forms of expressions from lines 13–27 to correct these statements.
   a) If you say that something is true and that people should act in accordance with it, you preach the bible about it.
   b) If conditions become difficult in a particular situation, the journey gets hard.
   c) A series of very bad events that might happen is a fateful narrative.
   d) A formal way of saying that something has happened is to say that it has come past.
   e) If a company does well after a period of doing badly, it undergoes a bounce.

4 True or false? (lines 13–42)
   a) The value of brands was completely destroyed during and after the recession.
   b) Companies that did not invest in their brands have been totally eliminated.
   c) The value of brands goes down during recessions.
   d) Companies with valuable brands do better than those without in the long run.

5 Which of the brand(s) mentioned in lines 43–82 ...
   a) relate to technology-based companies or their products?
   b) relate to non-technology companies?
   c) is top in the rankings?
   d) is technology-based, and below three other technology companies?
   e) are names of products related to a technology company?
   f) have grown partly because of the success of other brands?

6 Find expressions that refer to (lines 43–82) ...
   a) the thing that people think about most in relation to a brand. (8 letters, 14 letters)
   b) a period of success following a period of decline. (10 letters)
   c) makes you admire a person, brand, etc. (8 letters)
   d) a feeling of complete admiration, respect, etc. (8 letters)
   e) company founders who are still building their companies. (7 letters, 2 letters, 3 letters, 5 letters)
   f) companies such as Facebook and Twitter. (6 letters, 5 =)

Over to you 1

Look again at the list of brands that you made before you read the article. Compare it with the answers to question 5. Were there any surprises for you? If so, describe them.

Over to you 2

Which of the above brands will still be important 10 years from now, and which will have declined? Give your reasons.

GLOBAL BRANDS 2

Before you read

What are the top soft drink brands in your country? Which are international and which local?

Reading

Read this article from the *Financial Times* by Jonathan Birchall and do the exercises that follow.

FT

LEVEL OF DIFFICULTY ● ● ○

Coca-Cola targets more $1bn China brands

Jonathan Birchall

Coca-Cola already owns two of China's three best-selling sparkling drinks but by 2020 it wants to have four more $1bn brands in what has become its third-largest market by revenue. The ambitious target reflects Coca-Cola's confidence that its long-term plans to more than triple sales in China are secure both from domestic rivals and from potential political pitfalls.

Coca-Cola's revenues have grown by a compound annual rate of 19 per cent over the past five years and it claims to be widening its lead over its rivals. It says it has double Pepsi-Cola's total sales in China, supported in particular by its stronger presence in still drinks, water and juices. The company has also continued to expand its range of non-carbonated drinks where it competes with both local and international brands.

It has launched Glaceau enhanced water, as well as its first dairy and juice drink, Minute Maid Super Pulpy Milky, entering a 1 billion-case market where competitors include Wahaha, Danone's former joint venture partner. Coke and Sprite already each sell more than $1bn annually and Coca-Cola is forecasting that its Yuan Ye tea brand and its Ice Dew bottled water – both launched last year – will also be $1bn China brands by 2020, in spite of facing strong competition from Taiwan's Tingyi, which has about half the total ready-to-drink tea market.

In terms of political challenges, the world's largest soft drinks company suffered a blow this March when China's ministry of commerce blocked its planned $2.4bn takeover of China's largest juice company, Huiyuan. Since the setback, Coca-Cola has continued the kind of high-level commitment to China demonstrated by its sponsorship of the Beijing Olympics, recently announcing plans to invest $2bn in China over the next three years.

Muhtar Kent, chief executive, noted that at a meeting with Wang Qishan, China's vice-premier for economic affairs, Coca-Cola had been praised for being the only US company to have a pavilion at last year's Shanghai World's Expo. Mr Kent says he regards the potential obstacles to Coca-Cola's China ambitions coming from broader political pressures as China's growth could still fall short of expectations. He does not see this, including the threat of potential nationalist reaction to Coca-Cola's US brand identity. "Everyone's walking around with Nikes, and drinking Coke and wearing Oakleys. I think there's a difference between that and the view of the US – people don't worry at a consumer level, at a brand level," says Doug Jackson, head of Coke's China business unit.

1 Look through the whole article and find all the brands and company names mentioned.

2 Now look at your answers to question 1 and find:

a) two US soft drinks companies.

b) a French company (the article does not specifically say that it is French).

c) a Chinese company with which the company above had a joint venture.

d) a Chinese juice company.

e) a Taiwanese company.

f) two brands of water.

g) a brand of tea.

h) a brand of flavoured milk drink.

i) two non-drink brands, used here in their plural forms.

3 Look at lines 1–23 and say if these statements are true or false.

a) Coca-Cola owns the three best-selling sparking drinks in China.

b) Coca-Cola makes more than a billion dollars in sales in China from each of these brands.

c) China is Coca-Cola's biggest overseas market.

d) Coca-Cola's aim is to sell more than four times as much in China as it does now.

e) Coca-Cola's sales in China have grown by nearly a fifth each year for the past five years.

f) PepsiCola's sales in China are more than half of Coca-Cola's.

g) Coca-Cola until now has only sold Coke in China.

4 Match the verbs 1–7 with the things that they go with a–g in lines 24–53.

1	enter	a)	a blow
2	launch	b)	a takeover
3	suffer	c)	a commitment
4	block	d)	brands
5	continue	e)	plans
6	demonstrate	f)	a commitment
7	announce	g)	a market

5 Now match the verbs 1–7 in Exercise 4 with their meanings i–vii, as they are used in the article.

i) start selling

ii) give information about

iii) prevent

iv) negatively experience

v) show

vi) go into

vii) carry on

6 Choose the best alternative summary for the final paragraph.

Coca-Cola's chief executive thinks that …

a) Coca-Cola will definitely suffer if there is nationalist resistance to the company's future expansion in China.

b) the design of Coca-Cola's stand at the Shanghai World Expo was highly appreciated by the Chinese.

c) people think in terms of brands rather than nationalities, and Coca-Cola will not unduly suffer from nationalist resistance to foreign companies.

Over to you 1

How many of the brands mentioned in the article do you know? How strong are they in your country? What do you think of them?

Over to you 2

Has there been resistance to particular foreign brands in your country because of their national origins? Give some background and explain how this resistance came about.

WORKING FOR FREE

Before you read

Would you be willing to do pro bono work – that is, to work without being paid? Why? / Why not?

Reading

Read this article from the *Financial Times* by Rhymer Rigby and do the exercises that follow.

FT

LEVEL OF DIFFICULTY ● ● ○

The careerist: Pro bono work

Rhymer Rigby

Pro bono work is usually thought of as the preserve of lawyers, but organisations as varied as advertising agencies and professional services firms also donate their staff's time to good causes – either for free or for reduced fees. Although employees should do pro bono work for selfless reasons, your good deeds can also be rewarded in terms of your career.

How does pro bono work add to my experience?
If you are relatively junior, it can be a very good way to step up. "People who do pro bono work in the Accenture Development Partnerships typically take on more senior roles than they would in big corporate roles," says Royce Bell, a senior executive at the consultancy firm. "You get to see a lot of nuts and bolts and it's very good to get outside the normal cosy corporate world. You'd think that someone who sets up an IT system in Chad would have a broader view than a person who has only worked in Fortune 200 companies."

What about opportunities for building relationships?
Pro bono work often brings together people from different parts of organisations who might not otherwise meet. Phil Georgiadis, chairman of Walker Media, the London agency, says it can cut through hierarchies, too. "I'm about to do some work for the Great Ormond Street Hospital for Children and I'll enlist a couple of graduates to work with me – that'll be the account team. So suddenly you have a graduate who is reporting directly to the chairman, which is very rare," he explains.

What about job satisfaction?
Using your professional skills in the service of good causes often adds a kind of ethical dimension to your career and can be very motivating. Maya Mehta, a senior associate at Clifford Chance, the law firm, says that her inspiration for starting the Newham Asian Women's Project pro bono scheme came from reading about forced marriages: "It got to the point where I couldn't just turn the page. I wanted to do something about it." She says it is also one way of bridging the divide between Canary Wharf and the less privileged areas that surround it.

Pro bono work can be rewarding in other ways, too. Mr Georgiadis says you can be freer to be more creative with work done for charities: "You often have the opportunity to do some really interesting marketing and you have more freedom than you might have with, say, a breakfast cereal." Mr Bell adds that Accenture Development Partnership projects tend to be smaller and shorter than their corporate counterparts: "It's much easier to see overall results and understand the positive effect of what you are doing."

1 Look through the whole article and match these people with the organisations that they work for and the pro bono projects that they mention.

1 Royce Bell   **a)** Clifford Chance   **i)** the Great Ormond Street Hospital for Children

2 Phil Georgiadis   **b)** Accenture Development Partnerships   **ii)** the Newham Asian Women's Project

3 Maya Mehta   **c)** Walker Media   **iii)** an IT system in Chad

2 Choose the correct alternatives (lines 1–10).

1 'Pro bono', meaning 'for good', comes from which language?
 a) Greek   **b)** French   **c)** Latin

2 Working for reduced fees or no fee at all is …
 a) limited to the legal profession.
 b) only common in law and advertising.
 c) found in a range of professional services.

3 Normally, if you donate your time, you …
 a) charge for it.
 b) don't charge for it.
 c) charge twice as much as for other work.

4 This article uses 'donate' to mean …
 a) always charging nothing at all.
 b) charging nothing or sometimes charging a reduced fee.
 c) occasionally charging the full rate.

5 The opposite of 'selfless' is …
 a) selfish.   **b)** self-help.   **c)** self-service.

6 Which of these words is least similar in meaning to 'deeds'?
 a) doings   **b)** acts   **c)** thoughts

7 The reward for doing pro bono work comes in the form of …
 a) better career prospects.
 b) more job satisfaction.
 c) a better salary for your current job.

3 Where are these aspects of doing pro bono work mentioned in the article (lines 11–45)? Which are not mentioned?

You may have the chance of…
 a) seeing very practical aspects of projects.
 b) working with the chairman, even if you are a recent graduate recruit.
 c) getting a more rounded way of looking at things than you would in a large company.
 d) improving healthcare in the developing world.
 e) doing work with more responsibility.
 f) working on projects in the developing world.
 g) understanding how hierarchies work.

4 Match the verbs with the expressions that they go with (lines 46–77).

1 use   **a)** the divide
2 bridge   **b)** an ethical dimension
3 add   **c)** professional skills
4 start   **d)** more freedom
5 have   **e)** the project
6 have   **f)** the positive effect
7 see   **g)** the opportunity
8 understand   **h)** the overall results

5 Now match the opinions (a–e) to the people who might have expressed them (1–4). (One of these people relate to two of the opinions.) (lines 46–77).

1 Rhymer Rigby   **a)** 'I couldn't just ignore this social problem.'
2 Royce Bell   **b)** 'You really have a chance to work independently.'
3 Phil Georgiadis   **c)** 'You get to see the results of your own work more easily.'
4 Maya Mehta   **d)** 'It gives you the opportunity to know that you're doing good.'
   e) 'It allows us the chance to have contact with some of our neighbours.'

Over to you 1

Think about your organisation or one you would like to work for. What pro bono projects would it be advantageous for the organisation to carry out?

Over to you 2

Identify an area in which you personally might like to do pro bono work. Discuss the main points of your campaign.

DOING BUSINESS IN RUSSIA

Before you read

What advice would you give to a business visitor on building relationships in your country?

Reading

Read this article from the *Financial Times* by Isabel Gorst and do the exercises that follow.

FT

LEVEL OF DIFFICULTY ● ● ●

TEXT BANK

Hot and cold reception awaits Moscow's visitors

Isabel Gorst

When Russia first opened up to foreign investors in the 1990s, some puzzled international business people would take psychologists into negotiations to help fathom what was going on. Two decades later, the Russian business world seems outwardly accessible. Russian companies have built flashy corporate headquarters and have teams of English-speaking managers with western MBAs. But deep down, Russian business culture – a mix of the authoritarian and the free-wheeling – remains alien to foreigners. For their part, many Russian business people still regard outsiders with suspicion and prefer to work – and play – within close-knit circles.

The western practice of compartmentalising work and personal life has not caught on in Russia, where business carries on round the clock. Russian laws are unclear and dangerously open to interpretation, so business people prefer to strike deals on a comradely handshake rather than rely on written contracts.

Ivan Korsak, the trade commissioner at the Belgian embassy in Moscow, says: "Fifty per cent of doing business in Russia is about selling a product, and the rest is about building relationships. "The first thing is to convince Russians you have a value-added product and that you are a person they can trust. Price is secondary to all that," he says.

Responsibility for decision-making rests at the highest level in most Russian organisations. Doing a deal in Russia is about building trust with one or two people at the top, says Daniel Wolfe, a Moscow-based entrepreneur. "It's better to spend time figuring out how to get an audience with them than on devising flow charts and power-point presentations to sell your product."

Russian business people prefer face-to-face meetings, reflecting an ingrained suspicion that telecommunications are tapped. Nonetheless, fixing a high-level tête-à-tête can be frustrating. All too often, advance requests for appointments will be brushed aside with "Let's call each other when you arrive". "It's always a muddle right up to the last moment, but in the end everything always works out," says one expatriate banker in Moscow.

Russians address each other by first names and patronymics, leaving surnames aside. Nicknames add another layer of complexity providing fertile ground for gaffes. The Vladimir met in a boardroom can turn into Volodya by lunch or Vova in a late night bar. Russians know their language is difficult and are forgiving of foreigners' mistakes.

External appearances matter a lot. If you have to choose, a big car is more impressive than a fancy office suite. Business attire is a formal suit and tie. Clean shoes – the more expensive the better – are an absolute must. Chunky timepieces are part of the business kit.

1 Imagine that each paragraph has a heading. Put the headings in the correct order.

a) The use of names

b) The importance of appearances

c) Arranging meetings

d) Building trust

e) The (in-)accessibility of Russia

f) Personal and professional life

g) Talking to the right person

2 Find words (lines 1–20) that mean:

a) understand. (6 letters)

b) seemingly. (9 letters)

c) open. (10 letters)

d) attractive but not in good taste. (6 letters)

e) managed by a powerful person whose decisions are not questioned. (13 letters)

f) very different and hard to understand. (5 letters)

g) uncertainty about the honesty of others' motives. (9 letters)

h) describing a group, etc. where people know each other very well and others find it difficult to enter. (5 letters, 4 letters)

3 True or false? (lines 21–64).

If ...

a) you compartmentalise two things, you keep them together.

b) something catches on, a lot of people start do it.

c) a law is open to interpretation, it may have several meanings.

d) you strike a deal, you make one.

e) price is secondary, it's the most important thing.

f) a request is brushed aside, it is ignored.

g) a plan works out, it is not realised.

4 Match the two parts of these expressions. (lines 52–82).

1	ingrained	appearances
2	high-level	banker
3	advance	office suite
4	expatriate	requests
5	external	suspicion
6	fancy	timepieces
7	chunky	tête-à-tête

5 Now match the expressions above to these examples of them (a–g).

a) a one-to-one meeting with the head of Gazprom

b) a Hugo Boss suit and leather shoes altogether worth $1500

c) the idea, impossible to get rid of, that phone conversations are tapped

d) three very attractive connecting offices in an expensive business park

e) Rolex watches one centimetre thick

f) a French executive working for SocGen bank in Moscow

g) asking to see the head of Gazprom three weeks before your visit

Over to you 1

Look at the headings in question 1 above. Put your advice to a business visitor to your country under these headings. (You can repeat some of the advice you gave in 'Before you read' above if you wish.)

Over to you 2

'It's not what you know, it's who you know.' Is this true of your country and others that you know? If so, in what ways? If not, why not?

SUCCESSFUL WOMEN

Before you read

Who is the most successful businesswoman in your country? How did she become successful?

Reading

Read this article from the *Financial Times* by Lucy Kellaway and do the exercises that follow.

FT

LEVEL OF DIFFICULTY ● ● ○

A guide to being a successful female boss

Lucy Kellaway

Every year, the FT publishes a list of the top 50 women chief executives in the world who talk about the secrets of their success. The number
5 one woman, PepsiCo's Indra Nooyi, says you must work hard and have fun. Irene Rosenfeld of Kraft says you must follow your passion. The others talk about the importance of
10 having a mentor, of being yourself, of work-life balance, of teamwork and of being humble.

There was only one discordant note. This was sounded by Dong
15 Mingzhu, who runs Gree Electric Appliances, a Chinese manufacturer of air conditioners and is rated the ninth most important business-woman in the world. "I never miss,"
20 she says. "I never admit mistakes and I am always correct." I read this and laughed. It was so shocking, so out of line that I thought it a joke.

Yet Sister Dong, as she is some-
25 times known, has achieved results. Gree Electric Appliances has achieved total shareholder returns in the past three years of 529.5 per cent. One might argue that the Sister-
30 Dong-never-wrong school of management is something that only works in China, where the fondness for autocracy is considerable and theory of management is still about
35 making money and hasn't evolved to include such soppy practices as mentoring or 360-degree feedback.

Last week I went to see *The September Issue*, a documentary about
40 life at American Vogue, and can confirm that the Sister-Dong-never-wrong approach can work quite brilliantly in the most highly evolved and most competitive of industries:
45 fashion.

For 90 minutes, we see a not very personable woman who never praises anyone and hardly ever smiles telling her underlings their
50 work is ugly or boring. Yet for 20 years, this woman has hung on at the top of her business, while most CEOs – male and female – last four or five years before they are spat out
55 or squashed.

Pulling off the same feat with air conditioning must be harder. For Sister Dong, and for all the other CEOs who run complicated, global
60 businesses, it is terribly hard to tell if they are actually wrong or not. And in the meantime they have a choice. Either rule by fear - which still works in China and in fashion – or
65 rule by banging on about passion and mentors and hoping that if you are wrong, no one will notice.

1 **In lines 1–23, find reasons given by top women executives for their success.**

I ...

a) work ....

b) have ....

c) follow ....

d) believe in ....

e) try to ....

f) believe in ....-.......... ....

g) try to be ....

h) never ....

i) never ....

j) am always ....

2 **Now match each reason above to the executive who gave it and the company that she works for. (In some cases, no particular person or company is mentioned.)**

3 **Which three of the above reasons are 'discordant'? Why?**

4 **Which alternative could be used to replace the expression in *italics* without changing the meaning?**

1 Yet Sister Dong, as she is sometimes known, has *achieved* results.

a) fabricated   **b)** objectified   **c)** produced

2 GRE has achieved *shareholder* returns in the past three years of 529.5 per cent.

a) return on sales   **b)** return on equity

c) return on assets

3 ... in China, ... the *fondness* for ...

a) hatred   **b)** indifference   **c)** liking

4 ... *autocracy* is considerable ...

a) authoritarian management

b) democratic management

c) Scandinavian-style management

5 ... and hasn't evolved to include such *soppy* practices as mentoring or 360-degree feedback.

a) emotional   **b)** strong   **c)** soapy

6 ... the Sister-Dong-never-wrong approach can work quite brilliantly in the most highly *evolved* and most competitive of industries: fashion.

a) backward   **b)** developed   **c)** complicated

5 **Use correct forms of expressions from the lines 46–67 to complete these statements:**

a) Someone not that attractive or likeable is ....

b) People who work under someone else's authority are their ....

c) If you stay in a job when you might be expected not to, you .... there.

d) Someone rejected by an organisation is ....

e) Someone destroyed by an organisation is .... by it.

f) If you achieve something difficult, you ....

g) If you manage people by making them feel afraid, you ....

h) If you talk about something constantly, you .... it.

i) If people don't pay attention to something, they don't .... it.

6 **Which statement sums up the article best?**

Western ideas about management success ...

a) are all wrong.

b) may be right, or they may be wrong, but some women succeed in totally different ways.

c) may be right, but we don't really know.

Over to you 1

Go through the answers a–j to question 1 above.
What do you think of each of the 'secrets' of success?
Give your reasons.

Over to you 2

'In China, ... the fondness for autocracy is considerable.'
Is this true in your country's companies?
Why? / Why not?

SUCCESSFUL STRATEGIC CHANGE

Before you read

What advice would you give for successfully making changes in a) your professional life, b) your personal life?

Reading

Read this article from the *Financial Times* by Stefan Stern and do the exercises that follow.

FT

Master the mix of continuity and change

Stefan Stern

What makes winning businesses different from the also-rans? Having better products and services helps. Good leadership is essential. But the
5 strongest companies manage something else that is rare. They cope with crises and big strategic change without drifting off course. How rare is this?
10 Gerry Johnson, a professor at Lancaster University Management School, and two colleagues from the Rotterdam School of Management, George Yip, the dean, and researcher
15 Manuel Hensmans, have been studying companies that, over a 20-year period, achieved almost uninterrupted success while dealing with big changes. They have interviewed
20 senior executives (past and present) from some of these companies to find out what went on, how decisions were made and what the prevailing atmosphere was like.
25 The big danger, even for successful businesses, is strategic drift, Prof

Johnson says. Companies start out on the right track but they can all too easily lose their way. When things
30 become critical, existing leadership is kicked out, new leaders come in, and the cycle starts again. But not, in the case of a few exceptional businesses. Tesco, Cadbury and the
35 medical products group Smith & Nephew all dealt with big changes while avoiding disaster.

How? A combination of four characteristics, or traditions as the
40 researchers call them, seems to be crucial. The first is continuity. This involves "the reinvention of the company's distinctive business model" to fit in with prevailing mar-
45 ket conditions.

The second is anticipation. This is where it starts to get tricky. To build in anticipation, "alternative leaders" have to be allowed to start work on
50 the future shape and direction of the company but without undermining the current leadership. At Tesco in

the late 1960s and early 1970s, a new generation of managers (includ-
55 ing future boss Ian MacLaurin) began transforming the business under the nose of the founder Jack Cohen.

This leads to the third characteris-
60 tic of a winning business, which the academics call "contestation" or "respectful difference that grows out of conflict". This is vital. Dynamic, growing businesses benefit from the
65 creative tension of civilised disagreement. The Smith & Nephew culture was shaped by argument, Prof Johnson suggests. A witness to Tesco board meetings in the mid-
70 1980s told him that they were argumentative and confrontational "but like a family arguing rather than a group of enemies".

The final characteristic is mobil-
75 ity, meaning a flexible recruitment policy that tries to put the best person in the job, which prevents the growth of a time-serving culture.

TEXT BANK

1 Look through the whole article and find:

a) a professor of management in the UK.

b) two management researchers from the Netherlands.

c) a UK business school.

d) a business school in the Netherlands.

e) three successful companies.

f) two executives at one of these companies.

g) an unnamed person who went to board meetings at one of these companies.

2 Find the following in the first two lines 1–24:

a) a two-word expression, originally from horse racing, to refer to those who do not win a race

b) a verb that could be replaced by 'manage to deal'

c) the plural of 'crisis'

d) an adjective that can also describe important long-term decisions in a company

e) an adjective to refer to something that is not common or frequent

f) a two-word expression used in the context of organisations that do well over long periods

g) a two-word expression referring to the main feelings, culture, etc. in an organisation

3 Write questions relating to these answers from lines 25–45.

a) ....?

Strategic drift. They start out on the right track but they lose their way.

b) ....?

Existing managers are kicked out, new leaders come and the cycle starts again.

c) ....?

No, there are a few exceptional businesses like Tesco, Cadbury and Smith & Nephew that all dealt with big changes while avoiding disaster.

d) ....?

A combination of four characteristics or traditions.

e) ....?

Continuity.

f) ....?

The reinvention of the company's distinctive business model.

4 Now find nouns in the answers to the questions above that mean:

a) different things working together.

b) qualities.

c) finding something new to replace something that was also once new.

d) moving to places you don't want to go to.

e) a very serious failure.

f) the way a business operates in order to make money (two-word expression).

g) a good direction in which to go (two-word expression).

h) the ways things have long been done in a particular culture, organisation, etc.

5 Continuity is the first success factor mentioned. What are the other three?

6 What examples are given of the above three success factors?

7 What are the possible disadvantages relating to the first two of the above that Tesco avoided?

Over to you 1

Is contestation encouraged in your school or organisation? Why? / Why not?

Over to you 2

Think of a company that has been successful for a long time. How has it avoided drifting off course?

TEXT BANK

A JOB SATISFACTION SURVEY

Before you read
How easy is it for young people to get jobs in your country?

Reading
Read this article from the *Financial Times* by Brian Groom and do the exercises that follow.

FT

LEVEL OF DIFFICULTY ● ● ○

Unhappiness at work rises to record level

Brian Groom, Business and Employment Editor

Job satisfaction has dropped to a record low – with a particularly sharp fall among young people – as the pressures of recession take their
5 toll, according to a leading business group. A study of 2,000 workers by the Chartered Institute of Personnel and Development suggests that, even if official figures mark an end
10 to the recession, employees are still paying a high price in job insecurity and stress.

Evidence of unhappiness among young workers is disclosed after the
15 launch of the government's guarantee of a job, training or work experience place for every unemployed person aged 18 to 24 for six months. "We do not want to have the
20 lost generation of the 1980s," said the prime minister.

The government says that up to 470,000 opportunities will be created over 15 months, with 100,000
25 youngsters eligible straight away. BT, the telecoms group, announced 3,000 work placements in partnership with smaller companies. The CIPD's survey, conducted by You-
30 Gov, found job satisfaction levels had fallen from a net +48 last summer to +35. The job satisfaction score is the difference between those saying they are satisfied and those
35 who say they are not. In addition, fewer than one in 10 said their standard of living had improved in the past six months.

Job satisfaction among people
40 aged 18 to 24 fell from +44 to just +5. Happiness at work was higher among older age groups, with those aged 55-64 most satisfied. Claire McCartney, a CIPD adviser, said:
45 "Even though the economy is no longer flat on its back, the 'real economy' as experienced in the day-to-day lives of workers is crippled."

She said unhappiness among
50 young people may be partly explained by the fact they had grown up in an era of plenty and had not seen anything like this. "The lack of opportunities to learn new skills or
55 make their first steps up the career ladder is also likely to be grinding them down. The stagnant labour market means people are not moving on and up as they would like, leav-
60 ing many young people stranded in entry-level jobs."

Most workers surveyed said it would be difficult to find another job if made redundant, while a fifth
65 thought it likely they would lose their job. Public sector workers were more likely to report that their organisation had made, or planned to make, redundancies than in the pre-
70 vious quarter.

1 **Look through the whole article and find:**

   a) an organisation for professionals working in human resources.

   b) a telecoms company.

   c) an opinion poll organisation.

   d) someone who works for the organisation in a) above.

2 **Find nouns in lines 1–21 that refer to:**

   a) feelings of happiness and achievement.

   b) feelings of stress, unhappiness, etc. caused by something.

   c) damage that something can do.

   d) numbers.

   e) a period when economic activity goes down.

   f) not feeling safe.

   g) not feeling cheerful.

3 **Complete the table with words from lines 13–48, and grammatically related words.**

verb	noun
	disclosure
train	
launch	
experience	
	announcement
	fall
	improvement

4 **Match these numbers from lines 1–48 to what they refer to.**

1 2000   a) the change in the job satisfaction 'score' among all workers

2 470,000A   b) the number of job opportunities for young people to be created by the government immediately

3 100,000   c) the number of people in the CIPD survey

4 3,000   d) the age group where workers are happiest

5 +48 to +35   e) the number of people who said their standard of living had improved in the last six months

6 less than one in 10   f) the number of job opportunities for young people to be created by the government over the next 15 months

7 +44 to +5   g) the number of work placements to be created by BT

8 55–64   h) the change in the job satisfaction 'score' among 18- to 24-year-olds

5 **Look at lines 39–61 in order to find the correct expressions to replace those in *italics* below, using the same number of words.**

   a) If something is in a bad state, it is *down on the behind*.

   b) If something is functioning very badly, it is *creeping*.

   c) A period when everyone has all the things they want is an *area of plenitude*.

   d) Your first job is your first *landing* on the job staircase.

   e) If bad experiences make you more and more depressed, they *ground you downwards*.

   f) If you can't leave a place where you don't want to be, you are *abandoned* there.

   g) Jobs that people have when they join an organisation are described as *entrance-stage*.

6 **Read lines 49–70 to decide if these statements are true or false.**

   a) Young people have never known anything like the present economic situation.

   b) The employment market is growing now.

   c) Most people could easily find another job if they wanted to.

   d) 20 per cent thought that they might lose their jobs.

   e) Those working in the public sector thought it more likely that they would lose their jobs in the next three months than in the previous three.

Over to you 1

Imagine a similar survey in your own country. What do you think the findings would be about job satisfaction and security in relation to a) the 18 to 24 age group, and b) the 55 to 64 age group?

Over to you 2

In what ways are work placements for young people useful to a) employers and b) the young people themselves?

TEXT BANK

FLEXIBILITY

Before you read

Would it be possible to do your job, or one you would like to have, in four days a week? Why? / Why not?

Reading

Read this article from the *Financial Times* by Alison Maitland and do the exercises that follow.

FT

LEVEL OF DIFFICULTY ● ● ○

A different way of working

Alison Maitland

Lee Summersgill was initially con- cerned when he heard that his employer, KPMG, the professional services firm, wanted staff to volun-
5 teer for a four-day week to help minimise job cuts in the recession. The news coincided with the birth of his daughter in January last year, and he was worried about a reduction in
10 hours and pay. Then he considered the benefits of a change to his work- ing week so that he could share the childcare with his partner, a health visitor. Now he puts away his Black-
15 Berry every Thursday night and spends Friday with his two young children.

  "I've been doing it for a year and it's worked really well," says Mr
20 Summersgill, who advises clients on housing projects. "You have to be really disciplined and try to fit everything into four days. I think it makes you more loyal. Would any
25 other firm have the same level of flexibility and understanding? In the market I'm in, I don't think that would be there." Mr Summersgill's experience illustrates two growing
30 trends: fathers wanting greater flex- ibility to accommodate family life, and employers using flexibility to keep employees motivated, improve productivity and avoid large-scale
35 job cuts.

  Business leaders around the world have remained concerned about retaining good people, even in the depths of recession. A global survey
40 by Hay Group, a consultancy, con- cluded: "While employees fear losing their jobs, organisations fear the loss of top talent and critical skills." Amid signs of economic
45 recovery, but with cost constraints continuing, employers are looking at alternatives to financial incentives. Offering employees greater control over working time and location is
50 one such option.

  KPMG, for example, is examining new approaches, after the success of its "Flexible Futures" programme in signing up employees for taking a
55 year off or working reduced weeks. Roughly 85 per cent of the 10,000 UK staff volunteered at the start of last year. Approximately 800 people moved temporarily to four-day
60 weeks. The firm saved £4m last year, or the equivalent of 100 full-time jobs, says Michelle Quest, UK head of people.

  When the programme was
65 relaunched for this year, 71 per cent volunteered. "One of the softer ben- efits is moving the whole idea of flexible working up the agenda for everybody," says Ms Quest. The
70 firm is now considering more active promotion of job sharing, because this type of arrangement provides all-week cover for clients.

1 Which alternative could be used to replace the expression in *italics* from lines 1–17 so as to keep the same meaning?

1 Lee Summersgill was initially *concerned* …

   a) interested **b)** worried c) reassured

2 … when he heard that his employer … wanted staff to *volunteer* for a four-day week …

   a) offer to agree to **b)** refuse

   c) offer to discuss

3 … to help *minimise* job cuts in the recession.

   a) increase the number of

   b) reduce the psychological effect of

   c) reduce as much as possible the number of

4 The news *coincided* with the birth of his daughter in January last year, …

   a) came at the same time as **b)** came after

   c) came before

5 … Then he considered the *benefits* of a change to his working week …

   a) aspects b) advantages c) downsides

6 … so that he could share the *childcare* with his partner, a health visitor.

   a) schooling b) childminding c) healthcare

2 Answer these questions with one word nouns, or nouns related to verbs, from lines 18–35.

Have Lee Summersgill's new working arrangements …

a) increased his feelings of wanting to do his best for his employer?
– Yes, they've increased his ………. and …………

b) made him work in a more organised way, keep to deadlines and so on?
– Yes, they've increased his sense of ……….
about work.

c) shown that KPMG is willing to allow people to work in different ways?
– Yes, they've shown that they believe in job ……….

d) been criticised by KPMG?
– No, they have shown a high level of ………. in relation to his personal situation.

e) shown that KPMG understands the needs of families and is willing to help them?
– Yes, they've shown a high degree of ……….

f) and those of other KPMG employees shown that their output is less than before?
– No, their ………. actually increases.

3 Match the two parts of these expressions from lines 36–73.

1 top   skills
2 critical   constraints
3 economic incentives
4 cost   talent
5 financial   survey
6 global   recovery
7 active   promotion
8 all-week   sharing
9 job   cover

4 Which of the expressions above is each of these things an example of?

a) Growth this year is 4 per cent – last year it was minus 1 per cent.

b) Without people like these, the company would go out of business.

c) The best and the brightest people in the organisation.

d) Being able to respond to clients' requests Monday to Friday.

e) A report based on interviews in five continents.

f) A company regularly reminding employees about a particular programme.

g) Not having the budget to do something.

h) Antonia does this job on Mondays, Wednesdays and Fridays, and Hans does it on Tuesdays and Thursdays.

i) She can take a year off and she'll get full salary and benefits.

5 Read lines 36–73 again to decide if these statements are true or false.

a) In the recession, the only people who are worried about jobs are employees.

b) There are ways of keeping good employees that don't involve giving them more money.

c) KPMG is looking at this area for the first time.

d) Last year, fewer than half of its UK employees took up the offer of working less.

e) KPMG only saved £400,000 by doing this.

f) Fewer people were interested in the programme this year than last.

Over to you 1

Lee Summersgill's experience illustrates the trend of fathers wanting greater flexibility to accommodate family life. Is this a trend in your country? Why? / Why not?

Over to you 2

What is the attitude of your organisation, or one you would like to work for, to job flexibility?

REPUTATIONAL RISK

Before you read

Celebrity endorsement is when famous people appear in advertisements to promote particular products. Name as many as you can think of.

Reading

Read this article from the *Financial Times* by Paul J Davies and do the exercises that follow.

FT

LEVEL OF DIFFICULTY ● ● ○

When star power hits the rough

Paul J Davies

As Tiger Woods tees off at The Masters tournament, the humbled athlete is not the only one counting the cost of his fall from grace. The 34-year-old golfer's reputation as a clean-living and dedicated sportsman and husband was undone when his infidelities were spilled across television, newspapers and Internet sites after a mysterious car accident at his home.

Mr Woods' success on the course had enabled him to line up lucrative sponsorship deals off of it, with brands including Accenture, Nike, Gillette, Electronic Arts. Some estimates suggest that the arrangements made him the world's first sports star to make $1bn in career earnings.

But as his life became embroiled in scandal, those companies also took direct financial hits, from having to commission and produce new advertising to the costs of their own public relations campaigns explaining their actions in dropping the golfer and legal fees. According to a study by Christopher Knittel and Victor Stango, economists at the University of California, Davis, the collective loss in stock market value of all the companies that Mr Woods endorsed was worth $5bn–$12bn.

Of course, companies do not need a celebrity relationship to experience reputational damage. Toyota estimates that its global recall of cars had a direct cost of about $2bn (€1.5bn, £1.3bn). That figure does not take into account potential lost future sales, or Toyota's own stock price decline, which has knocked Y1,673bn ($17.8bn, €13.3bn, £11.7bn) off its market value even after a strong rebound in the past month.

In the wake of the Tiger Woods scandal, DeWitt Stern, the insurance broker, saw an opportunity to publicise a product it had launched to cover reputational risk, including how to deal with celebrity endorsers becoming engulfed in scandal. More recently, Lloyd's of London, the insurance market, held a conference on how to manage reputational risk and what cover – if any – might be available.

Companies are increasingly recognising that reputation is an important and valuable asset that is vulnerable and volatile, according to Anthony Fitzsimmons, chairman of Reputability, a consultancy focused on reputation and crisis strategy, risk and management.

"Reputation can be an organisation's most valuable intangible asset, though it appears in few balance sheets except as goodwill in acquisitions," he says. "People are generally aware of their brand values, but many have not worked out what matters most when things are going wrong. Few have made a systematic analysis of what might damage their reputation, let alone worked out how to keep their reputation strong through difficult times."

1 Look through the whole article. Which sport does the expression 'hit the rough' in the headline come from? Why is it used?

2 Find expressions in lines 1–19 to complete these statements.

If someone …

a) suffers from losing their good reputation, they have a ....

b) behaves very well in their marriage, their job, etc. they are described as ....

c) does not smoke, drink alcohol, etc. they are described as .... - ....

d) has a reputation that is destroyed, it is ....

e) signs deals that make them a lot of money, these deals are ....

f) makes a total of $1 billion from their job, these are their ....

3 Match these things from lines 20–46 with what they cost. (The cost of four of the things is not mentioned.)

1	the minimum estimated value of all the shares in all the companies whose products Tiger Woods endorsed	a)	$12 billion
2	the maximum estimated value of all the shares in all the companies whose products Tiger Woods endorsed	b)	about 1,700 billion yen
3	the legal fees of companies dealing with the damage done by Woods' actions	c)	$2 billion
4	the cost of producing new advertising following the damage done by Woods' actions	d)	$5 billion
5	the cost of Toyota's recall of cars so far		
6	the possible future costs of Toyota's recall		
7	the fall in the total value of Toyota's shares initially		
8	the fall in the total value of Toyota's shares at the time of writing		

4 Complete the table with words from lines 20–58, and grammatically related words.

noun	verb
commission	
	campaign
endorsement, endorser	
damage	
recall	
	decline
rebound	
publicity	
	cover

5 In lines 59–79, find:

a) an adverb meaning 'more and more'.

b) an adjective describing reputation as an asset in relation to the ease with which it can be damaged.

c) an adjective describing reputation as an asset in relation to possible changes in its value.

d) a two-word expression to talk about plans to deal with disastrous situations.

e) a two-word expression to talk about a business's property, but one that cannot be physically touched.

f) the value of this asset when the business is sold.

g) a two-word expression used to talk about what people associate with particular product names.

h) a two-word expression referring to a methodical examination of something.

Over to you 1

You head a consultancy specialising in reputation and crisis management. A car manufacturer comes to you for advice on what to do to recover its reputation following a recall of 100,000 of its cars because of a steering problem. (Luckily no accidents were caused by this, but there were some 'near misses'.) What would you advise the car company to do in relation to its communications and advertising following the recall?

Over to you 2

You are head of an oil company that has caused great environmental damage following an explosion on one of your oil rigs. What would you do to restore to try to your company's reputation?

TEXT BANK

CLIMATE CHANGE

Before you read

Is the weather getting more extreme than it was 20 or 30 years ago in your part of the world?

Reading

Read this article from the *Financial Times* by Sarah Murray and do the exercises that follow.

FT

LEVEL OF DIFFICULTY ● ● ●

TEXT BANK

Expensive picture of extreme climate

Sarah Murray

Images of the aftermath of the violent wind storms and tornadoes that swept across several US states this spring serve as a reminder of the
5 damage caused by extreme weather events. Changing patterns are prompting many businesses to shore up their operations and facilities. However, many have yet to address
10 longer term climate-related risks.

"Companies are looking at what should they do over the next few years to their infrastructure to increase the resilience of their opera-
15 tions," says Antonia Gawel, deputy director of energy and climate at the World Business Council for Sustainable Development. "But that's happening more than the longer term
20 planning."

Part of the reason lies in the difficulty of predicting weather patterns and the effects those might have far into the future. "The thing about the
25 sea level rising is that you don't really notice it," says Paul Dickinson, chief executive of the Carbon Disclosure Project, which asks businesses to monitor their carbon
30 emissions and publish the results for their shareholders. "But what does happen is that it causes an exponential increase in storm surge," he says. "And if there's a significant storm,
35 you might find the sea inundating further inland than it would otherwise have done."

This should prompt companies not only to establish procedures for
40 staff during hurricanes or to fit their facilities with more durable roofs and windows. It might also mean redesigning global supply chains or changing industrial processes.
45 Growing water scarcity is one reason to implement this type of planning. For companies that are highly dependent on water, this might mean relocating facilities or
50 rethinking the location of new investments.

Whether it is tackling water shortages or shoring a business up against disruptions from severe storms, Ms
55 Gawel emphasises the need to integrate climate adaptation into broader corporate risk management strategies that also cover areas such as terrorism, labour action or environ-
60 mental legislation.

"When you're taking an investment decision or looking to build infrastructure, it needs to be part of the whole due diligence and risk
65 management package," she says. "And it needs to bear sufficient weight within that decision-making process because, if it is just a standalone assessment, it might not have
70 as strong an impact as it would if it were integrated into a true strategy process."

1 **Look through lines 11–37 to find:**

   a) two organisations that are not companies.

   b) the names of two people working for them.

   c) their job titles.

2 **Read lines 1–20 and find:**

   a) two sentences about businesses and their reaction to the short-term effects of climate change.

   b) two sentences about businesses and their reaction to the long-term effects of climate change.

3 **Choose the correct alternative to replace the expression in *italics* so as to keep the same meaning. (lines 21–51)**

   1 Part of the reason lies in the difficulty of *predicting* weather patterns …

   a) analysing   b) identifying   c) forecasting

   2 "The thing about the sea level rising is that you don't really *notice* it,"

   a) see   b) watch   c) look for

   3 "But what does happen is that it causes an *exponential* increase in storm surge," he says.

   a) small   b) medium   c) huge

   4 "… you might find the sea *inundating* further inland than it would otherwise have done."

   a) flowing   b) flooding   c) running

   5 This should *prompt* companies not only to establish procedures for staff during hurricanes …

   a) prevent   b) cause   c) start

   6 Growing water *scarcity* …

   a) plenty   b) levels   c) shortage

   7 … is one reason to *implement* this type of planning.

   a) apply   b) reply   c) imply

4 **Match the two parts of these expressions from lines 38–72.**

   1 supply   diligence

   2 industrial   shortages

   3 water   chains

   4 climate   legislation

   5 environmental   adaptation

   6 due   process

5 **Now match the expressions to their meanings.**

   a) laws to prevent pollution

   b) actions by a business to ensure that it is doing the right thing

   c) all the businesses, etc. involved in providing an organisation with materials and parts

   d) all the steps involved in producing something

   e) periods when there is not enough water

   f) making changes so as to deal with long-term changes in the weather

6 **Give the infinitive forms of verbs in lines 52–72 that mean the same as the expressions in italics.**

   a) to deal with a problem

   b) to bring attention to an issue

   c) to make something stronger (phrasal ver**b**)

   d) to be relevant to a particular subject

   e) to include something in something else

   f) to make a decision

   g) to carry a particular load

Over to you 1

Give some risk assessment advice in relation to climate to a company setting up operations in your country (areas to avoid, and why, etc.)

Over to you 2

Thing of an organisation that you are interested in. Make a list of all the potential risks to its operations.

TEXT BANK

WOMEN MANAGERS

Before you read

Do women have a more collaborative approach as managers than men? Give your reasons.

Reading

Read this article from the *Financial Times* by Michael Skapinker and do the exercises that follow.

FT

TEXT BANK

Nature and nurture in the executive suite

Michael Skapinker

Women are calmer than men. They are more collaborative and they dislike self-promotion. It is all in their genes. Progressive thought once
5 held that men and women were essentially the same and that it was social conditioning that made men aggressive and women co-operative. Some writers still argue this way. In
10 an article in the Harvard Business Review, Alice Eagly and Linda Carli say the reason women managers generally adopt a softer style is unlikely to be genetic. They do it
15 because people react badly to aggressive women and a collaborative approach is how female managers assert their authority.

A new book, *Why Women Mean*
20 *Business*, is bolder: biology matters, it says. The authors, Avivah Wittenberg-Cox and Alison Maitland, approvingly cite recent research showing men's and women's brains
25 differ. This inevitably affects the way they manage. "Why would

differences in communication styles, biological rhythms, and brain functioning (to mention only a few)
30 stop just short of leadership styles?" they ask.

If companies want to succeed they will have to come around to women's way of doing things, the authors
35 argue. Faced with falling populations, companies in Europe will need more women in senior management. In the new knowledge-based economy, they say, companies need
40 collaborative managers who can persuade people to work in teams. There is no need for women to change their essential natures.

Why Women Mean Business is an
45 innovative and stimulating book. But the resort to biology raises problems. First, scans have indeed shown differences between male and female brain functioning. Newborn
50 girls look at human faces for longer than they look at mechanical mobiles, while boys do the opposite.

But the science is far from settled. We still do not know the precise mix-
55 ture of nature and nurture that makes men and women what they are.

Second, if you argue that women's empathetic nature makes them particularly suited to helping run
60 collaborative enterprises, a corollary would have to be that they are less well equipped for other tasks.

Third, the problem with characterising huge groups is that it takes no
65 account of the large variations within them. Women, on average, may be more empathetic than men, but we all know collaborative male managers and sharp-elbowed female
70 ones, just as we know boys who cannot turn plastic sticks into tractors and girls who do not listen quietly while others speak. Nature is important, but humans are endlessly
75 complicated.

1 **Read lines 1–31 and put these expressions from there, and some related expressions, under one of the two headings a) 'Nature' or b) 'Nurture'**

  1 'It's the way you're brought up.'

  2 'It's all in the genes.'

  3 'It's social conditioning.'

  4 'It's unlikely to be genetic.'

  5 'That's the way you're born.'

  6 'It all depends on your environment when you're growing up.'

  7 'Biology matters.'

2 **Now match each of the writers mentioned in lines 1–31 to a) the 'nature' argument and b) the 'nurture' argument.**

  1 Avivah Wittenberg-Cox

  2 Linda Carli

  3 Alice Eagly

  4 Alison Maitland

3 **Read lines 32–56 to decide if these statements about the expressions in *italic* are true or false.**

  If …

  a) you *come round* to an idea, you agree with it the first time you hear it.

  b) people are *collaborative*, they believe in working together.

  c) you *change your essential nature*, you behave in ways that you have to learn.

  d) a book is *stimulating*, it is boring.

  e) there is *resort* to a particular idea in your reasoning, you use that idea to support it.

  f) an argument is *settled*, it has not been decided.

4 **Which is the most important point in lines 32–43? Choose the best summary.**

  a) Women need to learn how to be collaborative in order to succeed as managers in the future.

  b) There are decreasing numbers of women who can become managers because of Europe's future population decreases.

  c) It is in women's nature to be collaborative and this will ideally suit them to be managers of the types of companies we will increasingly have in the future.

5 **Find words and grammatically related words in lines 44–75 to complete the table.**

noun	adjective
precision	
stimulation	
	empathetic
collaboration	
equipment	
	varied
	male
complication	

6 **Now match these definitions to the adjectives above.**

  Used to describe …

  a) people who understand others and what they are feeling.

  b) men and boys.

  c) something that is exact.

  d) something containing a lot of differences.

  e) people who are good at working together.

  f) people who have particular skills.

  g) something interesting.

  h) things that are complex.

Over to you 1

Is nature or nurture more important in the way people develop? Explain your reasoning.

Over to you 2

Is collaborative working valued in your organisation, or one you would like to work for? Why? / Why not?

THE FUTURE OF MANAGEMENT

Before you read
What is your definition of good management?

Reading
Read this article from the Financial Times by Julian Birkinshaw and do the exercises that follow.

FT

LEVEL OF DIFFICULTY ● ● ○

Managers need a makeover

Julian Birkinshaw

What is the way forward for managers during a period of economic recovery? Leadership is a process of social influence: it is concerned with
5 the styles and behaviours of individuals that cause others to follow them. Management is the act of getting people together to accomplish desired goals. In other words, we all
10 need to be leaders and managers. How does this line of thinking help you? For starters, it is interesting to note that almost all the well-known books on management were written
15 from the perspective of the manager, not the employee.

Here is a simple exercise. Ask some colleagues you work with about the last time they felt fully
20 motivated and engaged at work. What were the characteristics of that piece of work? Chances are, they will say some of the following: it was a challenging project, one where
25 they had to stretch themselves; they were given a lot of autonomy; they

had an opportunity to work collaboratively with others; and they felt the work was important to the
30 organisation. I am willing to bet there will be no mention of money; instead they will focus on the recognition and kudos they received from doing a project well.

35 Why is it so hard to do what we know to be right? It turns out that being a good manager is somewhat unnatural. We can do all the above things if we work on them. But it is
40 easy to lapse back into old habits, and as soon as things get busy or difficult at work we quickly revert to type – which usually means withholding information, telling our
45 employees what to do, and barking at them when they get it wrong. A small minority of people are "naturals" at good management. The vast majority of us have to work very
50 hard to do the job well.

The job of the senior leaders in an organisation is to put in place an

overall "management model" that encourages individuals to work
55 more effectively in their management activities. Many companies are experimenting with innovative management models along these lines, and when such innovations work,
60 they can be a real source of competitive advantage. A well-managed company is one that gets the most out of its people. An engaged workforce, in turn, is one that seeks out
65 opportunities to add value in creative and unforeseen ways, which then breeds responsiveness, innovation and resilience.

However, one thing is certain:
70 reinventing the practice of management is not going to provide your company with any short-term benefits. But that is the whole point. The road to recovery starts now, and it is
75 therefore a perfect time to put in place the basic changes that will accelerate over time.

1 Look at the headline. What types of change is 'makeover' normally most associated with?

2 Find the following expressions in lines 1–16.
   a) a period when business is improving (2 words)
   b) the way that people change because of what they see in others (2 words)
   c) what people typically do in particular situations (1 word)
   d) reaching particular objectives (1 word)
   e) a particular way of reasoning (3 words)
   f) the way you look at something (1 word)

3 Which alternative could not be used to replace the expression in *italics* from lines 17–34 so as to keep a similar meaning?
   1 'Ask some colleagues you work with about the last time they felt *fully* motivated and engaged at work.' (line 19)
      a) completely b) partly c) totally
   2 '... it was a challenging project, one where they had to *stretch themselves* ...' (line 25)
      a) work nearer the limits of what they were capable
      b) try harder than they normally did
      c) employ new people to help them
   3 '... they were given a lot of *autonomy* ...' (line 26)
      a) independence b) freedom c) advice
   4 '... they had an opportunity to work *collaboratively* with others ...' (line 27)
      a) together with
      b) towards the same goal as
      c) in parallel with
   5 '... instead, they will *focus on* the recognition ...' (line 32)
      a) concentrate on b) talk about
      c) emphasise
   6 '... and *kudos* they received from doing a project well.' (line 33)
      a) increase in salary b) increase in respect
      c) increase in status

4 Read lines 35–50 to decide if these statements are true or false.
   a) Being a good manager is a normal thing to be able to do.
   b) It's possible to apply all the advice given all the time.
   c) Managers can go back to their previous behaviour when under pressure.
   d) Two examples of typical behaviour of managers under pressure are given.
   e) There are a small number of people who are good managers without advice or training.
   f) Others can be good managers with just a little effort.

5 Replace the words in *italic* with nouns from lines 51–77. (One of the answers occurs twice.)
   a) *They* have a big role to play in improving managers' skills in their organisations.
   b) Senior managers are introducing *them* in organisations to give managers an idea of what to follow to improve their management skills.
   c) *This* can really be improved in relation to other firms if managers' skills get better.
   d) *This* helps to make people perform as well as they can.
   e) *This* means that people are always looking for ways to contribute in new, productive ways that haven't been predicted.
   f) *This* means that managers react more to problems and are more able to deal with them.
   g) You won't get *these*, but you will get longer term ones.

Over to you 1

Think of management from the point of view of employees. What are the three biggest improvements that managers could make to the way that they manage?

Over to you 2

'A small minority of people are "naturals" at good management. The vast majority of us have to work very hard to do the job well.' Do you agree? Why? / Why not?

SPORTS COACHING AND CORPORATE TEAM BUILDING

Before you read

How easy is it to transfer ideas for team building from sport to business? Explain your reasoning.

Reading

Read this article from the *Financial Times* by Paul Betts and do the exercises that follow.

FT

LEVEL OF DIFFICULTY ● ● ○

Capello's masterclass for on-the-ball Finmeccanica

Paul Betts

When Fabio Capello flew to South Africa as the England football manager to attend the 2010 World Cup finals, he stopped briefly in Rome on
5 his way to give the Italian defence and engineering group Finmeccanica a masterclass on leadership. Having previously managed one of the Italian capital's football clubs,
10 AS Roma, Mr Capello was inevitably the centre of attention. "So why are you doing this corporate coaching?" I asked at one stage. "I suppose because I have widespread interna-
15 tional experience having led teams such as Juventus and Real Madrid as well as Roma and now England and I know a thing or two about managing players, creating a team spirit, in
20 short leading," he said. Mr Capello clearly knows a thing or two about bringing discipline, direction and inspiration to the highest levels of his business.

25 Unlike in other countries, such as Brazil, he had to work hard to instil a hunger among some top English players to pull on an England shirt. Morale was pretty awful when he
30 took over. Not surprisingly, he was the star at Finmeccanica's convention attended by some 3,000 managers from around the world. And probably his biggest fan in the
35 audience was none other than his counterpart at Finmeccanica, Pier Francesco Guarguaglini. After all, the Italian group's veteran boss is also a fanatical supporter of Juventus,
40 where Mr Capello once worked his magic.

Finmeccanica under Mr Guarguaglini has prospered in recent years thanks to clear leadership and a
45 sense of purpose that previously was sorely lacking. Over the years up to Mr Guarguaglini's appointment, the partly state-owned Finmeccanica

had suffered badly from state inter-
50 ference that lacked any clear industrial vision for the group. More often than not senior politicians saw Finmeccanica primarily as a convenient place to park friends in top jobs
55 to the detriment of its commercial success.

It was the UK that Mr Guarguaglini chose as his starting point for Finmeccanica's renaissance. Within
60 two years he had acquired full control of AgustaWestland, the helicopter-maker where previously GKN had been his partner. Then he quickly moved on to buy out BAE
65 Systems from a joint venture in defence systems. All of a sudden Finmeccanica was the UK's second-largest defence contractor by sales, employing more than 10,000 Britons.

1 Look through the whole article and find:

a) two leaders – one in sport and one in business.

b) the names of the organisations led by each leader above.

c) the names of five football teams.

d) the name of a helicopter manufacturer owned by one of the organisations in b) above.

2 Complete these statements with appropriate forms of expressions from lines 1–24.

If ...

a) people notice you more than others, you are ....

b) you train managers, you give them ....

c) you have done something a lot, you have .... of it.

d) you get team members to work together better, you .... among them.

e) you have a lot of knowledge about something, you know a .... it.

f) you cause an organisation to acquire particular qualities, you .... these qualities to it.

3 Find nouns in lines 42–56 referring to ...

a) a team's feeling of enthusiasm caused by someone or something outside it.

b) team members obeying the rules.

c) a team's sense of where it is going.

d) a team's need to be successful and win.

e) the good or bad feelings that team members have at a particular time.

4 Find nouns in lines 25–41 illustrated by the examples (a–f).

a) the most famous person in a film

b) someone who admires e) above

c) the head of one company in relation to the head of another

d) someone who has worked for the same company for 35 years

e) the head of a company

f) someone who goes regularly to a team's football matches

5 Match the adverbs (1–8) from lines 25–69 with expressions that could replace them without changing the meaning (a–h):

1	surprisingly	a)	almost certainly
2	probably	b)	fast
3	previously	c)	badly
4	sorely	d)	partially
5	badly	e)	earlier
6	partly	f)	sorely
7	primarily	g)	unexpectedly
8	quickly	h)	mainly

6 Find the answers to these questions in lines 42–69.

a) Which two qualities have allowed both Capello and Guarguaglini to succeed?

b) Give the main cause and the resulting reasons for Finmeccanica's poor performance before Guarguaglini took over.

c) Where did Guarguaglini start to change his company's fortunes?

d) How is this change referred to?

e) Which two companies did Finmeccanica take over? Are they both named?

f) Did Finmeccanica have holdings in them before?

g) Is Finmeccanica the second biggest defence company in the UK in terms of the number of employees?

Over to you 1

What are the main differences between sports coaching and corporate team building?

Over to you 2

Look again at the answers to question 3 above. Describe the state of these things in relation to an organisation you know, for example a company or a sports team.

TEAMS OF FIVE AND TEAMS OF ONE HUNDRED

Before you read

Think of a business team or one you would like to work in. What would be the ideal number of people in it? Why?

Reading

Read this article from the *Financial Times* by Jonathan Moules and do the exercises that follow.

FT

Success and satisfaction

Jonathan Moules

The problem with expanding a business is that it only becomes harder to engage your staff. "It is the culture that will keep people working for
5 you," says Brian Chernett, founder of the Academy for Chief Executives, a leadership coaching club. "The difference between small and big business is that it is easier to
10 retain that culture in a small organisation than in a large one."

Andy Hooper quit his salaried job with a large corporation in 2004 to set up Westlakes Engineering, an
15 architecture and engineering consultancy on the west coast of Cumbria. At first, he found growth easy, largely because he could foster a culture where everyone wanted to be
20 a part of the company's success. By the time the company employed 20 people, however, Mr Hooper noticed that leading the team had become much harder work. "I found myself
25 increasingly stretched," he recalls.

"What worked for me when we were a team of five, six, seven or eight, I was finding too much when we got to 20 people."
30 When Mr Hooper asked his staff what they wanted, he realised he needed to delegate responsibility. Westlakes now has a board of five directors, promoted from within Mr
35 Hooper's team. "It is all about letting go," he says. "Everybody now has visibility of what we are doing and why we are doing it. We are using everybody's ideas."
40 Some companies consciously restrain the growth of their workforce to maintain the culture of their organisation. With almost 100 staff, George Davies, a Manchester-based
45 legal firm, is neither small nor especially large, but that is the way it wants to stay. Lisa Pearson, business development manager, says: "Our priority is to make sure everybody
50 who deals with this firm has the best

experience that you can have dealing with a law firm. We don't believe that if we expand, we would be able to give that level of service."
55 Unlike many law firms, George Davies discourages its employees from working long hours. Those that are parents are encouraged to spend more time with their families. Such
60 policies lead to a better office atmosphere and greater employee commitment, according to Ms Pearson, who notes many of the employees have been with George
65 Davies for more than a decade.

A company need not lose the vitality of a small enterprise as it grows, says David MacLeod, who co-wrote the government's report last year on
70 employee engagement. He claims businesses reach a "break point" when the head count passes 20 and an owner's personality alone can no longer be the sole driving force.

1 **Look through the whole article to find these people and organisations, and what they do.**

   a) Brian Chernett

   b) Andy Hooper

   c) George Davies

   d) Lisa Pearson

   e) David MacLeod

2 **Look at how the expressions in *italic* are used in lines 1–29 and choose the correct alternative meaning.**

   1 'The problem with expanding a business is that it only becomes harder to *engage* your staff.' (line 3)

   a) recruit   b) motivate and inspire

   2 '"It is the *culture* that will keep people working for you, ..."' (line 3)

   a) arts, music, painting, literature, etc.

   b) the way people think and do things

   3 'the Academy for Chief Executives, a leadership *coaching* club...' (line 7)

   a) training   b) schooling

   4 '"The difference between small and big business is that it is easier to *retain* that culture in a small organisation than in a large one."' (line 10)

   a) keep   b) remember

   5 '...he could *foster* a culture where everyone wanted to be a part of the company's success. ...' (line 18)

   a) adopt   b) encourage

   6 '"I found myself increasingly *stretched*," ...' (line 25)

   a) challenged and stimulated   b) made longer

3 **Correct, where necessary, the structures of these expressions used in lines 30–54.**

   1 to delegate down responsibility (line 32)

   2 to promote someone from within a particular department to the board of directors (line 33)

   3 to restrain the growth of the workforce of an organisation (line 41)

   4 to maintain up the culture of an organisation (line 42)

   5 to deal with an organisation (line 50)

   6 to expand up (line 53)

4 **Now match the verbs in the expressions above to their meanings.**

   a) limit

   b) keep the same

   c) talk to and work with

   d) give someone a more important job

   e) get bigger

   f) give someone more power

5 **Read lines 55–74 and decide if these statements are true or false.**

   a) George Davies encourages its employees to work longer hours than from 9 to 5.

   b) The firm likes all its employees to spend more time with their families.

   c) Family-friendly policies make employees more committed to the organisation.

   d) Most of George Davies's employees have been there more than 10 years.

   e) It's not inevitable for small companies to lose their dynamism as they grow.

   f) However big the firm, the owner's personality will be the only real factor in motivating people.

Over to you 1

Why is the role of the organisation's boss different in big and small teams?

Over to you 2

George Davies discourages its employees from working long hours and those that are parents are encouraged to spend more time with their families. Is this a possible way of working for all organisations? Why? / Why not?

TEXT BANK

WILLING AND LESS WILLING LENDERS

Before you read
If you had an idea for a business start-up, where would you go for finance?

Reading
Read this article from the *Financial Times* by Brian Groom and Jonathan Guthrie and do the exercises that follow.

FT

LEVEL OF DIFFICULTY ● ● ○

TEXT BANK

Small businesses and the banks

by Brian Groom and Jonathan Guthrie

The frosty relationship between business and banks over credit is at last showing tentative signs of a thaw. Business leaders warn, how-
5 ever, that bankruptcies could rise sharply in the next 12 months unless sufficient finance is available, especially for smaller companies, while banks say companies must over-
10 come their reluctance to borrow.

The EEF manufacturers' organisation reports on Monday an easing of credit conditions for the first time in more than a year. In a survey of 410
15 manufacturers, 33 per cent said the cost of finance had increased in the past two months – down from 47 per cent in the third quarter. Just one in five reported a decline in availability
20 of new borrowing, down from one in three.

Annika Bosanquet has been struggling to raise finance to fulfil orders worth more than £200,000. The
25 founder of upmarket packaging company Wrapology, which has cli-

ents such as Harrods and Armani, first approached HSBC for a letter of credit this summer but she was
30 turned down. The bank also declined to support a loan via the government's Enterprise Finance Guarantee scheme.

"HSBC said that the scheme was
35 thrust on them the day that the government announced it to the press and that they had no system for processing applications," Ms Bosanquet says. The bank also tried to halve
40 Wrapology's overdraft to £50,000, she says. The former anthropologist, who runs Wrapology with her brother Tom, did not fare any better with Barclays, which refused her
45 request for a letter of credit and said it could not extend any finance under the EFG because the scheme was "for refinancing, not working capital".

Ms Bosanquet, who is a board
50 member of Enterprise Insight, a government-sponsored body that promotes entrepreneurship, says: "It

is very depressing because we are not looking for unfunded borrowing
55 – we have confirmed orders." The company needs to pay for packaging orders made overseas before it can collect payments from its own customers, which include John Lewis,
60 the department store, and Monsoon, the fashion retailer.

HSBC says it has kept Wrapology's overdraft at £100,000 and denies threatening to reduce it,
65 "even though she has gone well over her overdraft limit". Barclays says it aims to lend "appropriately" and that it would be "irresponsible" to put up sums that clients might find hard to
70 repay. Ms Bosanquet set up Wrapology in 2001. Last year it had a turnover of £1.4m and according to the entrepreneur will make a profit this year. She says: "There is no
75 point the government fretting over economic policy if it cannot get money into the system."

1 Look through the whole article to find the names of:

a) an employers' organisation.

b) a woman entrepreneur.

c) her firm.

d) four of her clients.

e) a government organisation to back loans to entrepreneurs.

f) a bank.

g) the entrepreneur's brother.

h) a government-backed organisation to encourage entrepreneurship.

2 Read lines 1–21 and decide if these statements are true or false.

a) The relationship between business and banks is compared to weather conditions.

b) These conditions seem to be improving.

c) The number of bankruptcies will fall in the next year, according to business leaders.

d) Banks say that companies are unwilling to ask for loans.

e) More companies than before say that the cost of finance has gone up.

f) Fewer companies than before say that it's possible to borrow.

3 Complete these statements with appropriate forms of verbs and phrasal verbs from lines 22–48.

If ...

a) you .... to do something, you find it difficult.

b) you .... an order, you prepare and deliver it.

c) you .... an organisation, you make contact with it.

d) a request is ...., it is refused.

e) a request is ...., it is refused.

f) a task is given to you against your will, it is .... on you.

g) an organisation .... an application, it deals with it.

h) you .... well, badly, etc. in a particular situation, this is what happens to you in that situation.

i) a bank makes loans to firms, it .... finance to them.

4 Look again at lines 22–48 to find finance-related expressions that mean:

a) an agreement by a bank to give credit. (3 words)

b) an arrangement by a government to pay back loans when the borrower cannot, contained in the name of an organisation. (3 words)

c) when you take more money out of your bank account than you put in. (1 word)

d) when you get loans to replace earlier loans. (1 word)

e) the money needed to operate a business, for example to pay suppliers before you are paid by customers. (2 words)

5 Match what the people (a–e) might say (1–5), based on lines 49–77.

a) HSBC spokesperson
b) Annika Bosanquet
c) Monsoon spokesperson
d) Barclays spokesperson
e) UK government spokesperson

1 'I'm sad that we can't get finance. It's only because lenders don't really understand our situation.'

2 'It would be crazy to lend to businesses that can't repay.'

3 'We're doing everything we can to get banks to lend to businesses, whatever some entrepreneurs say.'

4 'We haven't reduced Ms Bosanquet's overdraft, whatever she says.'

5 'We've ordered goods from Wrapology, but we haven't paid for them yet.'

Over to you 1

What is the relationship between small businesses and banks in your country?

Over to you 2

Imagine you own a small business which is in need of finance. What are the advantages and disadvantages of a) raising money from banks, and b) asking family members to contribute? Compare and contrast the two approaches.

CROWDFUNDING

Before you read

Would you invest in a young company raising finance on the Internet? Why? / Why not?

Reading

Read this article from the *Financial Times* by Emma Jacobs and do the exercises that follow.

FT

LEVEL OF DIFFICULTY ● ● ○

Jumping into a funding model for the online age

Emma Jacobs

Earlier this year, Trampoline Systems, a London-based technology company founded in 2003, realised if they were going to further expand
5 the business, they would need some more money. So they sounded out a few venture capitalists. But, says Charles Armstrong, one of the company's founders, "it soon became
10 clear that it would be tough to raise finance this way". So Trampoline hit upon another route: "crowdfunding" – raising small stakes from a large group of investors, particularly
15 through online communities and social networks.

The crowdfunding concept derives from "crowdsourcing", whereby organisations ask the
20 public, usually via the Internet, to do jobs typically done by their employees. For example, The Guardian newspaper's website recently asked readers to trawl through 700,000
25 expense claims by British Members of Parliament to find acts of wrongdoing. Crowdsourcing and crowdfunding could, in theory, occur without the Internet, says Jeff
30 Howe, the man who coined the term

"crowdsourcing" and wrote a book on the subject, but "it certainly helps to accelerate the process".

Trampoline was encouraged by
35 the crowdfunding successes of the likes of SellaBand, a site which connects music fans with unsigned artists looking to record albums. Musicians post their profiles and
40 songs, and ask the site's users to buy shares, at a minimum of $10. As soon as an artist sells 5,000 shares, they can record the album and the proceeds are then split between the
45 artist, SellaBand and the artist's supporters, or "believers", as the site calls them.

Trampoline's effort is unusual, however, because the company is
50 already established – it employs 15 and raised £2m in seed capital from venture capitalists when it launched. But, says Mr Armstrong, with traditional venture capital funds
55 battening down the hatches in the current downturn, it seemed like the best option.

Deloitte's Global Trends in Venture Capital report notes: "The
60 second round of raising finance

where a business is still finding its legs … carries more risk given higher burn rates and the current uncertainty around future financ-
65 ings. So, we're seeing reduced investment levels as firms either invest smaller sums in very early-stage companies or invest traditional sums in fewer and much later-stage
70 companies. The middle ground has been largely vacated."

Trampoline hopes crowdfunding will avoid these obstacles and create new opportunities. "A typical ven-
75 ture capital funding would be half a dozen investors. I suspect there'll be about 60 or 70 investors," says Mr Armstrong. "The benefits of such a large investor network is that it will
80 bring in new contacts and experience and will build a stronger support system." The investment stakes for Trampoline are much higher than SellaBand. It is asking
85 investors to put in a minimum of £10,000 and they hope to raise £1m in total. They have not put a time limit on when they hope to achieve their target.

TEXT BANK

1 Choose the correct alternative to replace the expression in *italics* from lines 1–33 so as to keep the closest meaning.

1 '... they *sounded* out a few venture capitalists.' (line 6)

   a) listened to   **b)** approached   **c)** heard

2 '... "it soon became clear that it would be *tough* to raise finance this way". ...' (line 10)

   a) easy   **b)** straightforward   **c)** difficult

3 '... So Trampoline *hit* upon another route: "crowdfunding"...' (line 11)

   a) discovered   **b)** ignored   **c)** founded

4 '... raising small *stakes* from a large group of investors, ...' (line 13)

   a) investments   **b)** interest   **c)** bonds

5 '... particularly through online communities and *social networks*.' (line 16)

   a) e-commerce sites   **b)** email programmes

   c) sites like Facebook

6 '... The crowdfunding concept *derives* from "crowdsourcing", ...' (line 18)

   a) goes   **b)** originates   **c)** leaves

7 '... The Guardian newspaper's website recently asked readers to *trawl* through 700,000 expense claims ...' (line 24)

   a) examine in detail   **b)** fish through

   c) quickly read

8 '... "it certainly helps to *accelerate* the process".' (line 33)

   a) slow down   **b)** simplify   **c)** speed up

2 Use expressions from lines 34–57 to answer these questions.

1 Was Trampoline disappointed by the crowdfunding efforts of others? (line 34)
– No, it was .... by them.

2 Does SellaBand work with musicians who have not made commercial recordings? (line 37)
– Yes, it works with ....

3 Does SellaBand ask banks to invest in musicians on its site? (line 44)
– No, it asks the site's users to buy shares, and they divide the .... between them, the site and the musicians.

4 Is Trampoline a start-up? (line 50)
– No, it's already ....

5 How much did it raise when it was founded? (line 51)
– It raised .... of £2 million.

6 Are venture capital funds investing a lot at the moment? (line 55)
– No, they're ....

7 Was the economy booming in 2009? (line 56)
– No, we were in a ....

3 Among the answers to Exercise 2, find an expression that ...

   a) contains a word that can also refer to painters.

   b) could also relate to ships.

   c) contains a word that comes from farming.

   d) is also possible as the third person singular of a verb.

   e) contains a word that means 'bravery'.

   f) means the same as 'recession'.

   g) means the same as 'in existence'.

4 Combine words from the box below to make expressions from lines 58–71 that refer to the following:

   a) the second occasion on which companies look for finance, as it typically happens (3 word**s**)

   b) used to describe the situation when companies use the money they have raised quickly (3 word**s**)

   c) people not knowing at the moment what's going to happen in the future (3 word**s**)

   d) later occasions when firms will look for investment (2 word**s**)

   e) the amounts of money typically put into businesses (2 word**s**)

   f) firms that were founded longer ago than recent start-ups (3 word**s**)

   g) firms that are neither very new nor mature in their development (2 word**s**)

burn	classic	uncertainty	companies
second	current	financings	later-stage
rates	higher	round	ground
middle	investment	future	levels

5 What is the main point in lines 72–89? Choose the best alternative.

   a) Trampoline hopes to go into the music business by copying SellaBand's model and getting a larger investor network.

   b) By using crowdfunding, Trampoline hopes to get more investors than is usual, forming a stronger base for the company's development.

   c) Time is not important for Trampoline and it is willing to wait several years before getting the necessary investment to grow.

Over to you 1

Go back to the answer you gave in 'Before you read'. Have you changed your mind after reading the article? Why? / Why not?

Over to you 2

What types of business would be particularly suited to crowdfunding? Give your reasons.

OUTLET VILLAGES

Before you read

Retail outlet villages, out-of-town shopping centres selling branded goods at a discount, are becoming important around the world. Which outlet villages do you know?

Reading

Read this article from the *Financial Times* by Hannah Kuchler and do the exercises that follow.

FT

LEVEL OF DIFFICULTY ● ● ○

TEXT BANK

Bargain-hunting tourists find an outlet

Hannah Kuchler

Foreign tourists are fast becoming the primary customers for many of Britain's outlet villages. Some centres are even sending teams to [5] emerging markets to lure wealthy tourists to plan trips that snub London's Bond Street and opt for their discounted designer brands instead. The number of Chinese consumers [10] visiting Bicester Village in Oxfordshire has almost doubled in the past year, with tourists from China now making up more than a quarter of all shoppers at the village.

[15] Value Retail, which runs Bicester and eight other outlet villages throughout Europe, has a team of 30 people who market the centres to foreign consumers. They visit the [20] countries to give presentations to tourist companies and use social media to engage with shoppers directly. Bicester even has its own blog written in Chinese where it uses [25] competitions to entice Chinese bloggers to write for it. "Bicester is better known today in China than Selfridges or Harrods," says Scott Malkin, chairman of Value Retail.
[30] "We'll get information that a Saudi princess is coming with 50 other women so we'll create special accommodation for them and bring in Arabic-speaking staff," says Mr [35] Malkin. Tax-refunded sales, which are one way of tracking sales from outside the EU, increased 27 per cent in the West End of London last year, but rose 88 per cent at Bicester.

[40] McArthur Glen runs seven outlets in the UK and has seen international customers rise by 50 per cent in the past year, albeit from a lower base than at Bicester. "Our teams on the [45] ground noticed a shift in the number of tour buses, the Chinese became visible," says Heinrik Madsen, managing director for McArthur Glen in northern Europe.

[50] Even though they are choosing to buy brands at a discount, foreign customers are not counting their pennies: the average spend per visit of an international visitor to Bicester [55] is about £1,000 but it is not unusual for them to spend more than £10,000. Outlet village companies believe tourists are not embarrassed to buy discounted goods because of [60] the importance of genuine brands when counterfeited products are rife at home.

Mr Malkin thinks Bicester beats Bond Street not only because of its [65] prices but because it offers greater anonymity and the opportunity to visit Oxford or Warwick as part of a day out. To accommodate the new visitors, retailers have started stock-[70]ing smaller sizes and some are employing sales staff who speak foreign languages. Value Retail runs courses to teach store staff what Asian customers expect. "The level [75] of customer service has to be very precise because there's the language barrier, the customers take a lot of time and want to see a lot of products," says Jane Soper, store [80] manager for Jimmy Choo.

1 Look through the whole article and find:

a) a London shopping street

b) an outlet village not in London

c) two London department stores

d) two companies that own outlets

e) their chairman and managing director respectively

f) a retailer

g) a store manager

2 Look through the whole article and match these figures to the things that they refer to.

1 30   a) the increase in international visitors to McArthur Glen stores last year

2 50   b) the increase in tax-refunded sales at Bicester last year

3 27 per cent   c) the number of women that a Saudi princess may bring shopping with her

4 88 per cent   d) the amount that visitors to Bicester spend on average

5 50 per cent   e) what a visitor to Bicester might spend

6 £1,000   f) the increase in tax-refunded sales in the West End of London last year

7 over £10,000   g) the number of people employed by Value Retail to market it in Asia

3 Choose the correct alternative to replace the expressions in *italics* from lines 1–14, so as to keep the same meaning.

1 Foreign tourists are fast becoming the *primary* customers for many of Britain's outlet villages.

  a) first   b) main   c) youngest

2 Some centres are even sending teams to emerging markets to *lure* wealthy tourists …

  a) attract   b) trick   c) magnetise

3 … to plan trips that *snub* London's Bond Street …

  a) go to   b) ignore   c) take in

4 … and *opt* for their discounted designer brands instead.

  a) exclude   b) add   c) choose

5 The number of Chinese consumers visiting Bicester Village in Oxfordshire has almost *doubled* in the past year, …

  a) gone up by nearly 100 per cent

  b) gone up by nearly 200 per cent

  c) gone up nearly twice

6 … with tourists from China now *making up* more than a quarter of all shoppers at the village.

  a) consisting   b) consistent   c) constituting

4 Find the infinitive forms of verbs in lines 15–29 that could be replaced by these verbs, with no change in meaning.

a) manage

b) sell

c) go to

d) employ (occurs twice)

e) communicate

5 Look through lines 15–39 and 63–80. Which of these things are not mentioned as part of village outlets' customer service?

a) employing staff that speak foreign languages

b) employing Arabic-speaking staff

c) employing Chinese-speaking staff

d) giving language training to existing staff

e) getting Arab visitors to write a blog in Arabic

f) getting overseas visitors to use social media to talk about their experiences

g) training staff in what Asian customers expect

h) keeping smaller sizes in stock

i) keeping larger sizes in stock

6 Use appropriate forms of the expressions in brackets from lines 40–62 to answer these questions.

a) Is the rise in the number of overseas visitors to McArthur Glen's outlets directly comparable to the rise in numbers visiting Bicester? (lower base)

b) Is it the managers at head office who have noticed the increase in numbers with their own eyes? (on the ground)

c) Has the number of tour buses with Chinese visitors stayed the same? (shift)

d) Are overseas visitors watching how much they spend overall? (count their pennies)

e) Are visitors happy to buy discounted goods? (embarrassed)

f) Are there are a lot of counterfeit goods in the countries they come from? (rife)

Over to you 1

What could the retail outlets that you use do to improve their customer service?

Over to you 2

Value Retail runs courses to teach store staff what Asian customers expect. Imagine that you are running a course for a retailer that has a lot of visitors from your country. What would the course cover?

TEXT BANK

SOCIAL MEDIA

Before you read

Is it possible to have a personal relationship with a brand? Why? / Why not?

Reading

Read this article from the *Financial Times* by Tim Bradshaw and do the exercises that follow.

FT

LEVEL OF DIFFICULTY ● ● ○

Do you want to be friends with a brand?

Tim Bradshaw

When first faced with the prospect of marketing on social networks, many people ask a reasonable question: how many people want to be friends with a brand? The answer – surprisingly, perhaps – is: millions do, on a daily basis. More than 10m people each day become a "fan" of a brand on Facebook. The world's largest social network – with well in excess of 400m members globally – plays host to more than 1.4m branded fan pages on Facebook. BrandZ Top 100 brands such as Coca-Cola and Starbucks, along with other smaller brands such as Adidas that have each "befriended" millions of people.

Social media have matured rapidly in recent years. Sites such as YouTube, Facebook and Twitter offer scale and reach to rival Google – still the most dominant single site for online advertising – and many television channels. The best advertisers use social media alongside these traditional channels for a combination of brand-building, direct sales, customer service and PR. The worst simply ignore them, until they realise the complaints and accusations that unhappy customers are telling other would-be consumers.

"Social media have given consumers a voice to respond, as well as hundreds of channels through which to do so," says Debbie Klein, joint chief executive of Engine, a UK-based agency group. "These websites have fundamentally transformed marketing from a monologue to a dialogue. Brands cannot hide."

Eurostar, for instance, recently faced criticism for ignoring Twitter messages – which, unlike most Facebook posts, are usually made public for anyone to read – from angry customers trapped on trains between Paris and London. Eurostar had failed to grab its brand name on Twitter, and its main presence on the site – named "little_break" to tie into a wider marketing campaign – was still showing special offers rather than information on the disrupted service for some hours after the problems began.

In the fast-paced, "real-time" environment of Twitter, just a few hours is long enough for such criticism to spread widely, be chewed over by its users and, if it reaches a certain volume, be picked up and amplified further by the mainstream media. Kevin Smith, a film director, caused a similar Twitter storm when he complained to more than 1m followers that Southwest Airlines threw him off a flight for being overweight. Southwest later made two public apologies on its blog.

1 Read lines 1–17 to find this information.

The number of …

a) people who become 'friends' of a brand each day on Facebook.

b) people overall who are members of Facebook.

c) brand-related fan pages there are on Facebook.

d) friends that brands such as Coca-Cola and Starbucks typically have.

2 Complete these statements with correct forms of expressions from lines 1–17.

a) If you are ………. ………. ………. ………. of something, you may do it in the future, and you may or may not be happy about this.

b) Something that is normal and not strange is ……….

c) If a writer thinks that readers may not believe something, the writer can use the adverb '……….'.

d) Someone who likes and admires a film star, a brand, etc. is a ……….

e) Instead of using 'more than', you can say '………. ………. ……….'.

f) An adverb meaning 'all around the world' is '……….'.

g) A social website that contains particular pages ………. ………. to these pages.

h) If you make friends with someone, you ………. them.

3 Complete the table with words and grammatically related words from lines 18–41.

verb	noun
	maturity
reach	
rival	………. , ……….
use	
combine	
	complaint
	accusations
respond	

4 Now match the nouns in Exercise 3 to their meanings.

a) criticisms that may or may not be justified

b) using a number of things together

c) the number of people that you can communicate with

d) when a market starts to grow more slowly, there are fewer competitors, etc.

e) you make a ………. when you are not happy about something

f) when you apply particular methods, ideas, etc.

g) competition

h) when two people talk to each other

i) an answer

j) a competitor

5 Read lines 42–70 and decide if these statements are true or false.

Twitter …

a) and its potential have been cleverly exploited by Eurostar.

b) only showed advertising for short breaks from Eurostar even hours after the trains were delayed.

c) allows criticism to spread very quickly.

d) messages are always picked up by the mainstream media.

e) had a problem when Southwest Airlines threw an overweight customer off a flight.

f) has apologised about this.

6 What is the key point made by the article?

a) Every brand should have a presence on Twitter.

b) Brand marketing has become a dialogue, and companies have to be aware of this.

c) Twitter is a good way of handling complaints about customer service.

Over to you 1

Look at the customer complaints in paragraphs 5 and 6 again. What should Eurostar and Southwest Airlines have done respectively a) in relation to Twitter and b) more generally?

Over to you 2

Would you become a 'friend' of a brand on Facebook? If so, which one(s), and why? If not, why not?

TEXT BANK

CRISIS PR

Before you read

In your country do public relations firms specialise in either corporate or private work, or do they undertake both?

Reading

Read this article from the *Financial Times* by Matthew Garrahan and do the exercises that follow.

FT

LEVEL OF DIFFICULTY ● ● ○

The spin doctor of restructuring

Matthew Garrahan

Mike Sitrick has a book with hundreds of media contacts and is the spin doctor's spin doctor, helping clients cope with extreme media
5 scrutiny and advising them how to tell their side of the story. He says, however, PR is about much more than stories in newspapers. "We ask the client: who do you want to com-
10 municate with? Is it customers, employees, suppliers?" His talents are summed up in the title of his book *Spin: How to Turn the Power of the Press to your Advantage*. But
15 although most of his firm's work is for businesses in trouble, he is probably best known for his celebrity work.

Clients are often controversial – such as Chris Brown, the singer who
20 was arrested after assaulting his pop star girlfriend Rihanna, or Michael Vick, the football player who briefly became one of America's most reviled men for his involvement in a
25 dog-fighting ring. "We represent people trying to get their lives back in order," says Mr Sitrick. "I have to believe that even if they have done something wrong, they are trying to
30 turn their life around – or that allegations against them are false."

The celebrity work generates headlines but it is his corporate clients that generate most of the firm's
35 revenues – more than 90 per cent, according to Mr Sitrick. The company does not disclose its profits but in the past 12 months revenues were about $25m (€18.2m, £16.5m), he
40 says. His corporate work ranges from shaping the PR strategy for Exxon when it was being pummelled by negative headlines in the aftermath of the Exxon Valdez oil spill,
45 to advising the late Roy Disney and Stanley Gold when he orchestrated their campaign to remove Michael Eisner as chairman of Walt Disney in 2003. The campaign led to 43 per cent
50 of Disney shareholders withholding their support from him. Mr Eisner later stepped down voluntarily.

Mr Sitrick acted for Patricia Dunn, the former Hewlett-Packard chair-
55 man, who resigned in controversial circumstances after a boardroom spying scandal and put her up for a grilling on CBS's hard-hitting '60 Minutes' television programme.
60 "People said we were crazy," he says. "Some clients say to us: we'll talk, but only to a softball reporter. But that's wrong – you have to go in front of tough but fair reporters and
65 make your case." A California judge later dismissed all charges against her.

All his business comes by referral – "We don't even have a brochure" – and he tends to employ only for-
70 mer journalists: his staff have, between them, won seven Pulitzer Prizes. "I always felt it was easier to teach a journalist what PR was than teach a PR person what news was."

1 Read lines 1–17 and decide if these statements are true or false.

Mike Sitrick …

a) has a 'book' that is referred to in line 1 and this is the same as the one referred to in line 13.

b) is a spin doctor.

c) is not admired by others working in PR.

d) helps his clients to deal with the media.

e) tells clients to concentrate on communicating with customers.

f) is best known for his work with famous people.

g) earns most of his money from working with companies.

2 Use appropriate forms of expressions from lines 18–31 to complete these statements.

If someone …

a) does something that not everyone likes, they are ……….

b) is taken by the police to a police station, they are ……….

c) is hated and despised, they are ……….

d) tries to behave better in the long term, they try to get their lives ………. ………. ………. and turn their ………. ………. (2 expressions)

e) has ………. made against them, these are statements that may be true or false.

3 Answer these questions using the words given and correct forms of expressions from lines 32–52 of the article.

a) Does Mike Sitrick's corporate work generate most of his sales?
– Yes, even if it doesn't generate as many ……….

b) Does his corporate work cover a wide area?
– Yes, it ………. from work related to the Exxon Valdez disaster to work with Disney.

c) Did he work for Exxon a long time after the disaster?
– No, he worked for them in its ……….

d) Did he organise the campaign to remove Michael Eisner at Disney?
– Yes, he was the one who ………. it.

e) Did a large number of shareholders stop supporting Eisner?
– Yes, 43 per cent ………. ………. ………. .

f) Was Eisner fired?
– No, he ………. ………. ………. .

4 Use the expressions in the box to replace those in *italic* in the extract so as to keep the same meaning.

> journalist who asks easy questions   dropped
> mad   left her job   difficult interview   critical

Mr Sitrick acted for Patricia Dunn, the former Hewlett-Packard chairman, who resigneda) in controversial circumstances after a boardroom spying scandal and put her up for a *grilling* b) on CBS's *hard-hitting* c) *60 Minutes* television programme. "People said we were *crazy*, d) " he says. "Some clients say to us, "We'll talk, but only to a *softball* reporter e)." But that's wrong – you have to go in front of tough but fair reporters and make your case." A California judge later *dismissed* f) all charges against her.

5 Correct the structures of the expressions in *italics* as they are used in lines 53–74 and 5. (There is one word too many in each structure.)

a) *act up for* a client

b) *put someone on up* for a particular event

c) *go on in front* of an interviewer

d) *dismiss charges opposed* against someone

e) *employ on* someone in a job

f) *win up* a prize

g) *teach in* someone what something is

Over to you 1

If you were a PR professional, would you act for …

a) an oil company responsible for causing huge environmental damage?

b) a celebrity with a 'wild' private life?

Why? / Why not?

Over to you 2

Think of a recent corporate or celebrity scandal. Describe the situation and the way it was dealt with professionally in terms of PR.

TEXT BANK

ASSESSING RISK

Before you read

What was the latest 'scare story' in the news (e.g. a public health concern)?
Was the scare justified or not?

Reading

Read this article from the *Financial Times* by John Kay and do the exercises that follow.

FT

LEVEL OF DIFFICULTY ● ● ●

How our leaders get to grips with a scare story

John Kay

Do you remember swine flu? Or the millennium bug? The dangers of salmonella in eggs or of cheese made from unpasteurised milk?
5 These scare stories played for a time and were then forgotten, but cost large amounts of money and caused anxiety and loss to many individuals. Some scares catch on: others do
10 not. It is nonsense to claim that the dangers of the credit expansion of 2003–07 could not have been foreseen; those who did foresee problems could not attract public
15 attention or political support for their views. Those warning of the danger of easy availability of nuclear technology and of poor control of the former Soviet Union's nuclear
20 weapons have experienced something similar.

Successful promotion of a scare requires that some interest group benefits. Sometimes this is the scare-
25 promoters themselves. Scientists have learnt that exaggerated claims are a route to a media profile and research funding. There is little downside in predicting disaster: if it
30 does not materialise they can claim to have been instrumental in staving it off. Scares that thrive, such as the millennium bug and swine flu, have commercial interests that benefit
35 from their propagation. Naysayers in the credit boom, by contrast, were ignored in the rush to share the riches available to those who denied or disregarded the dangers.
40 The regulator, or politician, confronted with warnings of danger faces twin pressures of commercial interest and public opinion. Industries are a permanent lobbying
45 presence. Public concern, by contrast, is fickle: it may be strong when aroused, but unless supplied with a string of newsworthy events – dead
bodies, corporate collapses, scandal-
50 ous exposures – it soon fades.

When public and commercial interests operate in the same direction, the outcome is clear, but not when they conflict. That is why
55 swine flu produced an exaggerated response but no action was taken to restrain the credit boom. Public anger at bankers is now so great that it threatens to overwhelm even their
60 legendary lobbying capabilities.

We want our experts to talk certainties, not assess probabilities. The explanation "we thought an event might occur but underestimated its
65 likelihood or severity" is never acceptable: but that outcome does, and should, happen often to people who make decisions in complex environments. The political and
70 regulatory incentives are either to downplay risks or exaggerate them – or to do each at different times.

1 Match the two parts of the expressions from lines 1–21.

1	swine	stories
2	millennium	technology
3	scare	bug
4	credit	flu
5	public	expansion
6	political	attention
7	nuclear	support

2 Now match the expressions to their meanings.

a) dangerous events or possible dangerous events that may or may not be as serious as they sound

b) a disease

c) a possible problem with computers at the end of 1999

d) when politicians say that a problem is important, spend money to solve it, etc.

e) a way of producing energy

f) when banks increase the amount that they lend

g) when people believe that something is important

3 Read lines 22–39 and decide if these statements are true or false.

a) The words promotion and promoters are used in their normal senses here. (lines 22 and 25)

b) Exaggerated claims are objective and justified. (line 26)

c) If you have media profile, you are well known through newspapers, television, etc. (line 27)

d) A downside is an advantage. (line 29)

e) If you stave something off, you help to prevent it happening. (line 31)

f) If something thrives, it disappears quickly. (line 32)

g) The commercial interests that might have benefitted from two of the scare stories mentioned were IT companies and pharmaceutical companies. (line 34)

h) You can talk about the propagation of an idea, a rumour, etc. (line 35)

i) Naysayers are people who disapprove of something. (line 35)

j) If you disregard something, you pay attention to it. (line 39)

4 Find expressions in lines 40–60 that refer to:

a) someone who ensures that companies in a particular industry obey laws.

b) companies and their profit-making activities.

c) what the public thinks.

d) influencing politicians and the laws that they pass.

e) when companies go bankrupt.

f) things that are reported in newspapers and on TV, etc.

g) when people find out about and are shocked by illegal activities.

h) the famous power of banks to influence politicians.

5 Put these questions into the order in which they are answered in lines 40–60.

a) Which two examples show this?

b) Which of these two examples is now causing people to be very angry?

c) Which of these influences is stronger?

d) What two influences do regulators and politicians face when there is a possibly dangerous situation to deal with?

e) What happens when they are different?

f) What happens when the two influences go the same way?

g) What determines the strength of public concern about possible dangers?

6 What is the main point in lines 61–72? Choose the best alternative.

Experts …

a) can never know what is going to happen and deserve all the blame they get when they fail to prepare for disastrous events.

b) can say after a disastrous event that they did not think it would happen, or would be so serious, even if this does not seem to be an acceptable thing to say.

c) cannot be blamed when they fail to predict serious events, because regulators and politicians are either exaggerating or minimising the dangers all the time.

Over to you 1

Think of a recent scare story. How did the government in your country deal with it? Was this an overreaction? Explain your reasoning.

Over to you 2

'We want our experts to talk certainties, not assess probabilities.' After reading the last paragraph of the article, what do you think about this? Is the public ready to think in terms of probabilities?
Why? / Why not?

EXPANDING ABROAD

Before you read

What is the attitude in your country to takeovers of companies from abroad?

Reading

Read this article from the *Financial Times* by Robin Harding, Kathrin Hille and Song Jung-a and do the exercises that follow.

TEXT BANK

FT

LEVEL OF DIFFICULTY ● ● ●

Japan's Rakuten poised for overseas expansion

Robin Harding in Tokyo, Kathrin Hille in Beijing and Song Jung-a in Seoul

In its 13 years of existence, Japan's Rakuten has expanded from online shopping into everything from credit cards and stockbroking to golf reser-
5 vations and even a professional baseball team. So when president Hiroshi Mikitani says that he plans to expand into 27 foreign markets – 10 of them by the end of this year
10 – he deserves to be taken seriously. Rakuten's overseas push is part of a growing trend by Asian Internet companies to expand abroad as their domestic growth starts to slow
15 down. But in spite of the ambitions of Asia's young Internet billionaires, cultural barriers and entrenched local competition may prove impossible to overcome. There have been
20 a series of deals so far this year. In addition to Rakuten's tie-up with search engine Baidu to launch a Chinese version of its shopping site, South Korea's largest search engine
25 NHN has bought the Japanese Internet access portal Livedoor, and China's Tencent has invested $300m in Digital Sky Technologies of Russia.

Kentaro Hyakuno, the head of
30 Rakuten's international business, says his company stayed domestic on purpose while building up the eco-system of merchants that use its e-commerce site. Now it is ready to
35 expand abroad and, Mr Hyakuno says, "Japan is growing old, with less children, and if you want to keep growing as a corporation then you need opportunity."
40 South Korea, whose Internet companies began to venture abroad in the early 2000s, provides some evidence. Its portals and search engines have struggled to make inroads into
45 other countries, but its online game makers have become serious contenders in overseas markets such as China, Japan and the US.
Daum, the country's largest portal,
50 took over Lycos of the US in 2004 but had struggled to turn around the loss-making US business as it could not compete effectively with bigger rivals such as Google and Yahoo.
55 "They face high entry barriers to offer portal and search services in

foreign countries because such services are already dominated by big local players," says Wayne Lee,
60 analyst at South Korea's Woori Investment & Securities. "Language and culture are very important for Internet access portals and search services, compared with online
65 games. And it is not easy for foreign players to do well in offering such services based on local languages."
For Rakuten, as it contemplates its international blitz, the answer is to
70 look for markets where infrastructure such as broadband, credit cards and delivery logistics are improving but the market is not yet saturated with established players. "We evalu-
75 ated about 50 countries, we grouped them, and then we worked out the best approach," says Mr Hyakuno. So far that has included launches in Taiwan and China and an acquisition
80 in Thailand. India - a huge potential market – may be next on the list.

1 Look through the whole article and find:

a) a Japanese Internet company (with other activities too) and two of its executives.

b) a Chinese Internet search company.

c) a South Korean search engine and the Japanese Internet access provider that it has bought.

d) a Chinese company and the Russian company in which it has invested.

e) a South Korean Internet access provider and the US search engine that it bought.

f) a South Korean financial institution and someone who works for it.

2 Match the two parts of these expressions from lines 1–28.

1	online	barriers
2	domestic	trend
3	Internet	push
4	cultural	billionaires
5	entrenched local	shopping
6	overseas	growth
7	growing	competition

3 Now match the expressions above to their meanings.

a) strong companies in markets that you want to enter

b) increase in your home sales

c) efforts by a company to expand abroad

d) a tendency that is getting stronger

e) buying things on the Internet

f) ways of doing things in another market that make it difficult to enter

g) people who have made a lot of money from web businesses

4 Correct the expressions in *italic* as they are used in lines 29–48, using the same number of words.

a) If you do something intentionally, you do it with *purposeful*.

b) A company that enters foreign markets expansions *broadly*.

c) People and organisations that sell on the Internet are *merchandise*.

d) If a company starts trying to sell outside its home market, it *adventures* aboard.

e) If a company is not very successful in a foreign market, it *fights to do roads* on those markets.

f) Competitors new to a market can be referred to as *contentious*.

5 Match these questions and answers about lines 29–48.

1 Did Rakuten want to expand abroad earlier?

2 Is Japan's population getting younger?

3 Can Japanese companies expand in their domestic market?

4 Is the experience of South Korean Internet companies abroad typical?

5 Is the experience of South Korean game makers the same as that of Internet companies?

a) Yes, but for real opportunity they need to look abroad.

b) No, it stayed in Japan on purpose.

c) Yes, they have had trouble getting into other markets.

d) No, they've become serious competitors with overseas companies in at least three countries.

e) No, it's getting older.

6 Find the answers to these questions in lines 49–81.

Find ...

a) the first mention of the first reason for Daum's difficulties in making a success of Lycos.

b) the second mention of this reason.

c) the second reason for Daum's difficulties.

d) four aspects of overseas markets that Rakuten looks at before deciding which ones to enter.

e) three steps that Rakuten went through in assessing overseas markets before deciding which ones to enter.

f) three countries that Rakuten has already entered.

g) one country it might enter.

Over to you 1

'Language and culture are very important for Internet access portals and search services, compared with online games.' Why is this?

Over to you 2

Give advice on language and cultural issues to a foreign company that has acquired a company in your country.

SUCCESSFUL ACQUISITIONS

Before you read

Why do so many mergers and acquisitions fail to produce the promised results?

Reading

Read this article from the *Financial Times* by Rebecca Ranninger and Scott Moeller and do the exercises that follow.

FT

TEXT BANK

Is conflict inevitable in mergers and takeovers?

The Executive –
Rebecca Ranninger

Every business has a unique culture. Even when seemingly similar companies combine, some level of culture clash, along with the usual internal politics, is inevitable. These undesirable side-effects can be significantly reduced when there is clarity of purpose and honest communication by the right people. During my 17 years at Symantec, we have completed more than 60 acquisitions, and we still learn something new every time.

What has remained consistent, however, is the need for absolute agreement as to exactly what we are buying. Is it a particular technology? An established product? A brand? A particularly skilled group of engineers? A position in a given geography? Once this purpose has been established, consistent, honest, and well-thought out communications to the employees of both businesses, as early as possible, can go a long way to minimise some of the unavoidable friction.

While the acquiring company must clearly set the direction for the future business, the executive leadership of both companies must spearhead the communications. Employees can easily detect insincerity, so only those executives who are unequivocally dedicated to the success of the combined new business should deliver the future vision.

The writer is chief human resource officer, Symantec

The Academic –
Scott Moeller

Think back to your first love. Did it end because you tried to change each other or tried to embrace each other's personality? Of course, this isn't about romantic relationships, it's about the problem of bringing together two companies with established cultures. But a reality check is healthy, especially when you have just done a deal and are about to launch a costly integration campaign. With the failed romantic relationship, it didn't help to discuss what some combined personality could look like but it did help when you remembered what first attracted you to each other.

Back to business mergers: why waste time talking about common cultural aspects? Instead, focus on the goal. Winning business. Quickly. Note the success of Deutsche Bank with its marketing campaign of 'Leading to Results' after it acquired Bankers Trust, or Santander with Abbey. These days, looking at deals, you get the impression that the cultural aspect of deals is a bit over-engineered. You'll notice the internal communications teams are bigger than the external PR/marketing teams. Being internally focused gives your competitors a field day.

Leadership is key to successful mergers, and leaders go with their gut. Why did they buy the other company? Because of their culture? No. They were bought for their business. That's the message. The troops – and clients – will follow.

The writer is a professor at Cass Business School and co-author of Intelligent M&A

1 Match these adverbs from lines 1–41 with their expressions that could replace them with no change in meaning.

1	seemingly	a)	obviously
2	significantly	b)	apparently
3	exactly	c)	specially
4	particularly	d)	to a large extent
5	clearly	e)	without doubt or hesitation
6	easily	f)	precisely
7	unequivocally	g)	without difficulty

2 Use expressions from lines 1–29 to complete the answers to these questions.

a) Do all businesses share the same culture?
– No, each one is ....

b) In mergers and acquisitions, are culture clashes avoidable?
– No, they're ....

c) How can culture clashes be reduced?
– When there is .... and
....

d) Has all the thinking behind Symantec's acquisitions changed over the years?
– Some of it has, but one thing has remained
....

e) What is that?
– There must be total .... about the reasons for the acquisition.

3 What is Rebecca Ranninger's key point? Read lines 1–41 again and choose the best alternative.

In acquisitions, ...
a) communication is important, but in the end culture clashes are inevitable and you just hope that communication will minimise them.

b) executives who don't share the combined company's vision for the future should not be involved in the negotiations leading to the acquisition.

c) culture clashes are inevitable, but good communication about the combined company's vision for the future can overcome them.

4 Why does Scott Moeller refer to romantic relationships between people in lines 30–41? Choose the best alternative.

Because ...
a) they throw light on relationships between companies in mergers and the factors that bring merging companies together.

b) thinking about them prepares companies for the disappointment they will inevitably face when the merger fails.

c) they highlight the differences between people's relationships and those between companies.

5 Complete the table with words, and grammatically related words, from lines 44–60.

verb	noun
	launch
discuss	
	integration
	attraction
	focus
succeed	
	acquisition

6 Now match the nouns above with their meanings.

a) when one company buys another
b) when you concentrate on one thing in particular
c) when two things are combined
d) when one person or organisation likes another
e) when people talk about something
f) when actions produce positive results
g) when something is started

7 Which two examples of successful acquisitions are given in lines 61–76?

8 Match the expressions in *italics* from lines 61–83 with their meanings by choosing the better alternative.

1 '...you get the impression that the cultural aspect of deals is a bit *over-engineered*.' (line 72)
  a) downplayed   b) exaggerated

2 'Being *internally* focused ...' (line 75)
  a) concentrating on the functioning of the company
  b) concentrating on customers

3 '... gives your competitors *a field day*.' (line 76)
  a) a big chance to succeed
  b) the chance to fail

4 '...leaders go with their *gut*.' (line 78)
  a) follow their instincts   b) follow logical reasoning

5 'The *troops* – and clients – will follow.' (line 82)
  a) customers   b) employees

Over to you 1

How useful is it to compare romantic relationships with corporate ones in analysing successful acquisitions? Explain your reasoning.

Over to you 2

Why can the cultures of companies in the same industry be quite different? Give some examples from an industry you are interested in (perhaps your own).

TEXT BANK KEY

Unit 1
Corporate communication

1

verb	noun
collaborate	collaboration
collapse	collapse
define	definition
engage	engagement
explode	explosion
find	finding
prevail	prevalence
research	research

2 a) True
b) False – everything that companies do will communicate something, but the writer does not say they will be misunderstood.
c) True
d) False – all parts of an organisation are involved.
e) False – the writer mentions six points.

3 a) theme
b) value
c) values
d) stakeholders
e) philanthropy
f) being green
g) social values
h) initiatives

4 1e 2a 3f 4b 5d 6c

5 b

Twitter

1–2
1 social networking sites – d
2 bottom-line benefit – a
3 user experience manager – b
4 online spectacles retailer – c

3 a) devote precious resources
b) puts, in direct contact
c) engaging way
d) extremely proud
e) provide, immediate feedback
f) track, down
g) figure, what

4 a) False – it's not a financially important area for the business.
b) True
c) False – they have not yet found a way to make money from it.
d) False – three are mentioned: finding personnel, improving staff productivity and finding new customers.
e) True
f) False – she would not have founded it without Twitter.

5 a) hook up with
b) all the more surprising
c) inferior
d) face-to-face
e) workshop
f) launch
g) tweet

Unit 2
Global brands 1

1–2

noun	adjective
abruptness	abrupt – e
confidence	confident – d
health	healthy – a
finance	financial – f
severity	severe – b
value	valuable –c

3 a) If you say that something is true and that people should act in accordance with it, you preach the gospel about it.
b) If conditions become difficult in a particular situation, the going gets tough.
c) A series of very bad events that might happen is a Doomsday scenario.
d) A formal way of saying that something has happened is to say that it has come to pass.
e) If a company does well after a period of doing badly, it enjoys a rebound.

4 a) False – the worst predictions have not come true.
b) False – they are now regaining confidence.
c) True
d) True

5 a) Google, IBM, Apple, iPod, iPad, Microsoft, Oracle, Facebook, Twitter, Verizon, AT&T, iPhone
b) McDonald's, Marlboro, Starbucks, Coca-Cola
c) Google
d) Microsoft
e) Verizon, AT&T

6 a) defining characteristic
b) resurgence
c) inspires
d) devotion
e) keepers of the flame
f) social media

Global brands 2

1
Coca-Cola	PepsiCola
Glaceau	Minute Maid Super Pulpy Milky
Wahaha	Danone
Coke	Sprite
Yuan Ye	Ice Dew
Tingyi	Huiyuan
Nike	Oakleys

2 a) Coca-Cola, PepsiCola

162

b) Danone
c) Wahaha
d) Huiyuan
e) Tingyi
f) Glaceau, Ice Dew
g) Yuan Ye
h) Minute Maid Super Pulpy Milky
i) Nike, Oakley

3 a) False – it owns two of the three best-selling drinks.
b) True
c) False – it's the third biggest.
d) False – it plans to triple sales (sell three times as much).
e) True
f) False – Coca Cola has double Pepsi Cola's sales in China.
g) False – it already has a presence in still drinks, water and juices.

4–5
1 g vi
2 d i
3 a iv
4 b iii
5 c vii
6 f v
7 e ii

6 c)

Unit 3
Working for free

1 1 b iii   2 c i   3 a ii

2 1 c   2 c   3 b   4 b   5 a   6 c   7 a

3 a) "You get to see a lot of nuts and bolts …" (line 21)
b) "… I'll enlist a couple of graduates to work with me …" (line 40)
c) "…someone who sets up an IT system in Chad would have a broader view than a person who has only worked in Fortune 200 companies …" (line 24)
d) not mentioned
e) "People who do pro bono work … typically take on more senior roles than they would in big corporate roles …" (line 15)
f) " … an IT system in Chad … " (line 25)
g) not mentioned

4 1 c   2 a   3 b   4 e   5 g   6 d   7 h   8 f

5 1 d   2 c   3 b   4 a, e

Doing business in Russia

1 e   f   d   g   c   a   b

2 a) fathom
b) outwardly
c) accessible
d) flashy
e) authoritarian
f) alien
g) suspicion
h) close-knit

3 a) False – you keep them separate.
b) True
c) True
d) True
e) False – it's not the most important thing.
f) True
g) False – it's successful.

4–5
1 ingrained suspicion – c
2 high-level tête-à-tête – a
3 advance requests – g
4 expatriate banker – f
5 external appearances – b
6 fancy office suite – d
7 chunky timepieces – e

Unit 4
Successful women

1–2
a) I work hard. – Indra Nooyi, PepsiCo
b) I have fun. – Indra Nooyi, PepsiCo
c) I follow my passion. – Irene Rosenfeld, Kraft
d) I believe in having a mentor. – not mentioned
e) I try to be myself. – not mentioned
f) I believe in work-life balance. – not mentioned
g) I believe in teamwork. – not mentioned
h) I try to be humble. – not mentioned
i) I never miss. – Dong Mingzhu, Gree Electric Appliances
j) I never admit mistakes. – Dong Mingzhu, Gree Electric Appliances
k) I am always correct. – Dong Mingzhu, Gree Electric Appliances

3 i, j and k because they aren't like the reasons for success given by businesswomen in the West.

4 1 c   2 b   3 c   4 a   5 a   6 b

5 a) not very personable
b) underlings
c) hang on
d) spat out
e) squashed
f) pull off a feat
g) rule by fear
h) bang on about
i) notice

6 b

Successful strategic change

1 a) Gerry Johnson
b) George Yip and Manuel Hensmans
c) Lancaster University Management School
d) Rotterdam School of Management
e) Tesco, Cadbury and Smith & Nephew
f) Ian MacLaurin and Jack Cohen
g) 'A witness'

2 a) also-rans
b) cope
c) crises
d) strategic
e) rare

f) uninterrupted success
g) prevailing atmosphere

3 a) What is the big danger, even for successful businesses?
b) How do they lose their way?
c) Does this happen in all companies?
d) How do successful companies deal with big changes while avoiding disaster?
e) What is the first of these four characteristics or traditions?
f) What does continuity involve?

4 a) combination
b) characteristics
c) reinvention
d) drift
e) disaster
f) business model
g) right track
h) traditions

5 1 anticipation
2 contestation
3 mobility

6 1 A new generation of managers was developed – Ian Macaurin began changing the business while its founder, Jack Cohen, was still there.
2 There was confrontation and argument.
3 Putting the best person in the job, rather than recruiting someone just because it was their turn.

7 1 The new management did not undermine the old.
2 The idea of 'respectful difference' – board meetings 'were like a family arguing rather than a group of enemies'.

Unit 5
A job satisfaction survey

1 a) Chartered Institute of Personnel and Development
b) BT
c) YouGov
d) Claire McCartney

2 a) satisfaction
b) pressures
c) toll
d) figures
e) recession
f) insecurity
g) unhappiness

3

verb	noun
disclose	disclosure
train	training
launch	launch
experience	experience
announce	announcement
fall	fall
improve	improvement

4 1 c 2 f 3 b 4 g 5 a 6 e 7 h 8 d

5 a) flat on its back
b) crippled
c) era of plenty
d) step on the career ladder
e) grind you down
f) stranded
g) entry-level

6 a) True
b) False – it's stagnant.
c) False – most workers thought it would be difficult to find another job.
d) True
e) True

A different way of working

1 1 b 2 a 3 c 4 a 5 b 6 b

2 a) loyalty, motivation
b) discipline
c) flexibility
d) understanding
e) accommodation
f) productivity

3–4
1 top talent – c
2 critical skills – b
3 economic recovery – a
4 cost constraints – g
5 financial incentives – i
6 global survey – e
7 active promotion – f
8 all-week cover – d
9 job sharing – h

5 a) False – organisations are concerned about losing their most talented people, those with the most critical skills.
b) True
c) False – its previous 'Flexible Futures' programme was successful.
d) False – about 85 per cent of its UK staff volunteered.
e) False – it saved £4 million.
f) True

Unit 6
Reputational risk

1 From golf. It is used in relation to the difficulties of Tiger Woods, the golfer.

2 a) fall from grace
b) dedicated
c) clean-living
d) undone
e) lucrative
f) career earnings

3 1 d 2 a 3 not given 4 not given 5 c 6 not given 7 b 8 not given

4

noun	verb
commission	commission
campaign	campaign
endorsement, endorser	endorse
damage	damage
recall	recall
decline	decline
rebound	rebound
publicity	publicise
cover	cover

5 a) increasingly
   b) vulnerable
   c) volatile
   d) crisis strategy
   e) intangible asset
   f) goodwill
   g) brand values
   h) systematic analysis

Climate change

1 a) World Business Council for Sustainable Development, Carbon Disclosure Project
   b) Antonia Gawel, Paul Dickinson
   c) deputy director of energy and climate, chief executive

2 a) 'Changing patterns are prompting many businesses to shore up their operations and facilities.' and '"Companies are looking at what should they do over the next few years to their infrastructure to increase the resilience of their operations," … '
   b) 'However, many have yet to address longer term climate-related risks.' and '"But that's happening more than the longer term planning."'

3 1 c   2 a   3 c   4 b   5 b   6 c   7 a

4–5
   1 supply chains – c
   2 industrial process – d
   3 water shortages – e
   4 climate adaptation – f
   5 environmental legislation – a
   6 due diligence – b

6 a) tackle
   b) emphasise
   c) shore up
   d) cover
   e) integrate
   f) take
   g) bear

Unit 7
Women managers

1 1 b   2 a   3 b   4 b   5 a   6 b   7 a

2 1 a   2 b   3 b   4 a

3 a) False – you believe it after a period of not believing it.

   b) True
   c) True
   d) False – it is interesting.
   e) True
   f) False – it has been decided.

4 c

5–6

noun	adjective
precision	precise – c
stimulation	stimulating – g
empathy	empathetic – a
collaboration	collaborative – e
equipment	equipped – f
variation	varied – d
maleness/masculinity	male – b
complication	complicated – h

The future of management

1 changing someone's clothes and appearance, or changing the style of a room, its furniture, etc.

2 a) economic recovery
   b) social influence
   c) behaviours
   d) accomplish
   e) line of thinking
   f) perspective

3 1 b   2 c   3 c   4 c   5 b   6 a

4 a) False – 'It turns out that being a good manager is somewhat unnatural.'
   b) False – 'But it is easy to lapse back into old habits.'
   c) True
   d) False – three are given: '…withholding information, telling our employees what to do, and barking at them when they get it wrong'.
   e) True
   f) False – 'The vast majority of us have to work very hard to do the job well.'

5 a) senior leaders
   b) innovative management models
   c) competitive advantage
   d) A well-managed company
   e) An engaged workforce
   f) An engaged workforce
   g) short-term benefits

Unit 8
Sports coaching and corporate team building

1 a) Fabio Capello, Pier Francesco Guarguaglini
   b) England football team, Finmeccanica
   c) England, Juventus, Real Madrid, AS Roma, Brazil
   d) AgustaWestland

2 a) the centre of attention
   b) coaching
   c) widespread experience
   d) create a team spirit
   e) thing or two about
   f) bring

3   a) team spirit   b) discipline   c) direction
    d) hunger   e) morale

4   a) star   b) fan   c) counterpart
    d) veteran   e) boss   f) supporter

5   1 g   2 a   3 e   4 c   5 f   6 d   7 h   8 b

6   a) Clear leadership and a sense of purpose
    b) The main cause was state interference which
       meant that i) there was no long-term plan for the
       company and ii) politicians saw Finmeccanica
       mainly as a place to give top jobs to their friends.
    c) The UK.
    d) Finmeccanica's 'renaissance'
    e) AgustaWestland and BAE Systems' share of an
       unnamed joint venture.
    f) Yes.
    g) We don't know. The article only mentions that it's
       the second-biggest defence company by sales.

Teams of five and teams of one hundred

1   a) founder of the Academy for Chief Executives
    b) founder of Westlakes Engineering
    c) a law firm in Manchester
    d) business development manager at George Davies
    e) He was one of the authors of a government report
       on engaging employees.

2   1 b   2 b   3 a   4 a   5 b   6 a

3–4
    1   to delegate responsibility – g
    2   correct – e
    3   correct – a
    4   to maintain the culture of an organisation – b
    5   correct – c
    6   to expand – f

5   a) False – it discourages its employees from working
       long hours.
    b) False – those who are parents are encouraged to
       spend more time with their families.
    c) True
    d) False – many of them have been there for more
       than a decade, not most of them.
    e) True
    f) False – when the number of employees goes
       above 20, an owner's personality is no longer the
       main factor in motivating people.

Unit 9
Willing and less willing lenders

1   a) EEF
    b) Annika Bosanquet
    c) Wrapology
    d) Harrod's, Armani, John Lewis, Monsoon
    e) Enterprise Finance Guarantee scheme
    f) HSBC, Barclays
    g) Tom
    h) Enterprise Insight

2   a) True
    b) True
    c) False – they could rise sharply.
    d) True

    e) False – 33 per cent said this, compared to 47 per
       cent before.
    f) False – 1 in 5 said this, compared to 1 in 3 before.

3   a) struggle
    b) fulfil
    c) approach
    d) turned down
    e) declined
    f) thrust
    g) processes
    h) fare
    i) extends

4   a) letter of credit
    b) enterprise finance guarantee
    c) overdraft
    d) refinancing
    e) working capital

5   1 b   2 d   3 e   4 a   5 c

Crowdfunding

1   1 b   2 c   3 a   4 a   5 c   6 b   7 a   8 c

2–3
    1   encouraged – e
    2   unsigned artists – a
    3   proceeds – d
    4   established – g
    5   seed capital – c
    6   battening down the hatches – b
    7   downturn – f

4   a) classic second round
    b) higher burn rates
    c) current uncertainty
    d) future financings
    e) investment levels
    f) later-stage companies
    g) middle ground

5   b

Unit 10
Outlet villages

1   a) Bond Street
    b) Bicester Village
    c) Selfridges and Harrods
    d) Value Retail and McArthur Glen
    e) Scott Malkin and Heinrik Madsen
    f) Jimmy Choo
    g) Jane Soper

2   1 g   2 c   3 f   4 b   5 a   6 d   7 e

3   1 b   2 a   3 b   4 c   5 a   6 c

4   a) run
    b) market
    c) visit
    d) use
    e) engage

5   not mentioned: c,d,e,i

6   a) No, it started from a lower base.
    b) No, it's the teams on the ground.
    c) No, there's been a shift in the numbers of tour
       buses with Chinese visitors.

d) No, they are not counting their pennies.
e) Yes, they are not embarrassed about this.
f) Yes, counterfeited goods are rife there.

Social media

1 a) more than 10 million
b) more than 400 million
c) 1.4 million
d) millions

2 a) faced with the prospect
b) reasonable
c) surprisingly
d) fan
e) in excess of
f) globally
g) plays host
h) befriend

3–4

verb	noun
mature	maturity – d
reach	reach – c
rival	rival – j, rivalry – g
use	use – f
combine	combination – b
complain	complaint – e
accuse	accusations – a
respond	response – i

5 a) False – Eurostar has been slow to exploit its potential.
b) True
c) True
d) False – criticism only spreads widely if it reaches a certain volume.
e) False – Southwest Airlines had the problem.
f) False – Southwest Airlines has apologised.

6 b

Unit 11
Crisis PR

1 a) False – the first book contains his contacts and the second is one he published about PR.
b) True
c) False – he is 'is the spin doctor's spin doctor'.
d) True
e) False – it could be with customers, employees or suppliers.
f) True
g) True

2 a) controversial
b) arrested
c) reviled
d) back in order, life around
e) allegations

3 a) headlines
b) ranges
c) aftermath
d) orchestrated
e) withheld their support

f) stepped down voluntarily

4 a) left her job
b) difficult interview
c) critical
d) mad
e) journalist who asks easy questions
f) dropped

5 a) act for a client
b) put someone up for a particular event
c) go in front of an interviewer
d) dismiss charges against someone
e) employ someone in a job
f) win a prize
g) teach someone what something is

Assessing risk

1–2
1 swine flu – b
2 millennium bug – c
3 scare stories – a
4 credit expansion – f
5 public attention – g
6 political support – d
7 nuclear technology – e

3 a) False – they are usually used in advertising, etc.
b) False – they make something sound bigger, worse, etc. than it really is.
c) True
d) False – it's a disadvantage.
e) True
f) False – it continues to be 'successful'.
g) True
h) True
i) True
j) False – you ignore it.

4 a) regulator
b) commercial interests
c) public opinion
d) lobbying
e) corporate collapses
f) newsworthy events
g) scandalous exposures
h) legendary lobbying capabilities

5 d c g f e a b

6 b

Unit 12
Expanding abroad

1 a) Rakuten, Hiroshi Mikitani, Kentaro Hyakuno
b) Baidu
c) NHN, Livedoor
d) Tencent, Digital Sky Technologies
e) Daum, Lycos
f) Woori Investment & Securities, Wayne Lee

2–3
1 online shopping – e
2 domestic growth – b
3 Internet billionaires – g
4 cultural barriers – f
5 entrenched local competition – a

6 overseas push – c
7 growing trend – d

4 a) on purpose
 b) expands abroad
 c) merchants
 d) ventures abroad
 e) struggles to make inroads
 f) contenders

5 1 b 2 e 3 a 4 c 5 d

6 a) '…it could not compete effectively with bigger rivals such as Google and Yahoo.'
 b) '"They face high entry barriers to offer portal and search services in foreign countries because such services are already dominated by big local players," …'
 c) '"Language and culture are very important for portal and search services, compared with online games. And it is not easy for foreign players to do well in offering such services based on local languages."'
 d) '… broadband, credit cards and delivery logistics' and markets that are 'not yet saturated with established players'.
 e) '"We evaluated about 50 countries, we grouped them, and then we worked out the best approach," … '
 f) '…Taiwan and China and an acquisition in Thailand.'
 g) 'India – a huge potential market – may be next on the list.'

Successful acquisitions

1 1 b 2 d 3 f 4 c 5 a 6 g 7 e

2 a) unique
 b) inevitable
 c) clarity of purpose, honest communication
 d) consistent
 e) agreement

3 c

4 a

5–6

verb	noun
launch	launch – g
discuss	discussion – e
integrate	integration – c
attract	attraction – d
focus	focus – b
succeed	success – f
acquire	acquisition – a

7 Deutsche Bank's takeover of Bankers Trust, and Santander's of Abbey.

8 1 b 2 a 3 a 4 a 5 b

TEXT BANK – Key

Resource bank

Introduction
These Resource Bank activities are designed to extend and develop the material in the Course Book. The Resource Bank contains exercises and activities relating to:

Speaking
Each speaking unit begins with a language exercise that takes up and extends the language points from the Course Book unit, then applies this language in one or more activities. The speaking units are best done in the classroom. You have permission to photocopy the Resource bank pages in this book. In some units, you will give each student a copy of the whole page. In others, there are role cards which need to be cut out and given to participants with particular roles. These activities are indicated in the unit-specific notes below.

Listening
Students listen again to the interviews from the Listening sections in the Course Book and do further activities on comprehension and language development. These activities can be done in the classroom, but they have been designed in a way that makes it easy for students to do them on their own as homework. Make photocopies for the students. Follow up in the next lesson by getting students to talk about any difficulties that they had. You could play the recording again in the classroom to help resolve problems if necessary.

Writing
A model answer is given for the writing task at the end of each case study in the Course Book. There are then two or three extra writing activities. These can all be done as homework. Again, make photocopies for the students. Correct the writing exercises then go over in class the key points that have been causing problems.

Resource bank: Speaking

General notes
The language exercises at the beginning of each Speaking unit in the Resource Bank can be used to revise language from the Course Book unit, especially if you did the Skills section in another lesson. In any case, point out the connection with the Course Book Skills material. These language exercises are designed to prepare students for the role plays or discussions that follow and in many cases can be done in a few minutes as a way of focusing students on the activity that will follow.

When you go round the class helping students with exercises, work on the process of deducing the answers by looking at grammatical and sense clues. Do this again when you round up the correct answers with the whole class; don't just mechanically give the right answer and move on.

A typical two-person role play might last five or 10 minutes, followed by three to five minutes' praise and correction. An animated group discussion might last longer, and sometimes even longer than you planned. In this case, drop one of your other planned activities and do it another time, rather than try to cram it in before the end of the lesson. If you then have five or 10 minutes left over, you can always go over some language points from the lesson again, or better still, get students to say what they were. One way of doing this is to ask them what they've written in their notebooks during the lesson.

Revising and revisiting
Feel free to do an activity more than once. After one run-through, praise strong points, then work on three or four things that need correcting or improving. Then you can get learners to change roles and do the activity again, or the parts of the activity where these points come up. Obviously, there will come a time when interest wanes, but the usual tendency in language teaching is not to revisit things enough, rather than the reverse.

Fluency and accuracy
Concentrate on different things in different activities. In some role plays and discussions, you may want to focus on *fluency*, with learners interacting as spontaneously as possible. In others, you will want to concentrate on *accuracy*, with learners working on getting specific forms correct. Rather than expecting students to get everything correct, you could pick out, say, three or four forms that you want them to get right, and focus on these.

Clear instructions
Be sure to give complete instructions *before* getting students to start. In role plays, be very clear about who has which role, and give learners time to absorb the information they need. Sometimes there are role cards that you hand out. The activities where this happens are indicated in the notes which follow.

Parallel and public performances (PPP)
In pair work or small group situations, get all pairs to do the activity at the same time. Go round the class and listen. When they have finished, praise strong points and deal with three or four problems that you have heard, especially problems that more than one group has been having. Then get individual pairs to give public performances so that the whole class can listen. The performers should pay particular attention to these two or three points.

One-to-one
The pair activities can be done one-to-one, with the teacher taking one of the roles. The activity can be done a second time reversing the roles and getting the student to integrate your suggestions for improvement.

Unit 1 Communication

Dealing with communication breakdown

- With the whole class, look again at the expressions in the Useful language box on page 11 of the Course Book.
- Get students to work on the exercise individually or in pairs, working on the process of deducing the answers by looking at grammatical and sense clues.
- Go through the exercise with the whole class. Again, bring attention to the process of deducing the right answers through looking at the relevant clues, rather than just giving the right answer and moving on.
- Then get students to read the expressions here with realistic intonation.

1b	**2**f	**3**g	**4**a	**5**e	**6**c	**7**d

B

- Divide the class into pairs and hand out the role cards for Phone call 1. Get students to sit back-to-back to simulate the phone calls, or even better, get them to use real phone extensions.
- When the situation is clear, the role play can begin in parallel pairs.
- Circulate and monitor. Note language points for praise and correction, especially in the area of problem-solving.
- Praise good language points from the role play and work on three or four points that need improvement, getting individual students to say the correct forms.
- Hand out the role cards for Phone call 2.
- Follow the same procedure for monitoring and correction as above.
- Get one of the pairs to do a public performance of their role play for the whole class.

Unit 2 International marketing

Brainstorming

A

- Get students to look again at the brainstorming language on page 19 of the Course Book. Then ask them to correct the expressions here in pairs. Circulate and assist.
- With the whole class, ask students for the answers.

1 The <u>purpose</u> of the meeting this afternoon is to …
2 <u>What</u> we need to achieve today is to …
3 Our <u>objective</u> here is to …
4 I <u>suggest (that) we</u> brainstorm the problem.
5 That's <u>great</u>!
6 That's the <u>best</u> idea I've heard for a long time.
7 Don't <u>hold</u> back.
8 Say <u>whatever</u> comes to mind.
9 At this <u>stage</u>, we want all your ideas …
10 You're <u>absolutely</u> right because …

B

- Divide the class into groups of three or four, and appoint a leader for each group. Allocate a situation to each group.
- When it's clear what students have to do, the brainstorming sessions can begin.
- Circulate and monitor, but do not interrupt the flow of the brainstorming. Note language points for praise and correction, especially brainstorming-type language.
- Praise good language points from the discussion and work on three or four points that need improvement, getting individual students to say the correct forms.
- Ask representatives (not necessarily the most talkative members) of the different groups for a brief summary of their brainstorming discussions and conclusions.

Unit 3 Building relationships

Networking

A

- Remind students about the language of networking on page 27 of the Course Book.
- Divide the class into pairs. Cut up, shuffle and hand out the 'turns' to each pair. Obviously, be careful not to mix the different sets of turns, as this could lead to some surreal conversations!
- Get the pairs to piece together the conversation in parallel. Get students to concentrate on looking for clues in the logic of the conversation.
- You can hand out a complete conversation as printed in this book as a key and get students to read it in parallel pairs. Go round the class and assist with intonation, etc. where necessary.
- Ask for a performance of the conversation from one of the pairs for the whole class.

B

- Divide the class into pairs, give them time to absorb the information and get them to enact the conversation. Students could sit back-to-back.
- Circulate, monitor and assist with natural expression and intonation.
- Praise good language points from the role play and work on three or four points that need improvement, getting individual students to say the correct forms.
- Ask for a performance of the conversation from one of the pairs for the whole class.

C

- Divide the class into pairs and get them to rehearse the conversation.
- Circulate, monitor and assist with natural expression and intonation of the kind you hear between people who have just met.
- Praise good language points from the role play and work on three or four points that need improvement, getting individual students to say the correct forms.
- Ask for a performance of the conversation from one of the pairs for the whole class.

Unit 4 Success
Negotiating

 A

- Get students to look again at the expressions on page 41 of the Course Book, then do this exercise as a quick-fire whole-class activity.

> **1** b, e, h   **2** a, c, g   **3** d, f

B

- Divide the class into groups of four or six, each with two or three students on each side of the negotiation.
- Cut up and hand out the relevant role cards and give students a few minutes to study them.
- Explain the situation to the whole class, and that the points system is meant to represent the priorities of each side.
- Explain that each side will give reasons for its demands. For example, local government representatives might say that they prefer a new tram route to the airport, rather than a new road, for environmental reasons.
- When everyone is clear about the situation, the role play can begin. Circulate and monitor. Note language points for praise and correction, especially negotiation language.
- When the groups have reached a conclusion, bring the class to order and praise good language points from the role play and work on three or four points that need improvement, getting individual students to say the correct forms.
- Then ask a representative from each group for an account of what happened, and the final score. Compare and contrast the discussions and scores from each group.

Unit 5 Job satisfaction
Cold-calling

A

- Point out the connection with the expressions on page 49 of the Course Book.
- Ask students to do the exercise individually or in pairs.
- Check the answers with the whole class, discussing any difficulties.

> **1** David Rimini suggested <u>that</u> I call you.
> **2** They are <u>offering</u> a top salary and <u>great</u> benefits.
> **3** Why don't we <u>get together</u> to discuss their offer?
> **4** There's another thing you should <u>bear in</u> mind …
> **5** You can <u>look at</u> this in another way.
> **6** I <u>take your</u> point, but I'm happy with my current job.
> **7** Perhaps we should <u>discuss</u> this face-to-face?
> **8** Can you <u>give</u> me some more <u>details</u>?

B

- Divide the class into pairs. Cut up, shuffle and hand out the 'turns' to each pair. Be careful not to mix the different sets of turns.
- Get the pairs to piece together the conversation in parallel. Get students to concentrate on looking for clues in the logic of the conversation.
- You can hand out a complete conversation as printed in this book as a key and get students to read it in parallel pairs. Go round the class and assist with intonation, etc. where necessary.
- Ask for a performance of the conversation from one of the pairs for the whole class.

Unit 6 Risk
Reaching agreement

A

- Remind students about the expressions on page 57 of the Course Book then ask them to do the exercise individually or in pairs. Circulate and assist where necessary.
- Then check the answers with the whole class.

> **1** How do you feel ~~for~~ about this quality issue?
> **2** I can't see ~~into~~ what the problem is with quantities.
> **3** I think I ~~am~~ agree with you there on the need for better communication between us.
> **4** I couldn't ~~be~~ agree with you more that the key to reaching a deal is price.
> **5** I can't go along ~~on~~ with that – your demands are getting unrealistic!
> **6** We can consider paying more ~~for~~ as long as we get a commitment from you on early delivery.
> **7** How about ~~to~~ taking a break so we can each consider our position?
> **8** I don't want to repeat ~~again~~ myself, but we do want to do business with you.
> **9** So, we've agreed ~~for~~ that the contract will come into force on 1st January.
> **10** OK, let me ~~to~~ recap the key points of our discussion.

B

- Divide the class into groups of four: two buyers and two suppliers in each group.
- Explain the basic situation. The idea here is that students concentrate on clarification in a negotiation, rather than the other stages. The activity is an information exchange to clear up misunderstandings about what has been decided. Get the chief buyer in each group to start by saying:
  – 'Let's just run over what's been agreed'.
  Point out expressions for correcting, such as:
  – I don't think that's what we decided.
  – There's some sort of mistake there, surely, etc.

- When the situation is clear, the parallel clarification sessions can begin.
- Circulate and monitor. Note language points for praise and correction, especially in relation to the language of checking and clarification. Also, be strict with students saying numbers correctly. Work too on the stress and intonation of exchanges such as:
  – 'So we agree that we'll buy 25 Midijets at 40 million dollars each?'
  – 'No, it was 32 Midijets at 47 million dollars each.'
- Bring the class to order. Praise good language points from the role play and work on three or four points that need improvement, getting individual students to say the correct forms.

Unit 7 Management styles

Presentations

A

- Get students to work on answers individually or in pairs.
- Go round the class and assist where necessary.
- Go through the answers with the whole class.

> **1**e **2**b **3**c **4**h **5**f **6**d **7**g **8**a

B

- Divide the class into groups of three or four. In their presentation extracts, students can talk about subjects that they have already used in any earlier presentations they have given. The idea here is to concentrate on the key expressions.
- Get students to write out notes for their presentation extract integrating the expressions they are going to use. Circulate, monitor and assist. With weaker groups, it's probably a good idea to ask them exactly which expressions they are going to use and make sure they have them right.
- Students should also prepare one or two slides. If there is a computer and dataprojector in the room, you can get students to use PowerPoint. If there is an overhead projector, you could hand out transparencies and pens to the students.
- Give students time to practise giving their presentation extracts individually, based on their notes. Circulate and help with natural delivery. Don't tell them yet which member of each group is going to give the presentation.
- With the whole class, get individual students to come to the front and give their presentation extracts.
- The rest of the class has to spot and note down when the key expressions are used, and which heading they come under.
- After each presentation extract, get class members to say what the expressions were and which headings they come under.
- Keep the pace moving. If you have a very large class, get some students to give their presentation extracts now, and other students in later sessions.

Unit 8 Team building

Resolving conflict

A

- Draw students' attention to the link between these expressions and those on page 79 of the Course Book.
- Ask them to put the new expressions under the same headings.

> **1**c **2**g **3**b **4**h **5**f **6**a **7**e **8**d

B

- This is a whole-class activity role-playing a company meeting. The purpose of the meeting is to discuss proposed cost-cutting measures.
- Appoint two or three students as senior managers for Fun Bikes – they should come to sit at the front of the class to run the meeting.
- Before the class, make enough copies of the employees' role cards. (For example, if you have a class of eleven, you will have three managers and two each of employee A, two of employee B, two of employee C and two of employee D. There are no specific cards for the managers.)
- Give students the time to absorb the information. Go round and assist where necessary. Appoint one of the managers to lead the meeting, but tell the other two that they will also have to contribute to defend the company's plans.
- When students are ready, the role play can begin. Monitor the discussion. Note language points for praise and correction, especially in relation to language for resolving conflict.
- Bring the class to order. Praise good language points from the role play and work on three or four points that need improvement, getting individual students to say the correct forms.

Unit 9 Raising Finance

Negotiating

 A

- Point out the connection with the expressions on page 87 of the Course Book.
- Ask students to do the exercise individually or in pairs.
- Check the answers with the whole class, working on any difficulties.

1 Let's go over ~~on~~ what we've decided up till now.

2 Would it ~~to~~ be possible to outline your exact plans?

3 Do you have a plan B ~~on~~ if these negotiations were to collapse?

4 There are strict government rules on takeovers, so I'm afraid ~~of~~ that option is ruled out.

5 We want to ask ~~to~~ you something. If you do take us over, can you give guarantees on employment?

6 If your shareholders refuse ~~out~~ our offer we'll see what we can do to increase it.

7 What about ~~for~~ this? If you promise to keep the plants open, we will accept your offer.

B

- Explain the situation and divide the class into groups of four: two GFI executives and two Bradbury executives.
- Give students copies of the information for their side of the negotiation. Point out that the idea here is not to have a complete negotiation, but to apply the language seen above in A and in the Skills section of the Course Book, following the stages separated by continuous lines. (Explain 'deal-breaker' if necessary.)
- When the situation is clear, the role play can begin.
- Circulate and monitor, paying particular attention to the language relating to this unit. Note language points for praise and correction.
- With the whole class, praise good language points from the role play and work on three or four points that need improvement, getting individual students to say the correct forms.
- If there is time, reverse the roles and do the activity again, getting students to integrate corrections and improvements from the first run-through.

Unit 10 Customer service

Active listening

A

- Relate this to the expressions on page 101 of the Course Book.
- Get students to do the exercise individually or in pairs.
- With the whole class ask individual students for the answers.

1 Let's hear <u>the</u> complete version of events.

2 How terrible <u>to</u> think that they reacted like that!

3 How <u>did</u> you deal with the situation – the one that happened last week?

4 <u>Have</u> I got this correct – the cashier just ignored you?

5 So what you're really unhappy <u>about</u> is that you don't feel valued as a customer?

6 We believe customers should expect not just <u>to</u> be satisfied, but delighted. Do you?

7 What exactly do you <u>mean</u> by the expression 'customer orientation'?

8 Can <u>you</u> say more about that?

B

- Go through the situation with the whole class and explain it. In each group, one student will be a market researcher. There are two customers, and the fourth student is an observer, who will note down the language used by the interviewer and the customers in the interview, especially in relation to techniques for active listening.
- When the situation is clear for everyone, divide the class into groups of four and allocate the roles.
- When students have studied their role cards, the role play can begin in the parallel groups.
- Circulate and monitor, but do not pre-empt the task of the observer, who should be noting the stages in the interview and the language being used.
- When the interviews are over, ask the observer from each group to give an account of what happened and the language used.
- Praise good language points from the role play and work on three or four points that need improvement, getting individual students to say the correct forms.

Unit 11 Crisis management
Asking and answering difficult questions

A

- Relate this to the language for asking and answering difficult questions on page 109 of the Course Book.
- Get students to do the exercise individually or in pairs.
- With the whole class ask students for the answers.

1g 2d 3a 4h 5f 6e 7b 8c

B

- Tell students that the questions in A anticipated this discussion. Read the background with the whole class.
- Divide the class into groups of four or five. In each group, two students represent Taocars, and there is a journalist from each newspaper. Hand out the relevant role cards.
- Point out that in this discussion, the Taocars company managers are very defensive, trying to minimise the problem. The journalists are very persistent.
- When students have absorbed all the necessary information, the role play can begin.
- Circulate and monitor. Note language points for praise and correction, especially in relation to asking and answering difficult questions.
- Praise good language points from the role play and work on three or four points that need improvement, getting individual students to say the correct forms.

Unit 12 Mergers and acquisitions
Making a presentation

A

- Make the link with the Skills section on page 117 of the Course Book.
- Ask students to do the exercise individually or in pairs.
- Circulate and monitor.
- With the whole class, ask for the answers and explain any difficulties.

1 Futurology is concerned with three things: scenarios that are certain ~~up~~ to happen, scenarios that are probable and scenarios that are unlikely.

2 Firstly we'll look at some of the probable trends over the next century, then we'll look at their social implications, and finally at their implications for business. ✓

3 What are the key issues facing ~~the~~ humanity in the next 100 years?

4 As I said at the beginning ~~to~~ of my presentation, forecasting is difficult.

5 Of course, a three-metre rise in sea levels would ~~in~~ be catastrophic.

6 As one politician said, society must have a sharp focus on its key priorities: education, education, education. ✓

7 Let's look at one illustration ~~out~~ of this future trend: in fact, it's one that is already happening.

8 Are there any ~~of~~ questions?

B

- The idea here is for students to put into practice the language for ordering, referring back, etc. The points on different future trends have been provided as subject matter in which they can use the key language, but they are free to use other ideas.
- Hand out a subject card to each student. Emphasise to students that the points are suggestions, and that they should feel free to mention others.
- Allow time for students to prepare their presentation, concentrating on the language for the particular functions practised in part A.
- If short of time, tell students that they won't have to make the complete presentation, just be ready to illustrate the key phrases in context.
- Ask individual students to come to the front of the class and give their presentations, where necessary 'fast-forwarding' to the next point where they use a key expression. Ask them to outline quickly what they would be saying between the key expressions.
- Note language points for praise and correction, especially in relation to the language of presentations.
- Praise good language points from the presentations and work on three or four points that need improvement, getting individual students to say the correct forms.

UNIT 1 Communication

DEALING WITH COMMUNICATION BREAKDOWN

A Look again at the expressions for problem solving on page 11 of the Course Book. For each category 1–7, there is a new expression in a–g. Match each expression to its category.

1 Asking for repetition
2 Asking for clarification
3 Checking information
4 Problems with understanding
5 Asking for further information
6 Technical problems
7 Summarising the call

a) Sorry, you've lost me.
b) I didn't (quite) catch that.
c) You'rea up – I can't hear you very well.
d) Just to recap ...
e) Could you elaborate on that, please?
f) What do the letters ABS stand for?
g) So, to double-check ...

B Work in pairs on these phone calls.

Phone call 1

A You work as a regulator for the Bank Regulation Board (BRB). You phone the credit card division at the National Credit Bank (NCB) about regulations that you think the bank has not been observing in relation to the credit cards that it issues.

You think that the bank is breaking the rules for credit cards in these ways:

- Interest rate: max. 19 per cent per year – NCB charges 23 per cent
- Late payment fee: max. €20 – NCB charges €25
- Credit card cheques (where you write a cheque and the money is put on a credit card) should not be sent to people who have not asked for them; NCB regularly sends out cheques in mailings to all its cardholders
- Age limit: No cards to be issued to people under 20; NCB issues to those 18 and over

B You work for the National Credit Bank (NCB). You get a call from someone who works at the Bank Regulation Board (BRB).

- Note down the problems that the BRB regulator mentions.
- Say that you will check the situation with your manager, the head of the credit card division at NCB.
- Say you will phone back later when you've found out about the situation.

Phone call 2

A
- B phones you back.
- Note down B's explanations for each of the four points that you raised.
- Say if you agree to the solutions offered. (You are happy with B's explanations in relation to all points except the Late payment fee – you know the legal limit is €20 and you ask B to talk to their boss about this again.)

B
- You phone A back.
- Explain that you have spoken to your manager about the issues that A raised in the first phone call.
- Interest rate: Last month, the rate that NCB charges was changed from 23 per cent to 18.9 per cent, so this is now within the law.
- Late payment fee: Your boss's understanding is that the maximum legal limit is €25 and NCB will continue to charge this.
- Credit card cheques: NCB agrees to stop sending these to people who have not asked for them.
- Age limit: NCB will raise the age limit to 20.

RESOURCE BANK – Speaking

International marketing

BRAINSTORMING

A   Look again at the Useful language on page 19 of the Course Book. Then correct these expressions.

1   The purport of the meeting this afternoon is to ...
2   That we need to achieve today is to ...
3   Our object here is to ...
4   I suggest we to brainstorm the problem.
5   That's greatly!
6   That's the better idea I've heard for a long time.
7   Don't keep back.
8   Say however comes to mind.
9   At this stadium, we want all your ideas ...
10   You're absolute right because ...

B   Hold brainstorming meetings about these situations.

1   The lease on your company's headquarters in the city centre is ending and the firm must vacate the building. 80 managers and employees work there. Brainstorm a) the possible new locations for it and b) solutions which would not require an HQ building at all.

2   Your company has developed a new electric car that can go much further without recharging the batteries than existing models. Brainstorm an advertising campaign for the car.

3   A national sports team from your country (choose the sport) has, yet again, just done very badly at the world championships. Brainstorm ideas for changes to the way the sport is managed and organised.

4   The percentage of rubbish and unwanted goods sent for recycling in your country (paper, plastic, electrical goods) is much lower than in neighbouring countries. Brainstorm ways to increase this percentage.

5   The chief executive of your company is leaving after 10 years of excellent performance and results. You and your fellow directors at the company brainstorm unusual ideas to mark his/her retirement.

Building relationships

NETWORKING

A Look again at the useful language for networking on page 27 of the Course Book and rearrange the 'turns' that your teacher will give you into a logical conversation that takes place at a networking event.

DR: Hello. Haven't we met somewhere before? I'm David Rimini.

FD: Oh, hello. Yes, I think we met at that awful presentation at the conference in Singapore last year – we both left the room at the same time.

DR: Ah yes, that presentation – what a disaster! How could I forget?

FD: We had a coffee afterwards and I seem to remember we're in the same line of business.

DR: Yes, didn't you say you were in brand development, like me? But I'm sorry I can't remember your name.

FD: François Duval. I work on brand development on social networking sites in Canada.

DR: Right – I remember now. That's a coincidence – I have a colleague who was in New York but who's just moved to Toronto to start her own brand consultancy there, concentrating on Canadian brands.

FD: Toronto?

DR: Yes. She might be in need of some local expertise. Perhaps you'd be interested. Why don't you give her a call?

FD: Have you got her phone number by any chance?

DR: Yes, her name's Laura Brenton and I've got her number here somewhere on my mobile – ah yes, here it is – here, on the screen.

FD: I'll copy it down if that's OK.

DR: Yes, go ahead.

FD: Can I mention your name when I call her?

DR: Yes, of course. You might be able to do business together.

RESOURCE BANK – Speaking

NETWORKING

B This conversation takes place soon after the one above in A. Student A is François Duval. Student B is Laura Brenton. Student A phones Student B.

François

Phone Laura and say that David Rimini gave you her number.

Show interest and ask how long ago Laura opened her consultancy in Toronto.

Ask Laura how her new business is going.

Offer to go to see her at her office in Toronto. Suggest a time for a meeting next week.

Confirm the details and say goodbye.

Laura

Respond suitably and say that you worked with David for 10 years at a brand development agency in New York, and that you both specialised recently in brand development on social networking sites.

Reply (you've been in Toronto three months) and say that you are originally from there and wanted to move back to your home city.

Say that it's going well, but that you need someone with local knowledge and contacts – you have lost touch with your home country.

Accept the suggestion or suggest a different time.

C This is the conversation that takes place when Laura Brenton and François Duval meet.

Laura

Greet François at reception and say that you will go to your office. Ask if he found the address OK.

Say that you had it designed by a top designer.

Ask if François would like some coffee, tea or juice.

Mention your mutual contact, David Rimini.

François

Say hello, and say that it was no problem to find the address. Compliment Laura on the design of her office.

Show interest.

Respond appropriately.

Talk about the two occasions you met him. Then tactfully change the subject to ask how you might be able to help Laura develop her new consultancy.

NEGOTIATING

A Look at the expressions for 1) bargaining, 2) checking understanding and 3) signalling on page 41 of the Course Book. Then put each of the expressions a–h under the correct heading.

a) Sorry, could you repeat that please?

b) If you can provide faster delivery, we might be prepared to pay more.

c) I just want to check something – you did say 10 per cent discount for orders over 100,000 units?

d) How about taking a break so that each side can consider its position?

e) If we added more features to the product for the same price, would that make it more affordable?

f) I think we're getting off the point by talking about these minor details.

g) If I understand correctly, the goods won't be ready on time.

h) If you can make just one last small concession, I think we'll have a deal.

B A city's airport has been expanding. The local government authority is concerned about the nuisance already caused and potential future developments – the increase in aircraft noise, road traffic, etc. The airport's managers meet local government representatives to discuss the concerns.

Airport managers

You want the airport to expand as fast as possible. You must gain as many points as possible when reaching agreement on these issues.

- Number of night flights
  Future 50 per cent increase: +50 points
  Increase of 25 per cent: +25 points
  No change: 0 points
  Decrease of 25 per cent: -25 points
  Decrease of 50 per cent: -50 points

- Approval for new direct gangways to planes
  10 gangways or more: +30 points
  5-9 gangways: +15 points
  1-4 gangways: 0 points

- Access to airport
  New road: +25 points
  New tram route: -25 points

- Construction of new car park
  Approval: +50 points
  Refusal: -50 points

- Construction of new runway
  Approval: +100 points
  Refusal: -100 points

Local government representatives

You want to stimulate the local economy but you don't want the environmental 'price' to be too high. You must gain as many points as possible when reaching agreement on these issues.

- Number of night flights
  Future 50 per cent increase: -50 points
  Increase of 25 per cent: -25 points
  No change: 0 points
  Decrease of 25 per cent: +25 points
  Decrease of 50 per cent: +50 points

- Approval for new direct gangways to planes
  10 gangways or more: -30 points
  5-9 gangways: -15 points
  1-4 gangways: 0 points

- Access to airport
  New road: -25 points
  New tram route: +25 points

- Construction of new car park
  Approval: -50 points
  Refusal: +50 points

- Construction of new runway
  Approval: -100 points
  Refusal: +100 points

RESOURCE BANK – Speaking

Job satisfaction

COLD-CALLING

A   Look again at the expressions for cold-calling on page 49 of the Course Book. There are two wrong words or word forms in each of the utterances 1–8. Cross them out and write the correct words.

1   David Rimini suggested me to call you.

2   They are proposing a top salary and important benefits.

3   Why don't we going jointly to discuss their offer?

4   There's another thing you should carry to mind …

5   You can see on this in another way.

6   I receive the point, but I'm happy with my current job.

7   Perhaps we should discussing this face on face?

8   Can you hand me some more precisions?

B   Work in pairs. Rearrange the 'turns' that your teacher will give you into a cold-call conversation between Birgit Mueller, a headhunter, and Zuzanna Winograd, an executive in a medical equipment company.

BM:	Can I speak to Zuzanna Winograd, please.
ZW:	Speaking.
BM:	Hello. My name's Birgit Mueller. I work for PEER – Pan European Executive Recruitment. We're based in Munich, but we recruit senior executives from all over Europe. I was given your name by an ex-colleague of yours, Rajmund Sikorsky.
ZW:	Who? I don't know anyone of that name.
BM:	He told me that you worked together the 1980s. He spoke very highly of you.
ZW:	Oh right, Rajmund – I remember now. I haven't seen him for 25 years. Those were the days! Where is he now?
BM:	He's working for a company called Besser Elektronik in Germany, for their medical equipment division. They're looking for someone to head up their new central European manufacturing operation in Lodz, Poland.
ZW:	Aha …
BM:	Rajmund suggested that I call you to – this is all very confidential of course – to see if you would be interested in the job.
ZW:	I'm very happy with what I'm doing now. We're not the biggest manufacturers of medical equipment in the world, but all my family are here in Warsaw. I don't know if I want to move to Lodz.
BM:	People often tell me that they don't want to move, but BE are offering a top salary.
ZW:	How much?
BM:	Well into six figures. We're talking euros here, of course.
ZW:	Six figures! Perhaps we should discuss this face-to-face …

UNIT 6 Risk

REACHING AGREEMENT

A Look at the useful expressions for reaching agreement on page 57 of the Course Book. Cross out the extra, unnecessary word in each of the expressions 1–10.

1 How do you feel for about this quality issue?

2 I can't see into what the problem is with quantities.

3 I think I am agree with you there on the need for better communication between us.

4 I couldn't be agree with you more that the key to reaching a deal is price.

5 I can't go along on with that – your demands are getting unrealistic!

6 We can consider paying more for as long as we get a commitment from you on early delivery.

7 How about to taking a break so we can each consider our position?

8 I don't want to repeat again myself, but we do want to do business with you.

9 So, we've agreed for that the contract will come into force on 1st January.

10 OK, let me to recap the key points of our discussion.

B Buyers for a Chinese airline are negotiating with Brazilian aircraft manufacturers. They have been negotiating for a week. The chief buyer for the airline thinks they have reached agreement and summarises what he/she thinks has been agreed. The suppliers disagree and indicate this politely. Enact the exchanges in pairs.

Prices are given in US dollars, but the actual currency of payment is to be negotiated.

Buyers (airline)
You think you have agreed the following:
- Maxijets: 10 @ $60 million each
- Midijets: 25 @ $40 million each
- Commuter planes: 40 @ $25 million each
- Delivery: 25 per cent each year over the next four years for all planes
- Payment: 10 per cent of total order up front; then three payments of 30 per cent two, four and six months respectively after each delivery
- Currency of payment: Chinese yuan

Suppliers (aircraft manufacturers)
You think you have agreed the following:
- Maxijets: 15 @ $65 million each
- Midijets: 32 @ $47 million each
- Commuter planes: 48 @ $27.5 million each
- Delivery: 25 per cent each year over the next four years for Maxijets; 20 per cent per year over the next five years for the other two models
- Payment: 25 per cent of total order up front; then three payments of 25 per cent one, two and three months respectively after each delivery
- Currency of payment: Brazilian reais

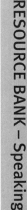

RESOURCE BANK – Speaking

PHOTOCOPIABLE © Pearson Education Limited 2011

Management styles

PRESENTATIONS

A Look at the presentations language on page 71 of the Course Book. Put each of the expressions 1–8 under one of the headings used there, a–h.

a) Stating the purpose

b) Involving the audience

c) Persuading

d) Changing the subject

e) Referring to visuals

f) Emphasising

g) Discussing implications

h) Exemplifying

1 Have a look at these maps showing the extent of polar ice – the one on the left in 1980 and on the right, in 2010.

2 I'm sure you've all noticed how much more extreme the weather has become over the last few years.

3 If you have any doubts about man's contribution to global warming, I think this slide will convince you.

4 Just one example of rising sea levels will suffice: in Bangladesh, there are places that were on the coast that are now three metres underwater.

5 Let me just underline again how serious the problem of global warming is.

6 OK, let's turn now to the problem of aircraft emissions.

7 The long-term outcome of the industrial revolution is a temperature increase in the atmosphere of at least three degrees.

8 Today I'm going to present the evidence that global warming is caused by human activity.

B Work in small groups. You will prepare a short extract of a presentation on a subject of your choice that one of you will then deliver.

- In giving the presentation extract, you will have to use four expressions – one each from four of the categories a–h above.

- Decide together which four expressions you are going to use (not necessarily exactly the ones that are above or in the Course Book). Prepare your extract and slides around these expressions. Your teacher will help with this.

- When you are ready, your teacher will tell you which person in each group is going to give the presentation.

- Other members of the class have to spot when the presenter uses each of the four expressions and state which heading it comes under.

RESOLVING CONFLICT

A Look again at the expressions for resolving conflict on page 79 of the Course Book.
Then put each of the expressions below 1–8 under one of the headings a–h.

a) Expressing your feelings	b) Making suggestions	c) Expressing satisfaction	d) Expressing dissatisfaction
e) Showing sympathy	f) Identifying the real problem	g) Resolving the conflict	h) Reviewing the situation

1 Yes, that's a brilliant idea.

2 What do you think would be the best way of going about this?

3 One idea might be to evaluate the cost savings objectively.

4 Let's wait six months and have a look at the situation again then.

5 Is this the real issue – the reduction in team-building activities?

6 I'm particularly upset about the closure of this service.

7 I can see how you must feel about the company restaurant, but we have no choice.

8 Getting rid of the annual bonus is a big mistake.

B After two years of disappointing profits, the management at Fun Bikes Ltd., a mountain bike distributor, wants to abolish a number of employee perks as part of a cost-cutting programme. You will role-play a company meeting to discuss the proposals.

- Close company crèche – employees will have to leave their children at commercial crèches
- Stop giving staff their annual Christmas bonus, equivalent to one month's salary
- End subsidy on company restaurant meals – restaurant to remain open and employees to buy meals at full cost
- End subsidy (30 per cent off usual retail price) for employees buying the company's products
- Reduce the number of 'away days' – team-building activity days out – from three to one a year
- Abolish the company bus service from the city centre to the business park where the company is situated – employees will have to use their own transport

Employee A
- You live a long way from the company – you don't have your own transport.
- You never go on the company team-building away days – you always find an excuse not to go.
- You don't have children.

Employee B
- You use the company restaurant every lunchtime – there is nowhere else to eat in the business park. You do not want to pay the full cost of meals.
- You do not have children – crèche and ending of subsidy on buying the company's products not a problem.

Employee C
- You have three very young children, all currently in the company crèche.
- You will miss the annual bonus.
- You buy a lot of the company's products for yourself and to resell to your friends.
- You don't use the company bus service – you cycle everywhere.

Employee D
- You are very sociable – the company away days are the high points of your year.
- You don't have children and you cycle to work.
- You usually bring your own sandwiches for lunch, but eat in the company restaurant on Fridays.
- You have no particular opinion about the subsidy on the company's products.

RESOURCE BANK – Speaking

NEGOTIATING

A Look again at the negotiations language on page 87 of the Course Book. There is one word too many in each of the expressions 1–7. Cross out the extra word in each expression.

1 Let's go over on what we've decided up till now.

2 Would it to be possible to outline your exact plans?

3 Do you have a plan B on if these negotiations were to collapse?

4 There are strict government rules on takeovers, so I'm afraid of that option is ruled out.

5 We want to ask to you something. If you do take us over, can you give guarantees on employment?

6 If your shareholders refuse out our offer, we'll see what we can do to increase it.

7 What about for this? If you promise to keep the plants open, we will accept your offer.

B The above expressions come from a negotiation between Global Foods, a US conglomerate, and Bradbury, a UK confectionery company (making chocolates, ice cream, etc.). Role-play part of these negotiations, following the instructions for each side.

Global Foods Inc. (GFI)	Bradbury Chocolate Co.
Summarise the situation so far: • GFI will make an offer of $55 per share for Bradbury. • GFI will guarantee 2,000 jobs at Bradbury's main plant. • Key issues remaining: jobs at other two UK plants (employing 1,500 people).	• Agree that summary is correct. • Argue that $55 per share offer is too low. • Say also that the company is looking for guarantees on jobs at all three plants.
• Say that you will come back to the issue of other plants later. • You may want to move some, but not all, production to plants in central Europe (e.g. plants you already own in Hungary, where labour costs are 60 per cent lower than in the UK).	• Say that you want answers on job losses soon.
• Say that you envisage long-term commitment in the UK, even if some production is moved abroad.	• Ask if GFI have considered the affection that UK public have for Bradbury products and potential anger if production is moved abroad.
• Avoid answering question directly – say all options are open, but decisions will be made according to strict business considerations.	• Repeat in a firm but friendly way that moving production abroad could be a deal-breaker for shareholders considering GFI's offer.

UNIT 10 Customer service

ACTIVE LISTENING

A Look at the useful language relating to active listening on page 101 of the Course Book. Then look at the expressions below and find the one word that is missing from each.

1 Let's hear complete version of events.
2 How terrible think that they reacted like that!
3 How you deal with the situation – the one that happened last week?
4 I got this correct – the cashier just ignored you?
5 So what you're really unhappy is that you don't feel valued as a customer?
6 We believe customers should expect not just be satisfied, but delighted. Do you?
7 What exactly do you by the expression 'customer orientation'?
8 Can say more about that?

B Work in groups of four. A market researcher is having a panel discussion with two customers who have recently opened business accounts at Natbank. The fourth student is an observer. Role play the discussion using the role cards that your teacher will give you. The observer notes down what happens in the discussion, especially in relation to techniques for active listening.

Market researcher

You want to find out about:

- Friendliness/efficiency/ professionalism of the account manager
- Ease of opening the account and speed/efficiency with which this was done. Accuracy of spelling of names and addresses, etc.? Mistakes?
- Level of overdraft allowed: sufficient?
- Statements (list of transactions received regularly by post or accessible online): accurate? Clear?
- Credit cards: spending limit high enough? Interest rate acceptable?
- Internet banking: ease and speed with which access to accounts was set up
- The overall 'customer experience'

Customer A

- The account manager was young and dynamic.
- You were able to open the account easily, with a minimum of fuss – there were no mistakes made.
- You were given a €10,000 overdraft facility, and this is more than enough for your purposes.
- The statements (list of transactions received regularly by post or accessible online) that you receive are accurate and clear.
- The account manager asked if you wanted a credit card, but at the time you said you wouldn't need one. You've now changed your mind and want to know how to apply for one.
- Internet banking was easy to set up.
- Overall, you are very satisfied with Natbank.

Customer B

- The account manager was OK but he called you by your first name, which you didn't like.
- The account was opened quickly, but there were spelling mistakes in your name and the name of the company – point out what these were.
- The overdraft limit was set at €1,000, which you think is very low for a business.
- The statements (list of transactions received regularly by post or accessible online) are confusing and arrive late.
- The credit card rate is very high (24.9%) and you think the bank is profiteering. You have decided not to use the card.
- You think that the Internet banking site is confusing. Payments into it do not appear until at least three days after they have been sent.
- Overall, you are not very satisfied with Natbank and are thinking of moving your account.

RESOURCE BANK – Speaking

185

Crisis management

ASKING AND ANSWERING DIFFICULT QUESTIONS

A   Look at the useful expressions on page 109 of the Course Book. Then match the two parts of these expressions.

1 Would you mind answering	**a)** your customers' safety, only your shareholders?
2 May I ask why the company	**b)** tests that you have been undertaking?
3 Isn't it true that you don't care for	**c)** not be paying compensation?
4 I would be interested in knowing what	**d)** did not react more quickly?
5 Do you deny that there	**e)** many cars are affected?
6 Could you tell us how	**f)** is a serious threat to public safety?
7 Could you clarify the results of the technical	**g)** the question? What is your policy on a general recall?
8 Are you saying that you will	**h)** Taocars has done to investigate the problem.

B   Role-play the television discussion programme where the above questions were asked. Students in Group A are senior managers at Taocars, a car company. Students in Group B are journalists and specialists.

Taocars has had to recall 100,000 cars because the brakes can suddenly fail. There have been dozens of reports of drivers not being able to stop – they put their foot on the brake and nothing happens.

Taocars managers

- You have investigated the problem and you maintain that it is limited – only half a dozen cars have been affected, and there have been no accidents.
- The fault is somewhere in the brake fluid system, which might develop a sudden leak, but this is a very rare fault.
- You maintain that only the half-dozen owners who have been affected will receive any compensation.
- You have decided to stonewall, in other words, to resist all attempts to make you admit that the problem is more widespread, or to compensate other owners.
- You do not plan a general recall of the model.

Chief presenter, _Geartrend_, a specialist TV programme on cars and driving

- Your impression is that the problem is much more widespread than Taocars admits.
- You have organised a survey on the programme's website, and 15,322 owners have said that they have had braking problems, causing 598 crashes – fortunately without fatalities or injuries, but the potential for disaster is there.

Journalist, _Quality Car_ magazine

- Laboratory tests have shown that there is a serious design fault in the braking system, which Taocars is aware of, but refuses to admit or discuss.
- You think there should be a general recall of the model.

Journalist, _Brake Systems International_ magazine

- You are a specialist in braking systems and you have personally dismantled one of the Taocar models to inspect the braking system.
- You are sure there is a serious problem and you think the model should be recalled.

© Pearson Education Limited 2011 **PHOTOCOPIABLE**

MAKING A PRESENTATION

A A futurologist is giving a presentation. In most of these extracts from the talk there is one extra word that does not fit. Cross out this word. Some of the extracts, however, are correct. If an extract is correct, put a tick (✓) against it.

1 Futurology is concerned with three things: scenarios that are certain up to happen, scenarios that are probable and scenarios that are unlikely.

2 Firstly we'll look at some of the probable trends over the next century, then we'll look at their social implications, and finally at their implications for business.

3 What are the key issues facing the humanity in the next 100 years?

4 As I said at the beginning to of my presentation, forecasting is difficult.

5 Of course, a three-metre rise in sea levels would in be catastrophic.

6 As one politician said, society must have a sharp focus on its key priorities: education, education, education.

7 Let's look at one illustration out of this future trend: in fact, it's one that is already happening.

8 Are there any of questions?

B You are a futurologist talking about what you think is going to happen in the future in a particular area. Some key ideas are given to help you, but you can mention others.

Climate change
- The degree of certainty (or uncertainty) that it is happening
- The effects of warmer temperatures
- The effects of rising sea levels
- The outcome in relation to cities
- How agriculture will evolve in different parts of the world

Consumer behaviour
- Explain how the Internet allows access to information that can influence large purchases (users' blogs, customer surveys, etc.).
- Say how this gives more power to consumers.
- Imagine future developments in this area (video discussions between users via the Internet, discussion between consumers and companies' marketers, etc.).

Education
- The place of the Internet and other technologies
- The relationship of teachers to technology. Will classrooms and teachers disappear?
- No more need for 'rote learning' (learning by heart) as everything available immediately online?
- In the longer term, brain implants for specific areas of knowledge, e.g. languages?

Leisure
- Will all leisure become 'virtual'? Will 'electronic' activities – video games, Wii, etc. become dominant? If not, why not? What indoor and outdoor activities will develop in particular?
- Will physical presence be needed to experience events like rock concerts, sports events, etc.?
- How will socialising and human interaction look 100 years from now? Will people still meet face-to-face?

RESOURCE BANK – Speaking

Communication

ALASTAIR DRYBURGH, HEAD OF AKENHURST CONSULTANTS

A 🔊 CD1.2 **Listen to this extract from part one of the interview and replace the seven mistakes in the transcript below with what Alastair Dryburgh actually says.**

I think the thing to remember is, the rules of communication haven't changed and I don't think there's anything included in technology that makes good communication easier. It can make it better but there are also many ways it can make it worse. So, I think there's four things that you need to bear in mind.

The first thing is that you've got to remember, people have limited capacity – if you like, limited bandwidth – which puts the burden on you as the communicator to think hard about what it is exactly you're attempting to communicate and make sure that you get it down as precisely as possible.

B 🔊 CD1.2 **Listen to the rest of part one. Find expressions to complete these statements.**

If a presenter …
1   gives too much information, they ………. ………. ………. of data on people.
2   has 41 slides, they shouldn't try to ………. ………. them all in 30 minutes.
3   puts too much information on slides, they are too ………..
4   reduces the information into a few key points, they ………. ………. ………. into a small number of points.
5   wants communication to be effective, there's got to be ………. ………. ………. ……….
     ………. in it.
6   uses technological tools, these tools could ………. ………. ………. ………..

C 🔊 CD1.3 **Listen to part two of the interview. Put these points into the order that you hear them.**

Amazon …
a) confirms your order.
b) is excellent.
c) has very good technology.
d) suggests things based on what you've bought in the past.
e) recommends books that you haven't heard of.
f) confirms when an order has been sent.
g) makes recommendations based on what you've looked at before.

D 🔊 CD1.4 **Listen to part three and find nouns that refer to the following:**

1   a system of recorded announcements (9 letters)
2   a system of paths where you easily get lost (4 letters)
3   a choice (6 letters)
4   a person (5 letters, 5 letters)
5   the importance given to something (8 letters)
6   how well and quickly something works (10 letters)

International marketing

A 🔊 CD1.9 **Listen to part one of the interview and match the verbs with the
expressions that follow them.**

1	adapt	**a)**	all over in the same format
2	market	**b)**	your product
3	sell	**c)**	global markets very fast
4	get into	**d)**	different markets with different product concepts
5	set up	**e)**	one product concept for the whole world
6	go into	**f)**	for local markets
7	manufacture	**g)**	production in Uganda

B 🔊 CD1.10 **Complete the table with words that Darren uses.**

verb	noun
market	
	development
	entry
	shape
practise	
assign	
report	
present	
brief	

Building relationships

ALISON WARD, HEAD OF GLOBAL CORPORATE RESPONSIBILITY AT CADBURY, THE CHOCOLATE MAKER

A 🔊 CD1.16 **Complete these statements with appropriate forms of expressions from part one.**

1 The ability of something to continue for a long time its *S*............

2 A person or thing that gives you new ideas for something you do is your *i*...........

3 The amount of crops that you obtain from land is its *y*........... between them.

4 The possible success, profit, etc. that you might get from something is its *P*............

5 If you look at one part of a situation, which has many parts, you look at a particular *a*......... of it.

6 The way you make money to live, or the money itself, is your *l*..............

7 The people and organisations that you work with on a project are your *P*...........

B 🔊 CD1.17 **Listen to part two. What do the words in italics refer to in each statement?**

1 *It* is something we're really proud of.

2 Alison met *these people*.

3 She saw *two things* that trade had given them.

4 *It* is powerful among both consumers and producers.

5 *It* has given power back to farmers.

6 Cadbury are very proud to be *this*.

7 The company is looking forward to helping *them*.

C 🔊 CD1.17 **Listen to part two again. Complete the table with words which Alison uses.**

noun	adjective
	beneficial
pride	
ethics	
privileged	
	powerful
	empowered

D 🔊 CD1.18 **Listen to this extract from part three of the interview and replace the eight mistakes in the transcript below with what Alison actually says.**

We see partnership as part of the way we do business and we also have a great relationship with our milk farmers in England. We use fresh milk in our chocolate and there's a combine of farmers who supply only milk that makes our UK chocolate. We've been co-operating with them on their carbon footprint, so that's the measurement that measures how much carbon is produced to make milk. And we found in our Cadbury Dairy Milk bars that 70 per cent of the carbon footprint comes from milk. So, by working with this co-operative, we've begun to help them and help us make some changes in our supply chain. So that includes different types of animal food, it includes investment, so that the lorry that brings the animal feed only comes once rather than three times, and actually helping them really make some changes on their farms, so it's more efficient.

Success

A 🔊 CD1.26 **Listen to part one of the interview. Are these statements true or false?**

1 A successful business is one that makes a profit.

2 You make a profit even if more money goes out of the business than comes in.

3 Isis Innovation always makes a quick profit.

4 Isis has a business plan that is based on a mature, established technology.

5 Isis will need more investment in the future.

6 Isis will not sell services.

B 🔊 CD1.27 **Listen to part two and answer the questions below.**

1 What does Tom say the most successful business stories are based on?

2 What three factors does Tom say lead to the creation of a successful business?

3 How many new university spin-out companies has Isis Innovation helped set up in the last ten years?

4 When did Tom and his team become involved in Natural Motion?

5 Tom feels lucky to have been involved working with the people who set up Natural Motion. Which four-word expression does he use to express this?

6 Complete the expression Tom uses to say that achieving success in the company hasn't been easy: '... *there have been some* ………. ………. ………. ……….'

C 🔊 CD1.28 **Match the two parts of these expressions from part three.**

1	alternative-energy	a)	consumption
2	carbon	b)	households
3	energy	c)	energy
4	global	d)	energy
5	domestic	e)	technologies
6	tidal	f)	challenge
7	wind	g)	emissions

D **Now match the expressions above with these examples.**

i) electricity generated by a river estuary dam

ii) people living in flats and houses (as opposed to corporate consumers)

iii) the problem of getting people to use alternative energy all over the world

iv) electricity generated by wind farms

v) carbon dioxide from car engines, for example

vi) electricity generated from solar, wind and tidal sources

vii) the amount of energy used

RESOURCE BANK – Listening

Job satisfaction

MADALYN BROOKS, DIRECTOR OF HUMAN RESOURCES, PROCTER & GAMBLE (UK)

A ◄)) CD2.4 Listen to the first section of part one. Match the verbs with the expressions that they relate to.

1	attract	a)	job satisfaction
2	retain	b)	people
3	motivate	c)	people
4	invest in	d)	them (people)
5	reward	e)	employees
6	recognise	f)	employees
7	drive	g)	employees

B ◄)) CD2.4 Listen to the second section of part one. Find words which mean the following:

1 A principle demonstrated by a company which employs many different types of people from different cultures, backgrounds, etc. *(n, U)*
2 The introduction of new ideas or methods *(n, U)*
3 The ideas, beliefs, etc. that a company has *(n, plural)* (2 words)
4 The core make-up of a company's managers and workers in terms of cultures, beliefs, etc. *(n, U)*
5 Expecting a lot of attention or expecting to have things in exactly the way you want them *(adj)*
6 Continually stimulated or tested in your skills or abilities *(adv and adj)* (2 words)
7 An organisation that provides a company with materials, services, etc. *(n, C)*

C ◄)) CD2.5 Listen to part two. In which order do you hear these adverbs?

a)	socially	d)	hugely
b)	really	e)	clearly
c)	initially		

D ◄)) CD2.6 Listen to part three. Choose the correct alternative to replace the expression in italics so as to keep the closest meaning.

1 I think we will see an increase in this desire for training. *Self-actualisation*, building self and skills will be a constant demand.
   a) keeping up to date   b) achieving one's potential   c) realising one's dreams
2 People are encouraged to be *lifelong learners*, ...
   a) to keep learning for the whole of their lives   b) to learn enough to last all their lives
   c) to learn that life has hard lessons
3 People want opportunity to grow through training, through opportunities of *challenging assignments* ...
   a) interesting homework   b) impossible tasks   c) difficult but achievable work projects
4 We are seeing, today, a drive for people's desire *to have time out*, ...
   a) to leave their jobs permanently   b) to take time off   c) to take more coffee breaks
5 They will want to be able to take time to do *voluntary work*, ...
   a) unpaid work for the good of society   b) unpaid work for the company.   c) unpaid overtime
6 ... such as working in schools, working in *local communities* and giving back.
   a) municipalities   b) groups of people who live in the same place   c) communes

STEVE FOWLER, MANAGING DIRECTOR, THE INSTITUTE OF RISK MANAGEMENT

A 🔊 CD2.10 **Listen to this extract from part one of the interview and replace the seven mistakes in the transcript below with what Steve Fowler actually says.**

Well, there are two ways of looking at risk. One way of looking at risk is to separate risks to an organisation between internal risks and external risks. Now, some examples of internal risks include wounds to employees within a factory or, alternatively, a fire in a warehouse, for example. Examples of external risks can include an earthquake or a tsunami affecting a site or, alternatively, a change in currency-rate mechanism.

Now, I mentioned there were two ways of looking at risk. The other way of looking at risk is to divide up risk into four categories – hazard, operating risks, financial risks and strategic risks. I will give some examples of each of those four.

Hazards can include natural events – storms, hurricanes, fires, floods and so on and so forth. Operational risks can include risks such as information technology, supply chain and employment risks. Financial risks include the non-availability of cheap credit or a lack of cash within an organisation.

B 🔊 CD2.11 **Listen to the five steps to managing risk that Steve mentions in part two and find two-word expressions that mean the following:**

1   an organisation's most important long-term aims
2   used to talk about looking at things from managers' point of view
3   used to talk about looking at things from the point of view of ordinary employees
4   a complete range
5   a list of possible risks
6   actions taken to prevent something from happening
7   legal agreements
8   a methodical examination

C 🔊 CD2.12 **Listen to part three and match the two parts of these expressions.**

1   systematic   a) implications
2   reckless   b) growth
3   massive   c) risk
4   economic   d) risk-taking
5   untold   e) media
6   great   f) risk-taking
7   digital   g) impact
8   ultimate   h) example

D **Now match the adjectives 1–8 above with their meanings.**

i)   without any sense of danger   v)   impossible to calculate or describe
ii) happening all the time   vi)   very good
iii) relating to money, finance, industry, trade, etc.   vii) very big
iv) the worst   viii) not analogue

RESOURCE BANK – Listening

LAURIE MULLINS, AUTHOR OF *MANAGEMENT AND ORGANISATIONAL BEHAVIOUR*

A 🔊 CD2.17 **Complete the table with words that Laurie Mullins uses.**

noun	adjective
manager	
compete	
volatility	
individual	
diversity	
challenge	
remoteness	

B **Now match the adjectives above to their meanings.**

a) not in the place where you are

b) difficult in an interesting or enjoyable way

c) describing a situation of rivalry

d) containing people from many different races, backgrounds, etc.

e) changing fast and unpredictably

f) relating to responsibility for the control of employees' work

g) relating to one person

C 🔊 CD2.18 **Listen to part two. Are the statements about the expressions in italics that Laurie uses true or false in relation to their context here?**

1 *Perceptions*: what you receive through the senses of sight, touch, etc.

2 *Consideration*: showing that you care about other people's feelings.

3 *Majority*: more than half the members of a group.

4 *Credit*: the ability to borrow money.

5 *Recognition*: when you see someone and you know who they are.

6 *Key feature*: one of the most important things about something.

7 *Emphasis*: special importance given to a word by saying it louder.

D 🔊 CD2.19 **Listen to the final part and find expressions that mean or refer to the following:**

1 an idea or principle (7 letters)

2 the way you feel about people before a particular event, etc. (14 letters)

3 a situation where things are done in a particular way and a particular order (7 letters)

4 a system of reward and punishment (6 letters-3 letters-5 letters)

5 ideas that people have without questioning them (11 letters)

6 combining things together (11 letters)

7 a situation where people discipline themselves (4 letters-7 letters)

Team building

A 🔊 CD2.25 **Listen to the first part of an interview and replace the eight mistakes with what Dan Collins actually says.**

The important thing with a team is that it is really just a group of people working towards a common objective. The leader's role in a team is to make sure that objective is well understood and is clear and then to encourage people along the way as they work towards that end. Where necessary, steer them back on track if they steer off, but a team is really a group of people who are feeling keen towards reaching the same objective and they are feeling supported by their leader throughout.

B 🔊 CD2.26, 2.27 **Use appropriate forms of the expressions from parts two and three to complete the answers to the questions.**

1 What's difficult for people to find time to do?
   – Most conversations are about a set subject, but there should be more conversations that are *s*........., *m*.......... and *s*............

2 What's important in team building, in addition to communication?
   – It's important to spend time discovering what each person's *s*.......... are and what they can *c*.......... to the team.

3 What types of people make up teams?
   – First there are people who take a leading role, either because they are *a*.......... or they are *n*.....................

4 What other types are there?
   – There are creative people who *t*.......... *o*.......... *o*.......... *t*.......... *b*.......... and there are others who solve problems creatively by using *a*.......... and *r*...........

5 What do 'gluers' do?
   – They hold the team together, but people tend to forget about the role. It is often o...........

6 What do 'doers' do?
   – They concentrate on *P*.......... and *P*.......... *m*...........

C 🔊 CD2.28 **Listen to part four. Are these statements about Dan's opinions true or false?**

1 Attitudes to leadership are the same everywhere.

2 Attitudes to leadership in Europe are identical to those in the US.

3 In the US, people are given detailed instructions about what to do.

4 In India and China, people are given detailed instructions about what to do.

5 One method of leadership is better than the other.

6 With different leadership styles, there are differences in team behaviour.

7 With different leadership styles, the way that team members relate to each other will not be the same.

RESOURCE BANK – Listening

UNIT **9** Raising finance

A 🔊 CD3.1 **Listen to part one. In which order do these adverbs occur?**

a) effectively   d) thirdly

b) effectively   e) probably

c) finally   f) secondly

B 🔊 CD3.2 **Listen to part two. Use the words in the box to make seven expressions that Simon uses, containing the number of words shown below.**

adjective	first word of compound noun	main noun
full	control	features
public	private	markets
significant	shareholder	markets
shareholder	capital	cost
dispersed	business	management
	executive	base
	debt	risk

1 When investment costs for a company are quite high: fairly ....

2 What shareholders must bear, which means they could lose all their money: ....

3 When there are a lot of shareholders, rather than just a few: ....

4 Where you can go to borrow money in the form of bonds, but you don't know who owns them: ....

5 Where you can get capital, other than in the public markets: ....

6 Ways in which shareholders can make decisions about a company: ....

7 The people who run a company: ....

C **Now match the expressions above to their meanings.**

a) the people who manage a company

b) when a company has a lot of different shareholders

c) a source of finance through bonds

d) a source of finance that is confidential

e) what shareholders in a company carry

f) investment that is quite expensive

g) what shareholders demand, so that they can influence a business that they invest in

D 🔊 CD3.3 **Listen to part three and find adjectives that describe:**

1 investors who now have such a large choice of things to invest in (6 letters)

2 investors who want a quick return (5 letters-7 letters)

3 the speed with which investment decisions can be made (10 letters)

4 loans that can be bought and sold between banks, investors, etc. (8 letters)

5 loans that are not bought and sold (6 letters)

RESOURCE BANK – Listening

UNIT 10 Customer service

A 🔊 CD3.10, 3.11 **Listen to parts one and two. Choose the best alternative so as to keep the closest meaning to the expression in italic.**

1 We are a 32-bedroom, luxury hotel with a *stunning* restaurant.
   a) good   **b)** delicious   **c)** beautiful

2 The *ethos* of the kitchen spreads into everywhere else in the house.
   a) values   **b)** ethics   **c)** menus

3 It is *a retreat from the norm* …
   a) a place that is well above average   **b)** a place where you can get away from the ordinary
   c) a place where you can withdraw from the world

4 … we try to *exceed* customers' expectations, …
   a) meet   **b)** satisfy   **c)** go beyond

5 … we have to have *empathy with* the client …
   a) complete understanding of   **b)** partial feeling for   **c)** sympathy for

6 We also must provide *consistent* standards of service.
   a) good and reasonable   **b)** unvaryingly good   **c)** changing but predictable

7 … 'the standards you *set* are the standards you get.'
   a) establish   **b)** legislate   **c)** appoint

B 🔊 CD3.12 **In what order is this information given in part three?**

The staff at Quat'Saisons …

a) are allowed to stay overnight to understand the guest experience.

b) can only go beyond customers' expectations if they understand what they are.

c) have a chance to eat in the restaurant.

d) get an idea of what customers expect through these two experiences.

e) go beyond customers' expectations.

f) must have a complete understanding of guests and their needs.

C 🔊 CD3.13 **Complete the table with words from part four and related words.**

verb	noun
require	
	expectation
increase	
	complaint
	change

RESOURCE BANK – Listening

CRAIG SMITH, PROFESSOR OF ETHICS AND SOCIAL RESPONSIBILITY, INSEAD IN PARIS

A 🔊 CD3.19 Listen to part one of the interview and match the verbs in brackets 1–7 to the tenses that Craig Smith actually uses, a–g.

1   ... the Toyota Motor Company (face) a huge crisis ...
2   ... there (be) some two thousand reported incidents ...
3   ... it was only September 2009 that the company really truly (acknowledge) there was a problem ...
4   ... we (have) a recall ...
5   ... the problem (put down) to a couple of causes ...
6   ... the classic advice here is (tell) it all and (tell) it quickly ...
7   ... people ... know that you (do) something about it.

a) present perfect
b) future with 'going to'
c) present continuous
d) present simple (passive)
e) imperative
f) present continuous
g) past simple

B 🔊 CD3.20 Listen to part two and decide if these statements about expressions that Craig uses are true or false.

1   An *approach* to a problem is a way of analysing it.
2   *Critical* activities are not very important.
3   The *likelihood* of an event is the degree of probability that it will happen.
4   If something is *avoidable*, it can be prevented.
5   If you *take out* insurance, you decide not to have it.
6   A *contingency plan* is something that prepares people to deal with a particular problem.
7   A *dedicated team* is usually one whose members change often and start to learn about the issues while they are dealing with them.

C 🔊 CD3.21, 3.22 Complete the questions and answers with words from parts three and four, and related words.

1   The first thing that needs to happen is to recognise that there is indeed a crisis, so crisis .... is an important first part of what takes place.
2   The second of the three .... during the crisis is .... Clearly you want to try and .... the crisis as best as possible.
3   This is where .... is very important.
4   And then thirdly, within the 'during' phase, it's .... the crisis.
5   It may be some clear .... in the product design or product materials.
6   The problem could be something to do with consumers and their .... of the product.
7   Once the crisis has passed, the 'after' phase if you will, then you've got the ....

Mergers and acquisitions

PROFESSOR SCOTT MOELLER, DIRECTOR, THE M&A RESEARCH CENTRE, CASS BUSINESS SCHOOL

A 🔊 CD3.27 **Listen to part one and replace the eight mistakes in the transcript below with what Scott Moeller actually says.**

It is true that somewhere between two-thirds and seven-eighths of all acquisitions fail, uh, so the success rate in acquisitions is evidently quite low. And the reason for that is due to a number of different causes. First off, inadequate planning. Uh, that is to say that the strategic plan behind the acquisition tends not to be anchored in too much of what the future strategy would be, but more of an opportunistic basis as to whether a company is able to be bought or not.

Secondly, the due diligence done on the target company tends to be carried out much too quickly, and in many cases doesn't concentrate on the key factors that are going to drive that particular deal to success in the future. More time should be spent trying to understand what it is that really makes that target company successful – if it is already successful – or why perhaps it has failed, uh, and whether that can be transformed if, in fact, the company is being acquired because, uh, it is a company that's now available, because of lack of success.

B 🔊 CD3.28 **Complete the table with words from part two, and related words.**

verb	noun (thing)	noun (person/organisation)
	assurance	–
	determination	–
	acquisition	
employment	employ	
	integration	–
	operation	
	appointment	appointee

C 🔊 CD3.29 **Listen to part three. Put these steps in a merger into the correct order.**

a) Managers and employees in both companies know which business will be kept, how the new organisation is going to work, who is going to run it, etc.

b) Put together a team of senior people from both sides, to decide who should run the merged company.

c) Agree that if the problems cannot be solved, the merger should not go ahead.

d) Identify potential problems very early.

RESOURCE BANK – Listening

RESOURCE BANK LISTENING KEY

Unit 1

I think the thing to remember is, the <u>principles</u> of communication haven't changed and I don't think there's anything <u>inherent</u> in technology that makes good communication easier. It can make it better but there are also many ways it can make it worse. So, I think there's four things that you need to <u>remember</u>.

The first thing is that you've got to remember people have limited <u>attention</u> – if you like, limited bandwidth – which puts the <u>onus</u> on you as the communicator to think hard about what it is exactly you're <u>trying</u> to communicate and make sure that you get it down as <u>succinctly</u> as possible.

1   dump vast amounts
2   get through
3   dense
4   distil the meaning
5   some sort of emotional connection
6   help or could hinder

b   a   f   d   c   g   e

1   voicemail
2   maze
3   option
4   human being
5   emphasis
6   efficiency

Unit 2

1b   **2**e   **3**a   **4**c   **5**g   **6**d   **7**f

verb	noun
market	market, marketing
develop	development
enter	entry
shape	shape
practise	practice
assign	assignment
report	report
present	presentation
brief	brief, briefing

Unit 3

1   sustainability
2   inspiration
3   yield
4   potential
5   aspect
6   livelihood
7   partners

B

1   achieving Fairtrade certification
2   farmers from the Fairtrade co-operative
3   empowerment and a helping hand out of poverty
4   The Fairtrade marque (brand)
5   The Fairtrade marque (brand)
6   a partner in the Faitrade project
7   farmers in Ghana

C

noun	adjective
benefits	beneficial
pride	proud
ethics	ethical
privilege	privileged
power	powerful
empowerment	empowered

D

We see partnership as part of the way we do business and we also have a great <u>partnership</u> with our milk farmers in <u>the UK</u>. We use fresh milk in our chocolate and there's a <u>co-operative</u> of farmers who supply only milk that makes our UK chocolate. We've been <u>working</u> with them on their carbon footprint, so that's the <u>metric</u> that measures how much carbon is produced to make milk.

And we found in our Cadbury Dairy Milk bars that <u>60</u> per cent of the carbon footprint comes from milk. So, by working with this co-operative, we've begun to help them and help us make some changes in our supply chain. So that includes different types of animal <u>feed</u>, it includes investment, so that the lorry that brings the animal feed only <u>delivers</u> once rather than three times, and actually helping them really make some changes on their farms, so it's more efficient.

Unit 4

A

1   True
2   False – '… you are getting more money in than is going out.'
3   False – 'it is going to take quite a few years for the company to go from those initial phases to actually having a product or service to sell.'
4   False – '[Isis is] creating businesses based on developing very early-stage technology.'
5   True
6   False – '… we are aiming for a product or service that we can sell …'

B

1   a great team of people
2   passion, vision, clarity of thought
3   sixty-five
4   at its start / at the beginning (2002)
5   had (have) the good fortune
6   challenges along the way

C – **D**

1   e)   vi)
2   g)   v)
3   a)   vii)
4   f)   iii)
5   b)   ii)
6   c)/d)   i)
7   c)/d)   iv)

Unit 5

A

1e   2f   3g   4d   5b   6c   7a

B

1   diversity
2   innovation
3   core principles
4   DNA
5   demanding
6   constantly challenged
7   supplier

C

c   b   a   e   d

D

1b   2a   3c   4b   5a   6b

Unit 6

A

Well, there are two ways of looking at risk. One way of looking at risk is to <u>divide</u> risks to an organisation between internal risks and external risks. Now, some examples of internal risks include <u>injuries</u> to employees within a factory or, alternatively, a fire in a warehouse, for example. Examples of external risks can include an earthquake or a tsunami affecting a site or, alternatively, a change in <u>exchange</u>-rate mechanism.

Now, I mentioned there were two ways of looking at risk. The other way of looking at risk is to divide up risk into four categories – hazard, <u>operational</u> risks, financial risks and strategic risks. I will give some examples of each of those four.

Hazards can include natural events – <u>typhoons</u>, hurricanes, fires, floods and so on and so forth. Operational risks can include risks such as information technology, supply chain and employment risks. Financial risks include the non-availability of <u>reasonably priced</u> credit or a lack of <u>liquidity</u> within an organisation.

B

1   strategic objectives
2   top down
3   bottom up
4   full spectrum
5   risk register
6   counter-measures
7   contractual arrangements
8   systematic analysis

C – D

1 d) ii)
2 f) i)
3 a) vii)
4 b) iii)
5 g) v)
6 h) vi)
7 e) viii)
8 c) iv)

Unit 7

A – B

noun	adjective
manager	managerial (f)
competition	competitive (c)
volatility	volatile (e)
individual	individual (g)
diversity	diverse (d)
challenge	challenging (b)
remoteness	remote (a)

C

1 False – here it's used to talk about what people understand and feel about a situation.
2 True
3 True
4 False – here it refers to praise that you give to someone for something they've done
5 False – in this context, it refers to showing that you know the value of something that someone has done.
6 True
7 False – here it means showing that an idea is particularly important.

D

1 precept
2 predisposition
3 routine
4 carrot and stick
5 assumptions
6 integration
7 self-control

Unit 8

A

The <u>key</u> thing with a team is that it is really just a group of people working towards a common <u>goal</u>. The leader's role in a team is to make sure that <u>goal</u> is well understood and is clear and then to encourage people along the way as they work towards that <u>objective</u>. Where necessary, steer them back on track if they <u>veer</u> off, but a team is really a group of people who are feeling <u>enthusiastic</u> towards <u>achieving</u> the same objective and they are feeling <u>encouraged</u> by their leader throughout.

B

1 spontaneous, meaningful, significant
2 strengths, contribute
3 appointed, natural leaders
4 think outside of the box, analysis, research
5 overlooked
6 process, project management

C

1 False – they vary from place to place.
2 False – they are increasingly similar, but not identical.
3 False – they are given an instruction and allowed to get on with it.
4 True
5 False – He doesn't know if one is better than the other.
6 True
7 True

Unit 9

A

e a f d b c

B – C

1 significant capital cost (f)
2 full business risk (e)
3 dispersed shareholder base (b)
4 public debt markets (c)
5 private markets (d)
6 shareholder control features (g)
7 executive management (a)

D

1 spoilt
2 short-termist
3 incredible
4 tradable
5 static

Unit 10

A

1c 2a 3b 4c 5a 6b 7a

B

f a c d e b

C

verb	noun
require	requirement
expect	expectation
increase	increase
complain	complaint
change	change

Unit 11

A

1c 2a 3g 4b 5d 6e 7f

B

1 True
2 False – they are very important.
3 True
4 True
5 False – you buy it.
6 True
7 False – its members don't change often and know about the issues they will be dealing with.

C

1 identification
2 considerations, containment, contain
3 communication
4 resolving
5 defect
6 misuse
7 recovery

Unit 12

A

It is true that somewhere between two-thirds and three-quarters of all acquisitions fail, uh, so the success rate in acquisitions is obviously quite low. And the reason for that is due to a number of different factors. First off, inadequate planning. Uh, that is to say that the strategic plan behind the acquisition tends not to be grounded in too much of what the future strategy would be, but more of an opportunistic basis as to whether a company is able to be acquired or not.

Secondly, the due diligence done on the target company tends to be done much too quickly, and in many cases doesn't focus on the key factors that are going to drive that particular deal to success in the future. More time should be spent trying to understand what it is that really makes that target company successful – if it is already successful – or why perhaps it has failed, uh, and whether that can be turned around if, in fact, the company is being acquired because, uh, it is a company that's now available, because of lack of success.

B

verb	noun (thing)	noun (person/ organisation)
assure	assurance	–
determine	determination	–
acquire	acquisition	acquirer
employment	employ	employee
integrate	integration	–
operate	operations	operator
appoint	appointment	appointee

C

d c b a

CASE STUDY WRITING TASK: MODEL ANSWER

Dear Ms. Ward,

Following your report on communications problems here at WCH, the directors have now discussed your recommendations.

On internal communications, the consensus was that weekly reports from the heads of department would be too time-consuming in relation to any benefits they might bring. However, the directors have approved the idea of appointing a Key Accounts Manager, and we will be advertising this position soon.

With regard to communication between Sales Reps and Head Office, it has been decided to issue BlackBerries to all reps, who will file daily reports on their activities to Head Office.

Following lengthy discussion, the directors also approved your recommendation of a new procedure for dealing with product complaints that have health and safety implications. All complaints of this nature will now be systematically forwarded to the Marketing, R&D and PR departments.

Thank you again for undertaking your report – as you see, most of your recommendations have been approved. I'll let you know the effects of these changes in due course.

Sincerely,*

Betty Friedman

Communications Director, WCH

* This is used in the US, rather than 'Yours sincerely'.

A Write a job advertisement for the position of Key Accounts Manager at WCH. Include the following:

- job title
- short description of company
- responsibilities
- likely background of applicants
- location
- salary and benefits
- how to apply

B It's six months later. Write another e-mail from Betty Friedman to Georgina Ward, describing the outcome of the changes that Ward Associates suggested. Include these points:

- Overall, communications at WCH are much better.
- Sales reps have happily taken to filing daily activity reports on their BlackBerries.
- Luckily there have been no customer complaints with health and safety implications recently, but the procedures are in place if such complaints are received in future.
- Unfortunately, the person appointed as Key Accounts Manager left after two weeks (give a reason). The post is being readvertised.
- Suggest a meeting to review the progress so far in more detail.
- End suitably.

UNIT **2**

Marketing meeting action minutes: *Physique*

Date: 3 November
Venue: Room 13, Head Office, Grasse
Present: Pierre Martin (Chief Executive), Carla Fernandez (Global Marketing Manager), Anne Dumont (Marketing assistant)

		Action	By
1, 2	**Target countries and product name** It was agreed that original target countries are suitable. Various alternative product names suggested, but no better name found.	–	–
3–5	**Positioning and packaging** Planned positioning of the product problematic – premium market overcrowded. We decided to go with mass market: men aged 30 to 55. Packaging design to be taken downmarket. We will take the brainstorming ideas that emerged at the meeting further in conjunction with our design consultancy.	AD	30 Nov
6, 7	**Price and distribution** Recommended retail price to be reduced by 40 per cent. Major Asian mass market retailers to be contacted.	CF	15 Dec
8	**Promotion** There are male French stars who are well-known worldwide. Our chief executive agreed to take personal charge of finding suitable ambassador(s) for *Physique*.	PM	31 Jan
9	**Slogan** Various suggestions made at meeting. AD to research linguistic and cultural acceptability of them in different languages and come up with a shortlist of four possible slogans, in conjunction with our advertising agency.	AD	15 Feb
10	**Manufacturing** It was agreed to keep manufacturing of *Physique* in Grasse, as originally planned, so as to keep control of the formula and the process despite lower costs elsewhere. PT to co-ordinate with production department on production requirements to build up product stocks for launch in September next year.	PT	15 Dec

A It's twelve months after the successful launch of *Physique*, with sales of more than twice the original targets. Write an e-mail from Pierre Martin to Anne Dumont, containing these points:

- Congratulate her on contributing to the success of *Physique*.
- Underline the importance of her work in helping to find the right internationally acceptable slogan.
- Offer her promotion to the new post of assistant marketing manager, working under Carla Fernandez.
- Tell her that the salary for this position will be €62,000 per year.
- Ask her to let you know as soon as possible if she accepts the offer.

RESOURCE BANK – Writing

Building relationships

CASE STUDY WRITING TASK: MODEL ANSWER

Dear Ms Wise,

Introducing the Superspa Card

I'm writing to you as one of our most loyal customers, to let you know about an exciting special offer that we are making to our most valued guests.

The new Superspa Card gives you:

- 15 per cent discount on standard room rates

- 5 per cent discount on all meals and drinks

- complimentary drinks in your room on arrival

- exclusive access to our new Superspa rooms – specially reserved areas for relaxation, including spa treatments and jacuzzis, open only to Superspa cardholders.

What's more, when you check in at any of our hotels or use any of the facilities, there will be no need to fill in the usual forms – we'll keep your details on file.

We're looking forward to seeing you at one of our hotels soon.

Vanessa Schultz

Vanessa Schultz

Director of Customer Relations, Al-Munir Group

A Write an e-mail from **Marion Wise** to **Vanessa Schultz**, with these points.

Marion Wise …
- thanks Ms Schultz for her letter about the Superspa Card.
- returned a month ago from a stay at one of Al-Munir Group's hotels in the Gulf. (She had planned to stay a week, but changed hotel after two days.)
- says she had a terrible experience – she has three complaints. (Specify them.)
- says she complained about these things to the hotel manager, but he did not take the complaints seriously, and even joked about them.
- has noticed a general decline in standards at the group's hotels over the last few years.
- will not be staying at any Al-Munir Group Hotel again.
- End suitably.

B You are the **Human Resources Director at Al-Munir Group**. Write some employee guidelines that will be displayed in the staff areas of all group hotels. Include:

- attitude to guests (politeness, helpfulness, responding to guests' questions, etc.)
- standards of dress among staff
- cleanliness of facilities (not just the responsibility of cleaning staff)

(See the Writing file, Course Book page 129, for the format of guidelines.)

CASE STUDY WRITING TASK: MODEL ANSWER 1

Press Presse Prensa

Kensington United plc

For the general and sports press
29 October

Universal Communications sponsorship deal

We are delighted to announce a five-year sponsorship agreement between
Kensington United (KU) and Universal Communications (UC).

At a signing ceremony and joint press conference at the club's ground in west
London, Raj Krishnamurthy, UC's chief executive and KU's commercial director, Ingrid
Tauber, outlined the terms of the agreement. 'This agreement will allow us to make
some major investments over the next few years, including the purchase of more
world class players,' Ms Tauber said.

Mr Krishnamurthy said, 'Our agreement goes much further than previous deals of
this type. We are pioneering new forms of commercial sponsorship for football in this
country, and indeed around the world.'

For additional information, visit our website www.kensingtonunited.co.uk.

CASE STUDY WRITING TASK: MODEL ANSWER 2

Dear Ms Tauber

I'm writing to say how much I regret that we were not able to reach a deal following our
recent discussions. The commercial logic for such an agreement between KU and UC remains
very strong. I will always be open to the idea of recommencing negotiations about
sponsorship or other commercial arrangements. Please feel free to contact me at any time.

Meanwhile, I wish you and your colleagues every success with Kensington United.

Yours sincerely

Raj Krishnamurthy

A Write a positive reply from Ingrid Tauber to Raj Krishnamurthy to the above letter.

B Write a negative reply from Ingrid Tauber to Raj Krishnamurthy, giving reasons for not wishing to
recommence negotiations. (Give examples from the recent negotiations – not necessarily ones
from the role play in which you participated – of why you think a future deal will not be possible.)

RESOURCE BANK – Writing

CASE STUDY WRITING TASK: MODEL ANSWER

Techno 21

To: All board members

From: Veronica Simpson, HR Director

Suggested Company Guidelines

Following recent incidents in the company that have adversely affected its performance, I suggest that we issue the following guidelines to staff regarding relationships between staff members. Of course, we cannot prevent employees having relationships with each other, but we need clear guidelines about behaviour. I suggest the following guidelines: (These can be discussed at our next board meeting. If board members have any other suggestions for guidelines, please let me know.)

- Employees and managers should think very carefully before entering into relationships with each other.

- They should consider the implications of any relationships for their future career with the company.

- Any relationships that do occur between company employees should be conducted with the utmost discretion. For example, there should be no overt displays of affection on company premises.

- If line managers, senior managers or the HR department consider that Techno 21's performance or morale are being negatively affected by relationships between staff, the company reserves the right to take appropriate action.

(See the Writing file, Course Book page 129, for the format of Guidelines.)

A Look again at the article on Marriot on page 47 and the one on KPMG on page 135 of the Course Book. Write an e-mail or letter to one of the companies, asking them for a job there.

- Say briefly that you have seen positive reports about conditions at the company, rather than any specific job advertisement.

- Say what kind of job you would like to apply for, and what you have to contribute.

- Mention that you are attaching your CV – there is no need to write this, but point out any qualifications or experience that you have that would be relevant to working for Marriot or KPMG.

- End suitably.

B Look again at the Skills section, Course Book page 49, and the script of the conversation between Patricia Evans and Felipe Gonzales, CD1, Track 37, on page 155.

- It is now three days after their meeting at the Chamberlain hotel.

- Write an e-mail from Felipe Gonzales to Patricia Evans, either accepting or refusing her job offer, giving reasons.

- End suitably.

WCM/AZT joint venture: RISK ASSESSMENT

Executive summary
WCM has been negotiating with AZT with a view to entering into a joint venture with them. WCM directors have thoroughly assessed the risks associated with this joint venture and their findings were discussed at a recent board meeting.

Exploitation risk
Site 1 (Kango): Good quantities of copper and basalt have been mined in the past. Risk: low

Site 2 (50 km from Kango): has produced large quantities of coltan, important in cell phones and DVD players. Risk: low

Site 3 (85 km from Kango): diamond deposits, but potential unproven. Risk: high

Health risk
There is a danger of high legal and remedial costs related to industrial emissions and water and soil contamination. Risk: very high

Economic risk
The cobalt and bauxite markets are booming at present, but the international industrial metals market is volatile. Overall long-term risk is low, as demand for the metals will no doubt recover.

The slowdown in the Chinese economy is continuing to have an effect on commodity prices. The longer-term risk is low as Chinese economy will certainly pick up.

There will be a general election in the country in six months' time. There is potential for disruption if the results are disputed, which is probable. Risk: very high

Security risk
The country is unstable with high levels of crime. Civil disturbances are also likely following the upcoming election (see above). Risk: very high.

Recommendation
Given the overall high risk levels, the Board do not recommend proceeding with this joint venture.

(See the Writing file, Course Book page 131, for the format of reports.)

A Write a formal letter from Daniel Habersham, WCM chief executive, to Robert Achebe, president of AZT informing him of your company's decision in relation to the planned joint venture.

- Open the letter formally.
- Give reasons for not going ahead with the joint venture project (be tactful).
- Express your regret for this.
- Say that if conditions change, WCM will re-examine the idea.
- End suitably.

B You are a mid-ranking operations manager at WCM, currently based at a bauxite mine in Canada. You have agreed to go Bolivia, South America, to work as senior operations manager at one of the company's mines there. Write an e-mail to a friend, telling them about the move and the promotion, inventing any necessary details. Write about:

- your family's attitude to the move
- what it will mean for your career
- the Spanish evening classes that that you have been going to
- how you imagine you will spend your leisure time in Bolivia.
- End suitably, telling your friend that they will be very welcome to visit you in Bolivia.

RESOURCE BANK – Writing

Management styles

PROJECT MANAGEMENT REPLACEMENT

Following our decision to replace Paul Johnstone as manager of the international project, we had informal talks with four shortlisted candidates.

Ruth, Central Europe Sales Manager

Seemed to be very assertive in talking about her direct, no-nonsense management style. However, I'm worried that this might upset some members of the project team who are used to a more consensual approach.

Eduardo, Manager, New Business

Describes himself as consensual. He says he is a good listener, and good at sorting out staff problems. However, his need to be liked may be a weakness when he's dealing with difficult people.

Kazuo, Manager, Business Support unit

There's no question about his loyalty to the company (which is great for us, but might seem over-the-top to some!). There seems to be a contradiction between his stated wish to consult staff on all decisions, but not to permit disagreement/argument.

Martina, Manager, IT department

Martina says that she sets goals and then lets people decide how to get the job done. So when she says that she expects people to carry out her instructions to the letter, I guess she means that the instructions are quite general, and she lets people reach objectives using their own methods.

Recommendation

The other candidates all have their strengths and weaknesses, but I like Martina's combination of wanting to give clear goals, while at the same time allowing people to work in their own way in order to achieve them. I think she's realistic in wanting to use the bonus system as a motivational tool. I also agree with her that staff appraisal interviews are usually a waste of time. For these reasons, I would recommend appointing Martina to head the international project team.

(See the Writing file, Course Book page 131, for the format of reports.)

A Write an e-mail to the person you chose to take over the project leader job, including the following points:

- Thank them for coming for the informal talk.
- Congratulate them on making such a good impression on the directors.
- Confirm that you are offering them the job. You hope that they will start asap.
- Give details of remuneration (salary increase, bonus on successful completion of project, etc.).
- End suitably.

B Write the standard e-mail that you will send to the unsuccessful candidates, including appropriate forms of these expressions.

- enjoyed meeting
- interesting discussions
- very strong candidates
- unfortunately
- hope you will continue to contribute to the success of the company in your existing role

RESOURCE BANK – Writing

CASE STUDY WRITING TASK: MODEL ANSWER 1

Dear Ms Wilton

I'm writing about the recent problems with members of the salesforce. Here is the update you requested about the actions that my fellow-directors and I have decided to take.

After a lot of discussion, we have decided to keep David Seymour in his post for another three months and to review the situation then. Some directors felt that he should go now, but most were of the opinion that he should be given one last chance to turn the situation round.

We have approved most of David's plans for improving the situation – please see the attached document. We have given the go-ahead for points 1–4 and 6 (end of year bonus, omissions based on monthly performance, prize for biggest six-monthly improvement, monthly sales figures for each salesperson to be posted at head office and twice-monthly webinars). However, we have told him not the proceed with point 5 (photo in the company newsletter of the salesman/woman of the month – the novelty will quickly wear off), nor point 7 (weekly sales reports) as we do not want sales staff to have to do more paperwork than they have already. On point 8, David will be free to organise informal lunches/dinners with salespeople as he sees fit.

As I say, we will review the situation again three months from now.

Yours sincerely

CASE STUDY WRITING TASK: MODEL ANSWER 2

Dear Hank

Following our recent discussions about the performance of the sales team, I am writing to let you know about some of my concerns.

My colleagues and I recognise that you have some of the best sales results, that you are very good at bringing in new business and that you are excellent at presenting new products. However, I find your argumentative attitude at meetings extremely disruptive, with negative effects on the rest of the team. In particular, your behaviour towards Max, who is after all our most senior salesperson, is unacceptable. Also, your attitude to paperwork leaves a lot to be desired, both in terms of its lack of accuracy and frequently overdue delivery.

This is a formal warning that if you do not take steps to improve your attitude and behaviour, we will have to consider your position in the company.

Yours sincerely

Dietrich Braun

Dietrich Braun

Acting UK Sales manager, DKP

A You are Hank, salesman at DKP. Write a reply to the second letter above, responding to the points in it, and saying how you will try to improve your attitude and behaviour.

B Look again at the Reading section on page 77 of the Course Book. You went on a team-building cookery course like the one in the article. Write an e-mail to a colleague about your experiences, and either a) recommending the course to your colleague, or b) advising them not to go on a course like this, giving reasons.

RESOURCE BANK – Writing

Raising finance

CASE STUDY WRITING TASK: MODEL ANSWER

RESOURCE BANK – Writing

To:	roberta.dimaggio@concordia.com
From:	charles.williams@yahoo.com
Subject:	Film project

Dear Ms Dimaggio,

It was very nice meeting you here in Paris. Thank you so much for agreeing to back our film. This e-mail is to confirm the outcome of our recent discussions.

1 Financial terms: We will repay you 110% of your investment (2 million euros) within five years of the launch of the film plus a share of the net profits (65% for you, 35% for us).

2 Film title/location: I'm glad that you accepted our idea of shooting in Paris, rather than Berlin.

3 Payments of instalments: Gunnar and I reluctantly agreed to the following: 10% when Pre-production begins, 45% at the start of Production, 35% at the beginning of Post-production; 10% reserved for Marketing and Promotion. (It would have been good to get more money earlier in the production process, of course.)

4 Director/Scriptwriter/Music: I will direct, using Gunnar's script – thank you for agreeing to this. We agreed to use commercially available music due to the high costs of special recordings.

5 Cinematographer/Camera Assistants: We finally agreed to use an experienced cinematographer (we look forward to hearing your suggestions). We will provide three fellow students from the Film Studies course as camera assistants. (The people we will use are very good and, what's more, they will work for free!)

6 Actors: You accepted the idea of using mainly unknown actors, with our friend, the actress Hannah Schumann, performing for a low fee – I will approach her to find out exactly how much she will charge.

7 & 8 Marketing, promotion and product placement: 10% of the budget will be for marketing costs, as specified above. We agreed to limit the number of product placement opportunities in the film to five. You agreed to approach companies who might be interested.

9 The way the film ends: This caused a lot of disagreement, as I'm sure you'll agree(!), but we decided to go with the 'up-beat' ending that you suggested. However, Gunnar and I are of course open to the idea of going back to the bittersweet ending that we would have liked. (We will film both endings so that we can decide which one we finally want to use at a later date.)

Thank you again for agreeing to back this project – you won't regret it! We will be in touch again soon to discuss the next stage.

Best regards,

Charles Williams

A Go back to the answer you gave to Starting up, Exercise D. Write a letter to someone involved in the source of finance that you chose, asking for them to back you. Give details of:

- the project that you need the money for
- how much you need
- where the money will come from in your business activities for repayment of the financial backing
- how much equity you would be willing to grant in the project, if the type of financial backing you choose requires this.
- End suitably.

B Look again at the article in the Reading section on page 85 of the Course Book. Write a summary of it to about a third of its original length. (See the Writing file, Course Book page 129, for the guidelines on writing summaries.)

CASE STUDY WRITING TASK: MODEL ANSWER

To: Director of Customer Services

Re: Recent complaints
This report will outline some of the types of complaints that we have had recently and ways we could deal with them better.

Baggage charges and lost baggage
Hurrah should underline that there are strict limits on the maximum weight of baggage per passenger and that excess charges will be strictly enforced. We should also communicate better with passengers about efforts to trace lost luggage. In addition, we should make it clearer that a) we will only pay out $200 for each lost bag, b) passengers should not put valuables in their baggage and c) they should also claim through their travel insurance for any losses.

Flight changes
We should make the charges for changing flights more transparent. There needs to be a page on the website that specifies them in relation to a) each fare type and the flexibility it gives, if any, as to whether there is a charge for the change and b) reasons for having to change flights that are beyond customers' control, e.g. advice from the government not to travel to particular countries because of unrest there, where Hurrah will not compensate customers.

Disabled customers
This is a very sensitive area and negative coverage in the press is very damaging for the airline. We should provide wheelchairs free of charge, and our new policy should be made clear to ground staff at all airports where we operate.

Pre-booked seating
Customers may pre-book specific seats for an extra charge of $20 per seat, but there have been cases where cabin staff have not taken the pre-bookings into consideration, causing upset among some passengers. Staff training should put more emphasis on respecting these pre-bookings – staff should tactfully ask passengers who are sitting in someone else's pre-booked seat to vacate the seat and move to another where necessary.

Delayed and cancelled flights
There should be better communication with passengers when flights are cancelled or delayed. The website should give details of cases where compensation will be paid and where it will not. We should emphasise that we are a low-cost airline and will only apply legal minimum amounts when compensating passengers.

Cabin service
Cabin staff should never lose sight of the fact that our customers pay their salaries and they should be the number one priority at all times – some customers complain that staff seem more interested in chatting among themselves and uninterested in explaining the entertainment system, etc. There have been one or two complaints about food freshness and hygiene – staff should be made more aware of not selling food after its sell-by date.

Conclusion
It's not all bad news – there has recently been some good feedback, for example in relation to the friendliness of our pilots and cabin crew. But we should aim for all of our customers to have a consistently good experience. By addressing the issues above, we should be able to achieve this.

A Write an e-mail from Hurrah in reply to one of the complaints in the case study in the Course Book, pages 102–103.

B A group of entrepreneurs decides to launch an airline exclusively for business passengers. They decide to eliminate all the things that usually irritate air passengers. Write a press release announcing the launch, giving details of how it will be different from other airlines.

(See the Writing file, Course Book page 128, for the format of press releases.)

RESOURCE BANK – Writing

Crisis management

CASE STUDY WRITING TASK: MODEL ANSWER 1

VIDEO-GAMES BOSS HOLDS UP UNDER FIRE

Linda Davis, chief executive of ExtremAction, famous for its realistic and violent video-games, today defended her company's actions in launching its latest potential blockbuster *In Range*.

The launch comes at a time when violent video games are under increasing criticism from psychologists and legislators alike. Leading US politicians have argued for a ban on sales of ultraviolent games to youngsters under 21. Educators have spoken against advertising them near schools, arguing that the games desensitise young people to violence and make them more aggressive.

At a news conference, Ms Davis said, 'I am aware of the research into the so-called harmful effects of video-games, but we have commissioned our own research that shows the opposite: if kids can release their frustrations in a video-game environment, they are less likely to be violent in real life.'

Asked if ExtremAction would consider cancelling the launch, or delaying the launch of *In Range* to give time to redesign it to make it less violent, Bob Morgan, the company's director of public relations said, 'We have listened carefully to all the arguments, and we have decided to go ahead with this launch.'

The company can only be praised for the way it has handled the crisis. By commissioning its own research, ExtremAction has been able to challenge the generally held ideas about video-games ...

CASE STUDY WRITING TASK: MODEL ANSWER 2

To: Media Watch

From: ExtremAction directors

Report on the launch of *In Range*

Background to the crisis

Over the past few years, politicians, educationalists, etc. have been increasingly hostile to the games industry as a whole and ExtremAction in particular. When we announced the launch of *In Range*, we knew that there would be controversy, but we were prepared for it. Our CEO, Linda Davis, our PR director Bob Morgan and other directors drew up contingency plans.

Our actions

We were aware of increasing concern, even panic, over the last few years in relation to so-called violent videogames, and we have commissioned our own research into their effects. Our research shows that they are entirely harmless to users aged 12 and above. The games provide a release from the stresses of the real world, and make people less violent, not more.

Conclusion

For these reasons, we decided to go ahead with the launch, and coverage of our actions in the press has been favourable on the whole. We are happy for further research to be done into the effects of video games, but we believe that it will confirm the research we have already undertaken.

A Look again at the Skills section, Course Book page 110, and the script (track 2.33, page 161). Write an e-mail of complaint to TG Products from a parent whose child has been affected by the defective toy, giving exact details of the problem and the compensation that the parent would consider to be fair.

B In the end, TG Products decide to recall the defective toy. Write a press release with these details:

- the product concerned and where customers should return it
- how they will be refunded
- a helpline number that they can call of they wish
- End by apologising for any inconvenience to customers.

(See the Writing file, Course Book page 128, for the format of press releases.)

CASE STUDY WRITING TASK: MODEL ANSWER

To: Chief Executive, Rinnovar International

ACQUISITION TARGETS

Executive summary

Rinnovar's growth strategy is based on making acquisitions rather than organic expansion. Following our recent research into four possible targets, here are our findings and our recommendation.

Mumbai Herbal Products (India)

Positives: The company has a strong position in bath and shower products, very good R&D, and quality products for the world market. Its client base is made up of airlines, hotel groups, embassies, top department stores, etc. It has made good profits recently.

Negatives: MHP has started to sell overseas, but sales have recently slowed. The company may be unable to face strong international competition, as the family-dominated board needs more business expertise (which we could provide). The owners will want to keep half-ownership of the company.

Good Earth (Brazil)

Positives: They have a wide range of mass market products in hair, skin and body care and a strong position in cosmetics and fragrances, distributed through direct selling. It has a strong sales force and is highly ethical. The Brazilian market is growing fast.

Negatives: This is another family-run business, but with some entrepreneurial members. Growth is slowing and profits suffering because of high investment in overseas plants (but these should boost profit in future). The family would want to remain as majority shareholders, unless we make a particularly attractive offer.

Hondo Beauty Products (Korea)

Positives: The company has a wide range of 'green' cosmetics, bath and shower products supplied to major cosmetic companies and a wide range of markets worldwide. It has extremely modern production methods and high quality. It benefits from overseas partnerships. The firm has had fast profit growth recently.

Negatives: Hondo faces the threat of increasing competition from China, India and other low-cost producers that could reduce its profit margins. Decision-making is slow. The family might accept a full takeover by Renova, but they have the reputation of being hard bargainers.

Sheen Hair Products (US)

Positives: It has a good range of shampoos, hair colours and hair care products sold to beauty salons. All its production is located in low-cost developing countries (but see below). It has the great advantage of being relatively easy to take over as it's a public company.

Negatives: a narrow range of customers (salons only – but new types of customer could easily be found), slow growth, declining profit margins, bad press for its overseas operations (but its image could easily be improved with a good public relations agency) and no experience of international markets.

Recommendation

I recommend that Sheen should be our main acquisition target. It's a publicly quoted company, the takeover would be under Florida law (which our lawyers understand), and we would avoid the uncertainties of family-owned companies in places that we do not know, and where the family members might want too much influence after the acquisition.

We could easily bring in new management to develop the customer base beyond the current one of hair salons, extend the product range and develop the worldwide market.

A You are a mid-level manager in Sheen's marketing department. You have heard rumours about a possible takeover by Rinnovar. Write an e-mail to a friend saying what you have heard about Rinnovar's plans for Sheen and how you think the takeover will affect you.

B Rinnovar successfully acquires Sheen Hair Products. Write a press release announcing the news. (See the Writing file, Course Book page 128, for the format of press releases.)

RESOURCE BANK – Writing

Pearson Education Limited
Edinburgh Gate
Harlow
Essex CM20 2JE
England
and Associated Companies throughout the world.

www.pearsonELT.com
www.market-leader.net

First published 2001

Third edition 2011

Sixth impression 2017

ISBN: 978-1-4082-6803-2

Set in MetaPlus 9.5/12pt

Printed in Slovakia by Neografia.

Acknowledgements
*We are grateful to the following for permission to reproduce
copyright material:*

Figures
Figure 9.a from "Businesses see credit conditions ease", *The
Financial Times*, 30/11/2009 (Bank of England: ONS), copyright
© Bank of England

Text
Extract 6.b from "Weather events: Expensive picture of extreme
climate", The Financial Times, 17/04/2009 (Murray, S.),
copyright © Sarah Murray

The Financial Times
Extract 1.a from "Time for communication to move towards centre
stage", *The Financial Times*, 29/12/2009 (Argenti, P.), copyright
© Professor Paul Argenti; Extract 1.b from "To tweet or not to tweet
is a business question", *The Financial Times*, 15/01/2010 (Moules, J.)
copyright © The Financial Times Ltd; Extract 2.a from "Big names
prove worth in crisis", *The Financial Times*, 28/04/2010 (Gapper, J.)
copyright © The Financial Times Ltd; Extract 2.b from "Coca-Cola
targets more $1bn China brand", *The Financial Times*, 22/11/2009
(Birchall, J.), copyright © The Financial Times Ltd; Extract 3.a from
"The careerist: Pro bono work", *The Financial Times*, 07/03/2010
(Rigby, R.), copyright © Rhymer Rigby; Extract 3.b from "Russia:
Hot and cold reception awaits Moscow's visitors", *The Financial
Times*, 27/03/2009 (Gorst, I.), copyright © The Financial Times Ltd;
Extract 4.a from "How to be a top female boss", *The Financial Times*,
27/09/2009 (Kellaway, L.), copyright © The Financial Times Ltd;
Extract 4.b from "Master the mix of continuity and change", *The
Financial Times*, 18/01/2010 (Stern, S.), copyright © The Financial
Times Ltd; Extract 5.a from "Unhappiness at work rises to record
level", *The Financial Times*, 26/01/2010 (Groom, B.), copyright
© The Financial Times Ltd, .; Extract 5.b from "A different way of
working", *The Financial Times*, 22/03/2010 (Maitland, A.), copyright
© The Financial Times Ltd; Extract 6.a from "When star power
hits the rough", *The Financial Times*, 08/04/2010 (Davies, P.J.),
copyright © The Financial Times Ltd; Extract 7.a from "Nature and
nurture in the executive suite", *The Financial Times*, 26/02/2008
(Skapinker, M.), copyright © The Financial Times Ltd; Extract 7.b
from "Managers need a makeover", *The Financial Times*, 23/02/2010
(Birkinshaw, J.), copyright © Professor Julian Birkinshaw; Extract 8.a
from "Capello's masterclass for on-the-ball Finmeccanica",
The Financial Times, 02/12/2009 (Betts, P.), copyright © The
Financial Times Ltd; Extract 8.b from "Success and satisfaction", *The
Financial Times*, 22/03/2010 (Moules, J.), copyright © The Financial
Times Ltd; Extract 9.a from "Businesses see credit conditions
ease", T*he Financial Times*, 30/11/2009 (Groom, B.), copyright ©
The Financial Times Ltd; Extract 9.b from "Jumping into a funding
model for the online age", *The Financial Times*, 29/07/2009 (Jacobs,
E.), copyright © The Financial Times Ltd; Extract 10.a from "Bargain-
hunting tourists find an outlet", *The Financial Times*, 15/05/2010
(Kuchler, H.), copyright © The Financial Times Ltd; Extract 10.b
from "Social media: Big names are all a-Twitter over Facebook",
The Financial Times, 28/04/2010 (Bradshaw, T.), copyright ©
The Financial Times Ltd; Extract 11.a from "The spin doctor of
restructuring", *The Financial Times*, 17/03/2010 (Garrahan, M.),
copyright © The Financial Times Ltd; Extract 11.b from "How
our leaders get to grips with a scare story", *The Financial Times*,
20/04/2010 (Kay, J.), copyright © The Financial Times Ltd;
Extract 12.a from "Japan's Rakuten poised for an international blitz",
The Financial Times, 04/05/2010 (Harding, R., Hille, K. and Jung-a,
S.), copyright © The Financial Times Ltd; Extract 12.b from "Is tribal
conflict inevitable in mergers and takeovers?", *The Financial Times*,
15/07/2008 (Ranninger, R., Coughlin, R., Moeller, S. and Hedges,
N.), copyright © The Financial Times Ltd

In some instances we have been unable to trace the owners of
copyright material, and we would appreciate any information that
would enable us to do so.

Project managed by Chris Hartley